CONGRESSIONAL COMMITTEES, 1789–1982

Recent Titles in
Bibliographies and Indexes in Law and Political Science

Scottish Nationalism and Cultural Identity in the Twentieth Century: An
Annotated Bibliography of Secondary Sources
Compiled by Gordon Bryan

Edwin S. Corwin and the American Constitution:
A Bibliographical Analysis
Kenneth D. Crews

Political Risk Assessment: An Annotated Bibliography
Compiled by David A. Jodice

Human Rights: An International and Comparative Law Bibliography
Compiled and Edited by Julian R. Friedman and Marc I. Sherman

Latin American Society and Legal Culture
Compiled by Frederick E. Snyder

CONGRESSIONAL COMMITTEES, 1789–1982

A Checklist

Compiled by Walter Stubbs

Bibliographies and Indexes in Law and Political Science,
Number 6

Greenwood Press
Westport, Connecticut • London, England

Library of Congress Cataloging-in-Publication Data

Stubbs, Walter.
  Congressional committees, 1789-1982.

  (Bibliographies and indexes in law and political
science, ISSN 0742-6909 ; no. 6)
  Bibliography: p.
  Includes index.
  1. United States.   Congress—Committees—History—
Handbooks, manuals, etc. I. Title.   II. Series.
JK1029.S78   1985   328.73'0765'09   85-10007
ISBN 0-313-24539-8 (lib. bdg. : alk. paper)

Library of Congress Catalog Card Number: 85-10007
ISBN: 0-313-24539-8
ISSN: 0742-6909

First published in 1985

Greenwood Press
A division of Congressional Information Service, Inc.
88 Post Road West, Westport, Connecticut 06881

Printed in the United States of America

The paper used in this book complies with the
Permanent Paper Standard issued by the National
Information Standards Organization (Z39.48-1984).

10   9   8   7   6   5   4   3   2   1

CONTENTS

INTRODUCTION

Congressional committees have figured prominently in the actions taken by Congress since the beginning of constitutional government in the United States. Most of the work of Congress is now done at the committee level, and they are a permanent part of Congressional organization.

Since the first Congress, the work of Congressional committees has steadily grown, both in importance and in volume, but there has not been any single source for identifying all of the many committees that have existed over the years. There have been over 1500 committees in existence at one time or another, but only the most prominent can be readily found in the standard printed sources.

Congressional Committees, 1789-1982 rectifies this omission by assembling all the data needed to answer such questions as:

What Congressional committees have existed?

What were the dates of establishment and termination of these committees?

What legislation--resolution numbers, Public Laws, etc.--have been responsible for establishing or abolishing the committees?

What major name changes have the committees experienced?

The volume is offered as a necessary starting point for the scholar doing many kinds of research on the Congress. Studies of the effectiveness of the committee system, of the impact of certain individuals on committees, etc., will all find the work useful. It can also be used as a starting point for anyone seeking the hearings and reports of the various committees: once the dates of the committees are known, the various chronological indexes available are easier to consult. Documents librarians will find it an aid in making more effective use of their collections.

The volume identifies more than 1500 committees and supplies references to the most frequently needed information about each. The citations for the founding of the committee will lead to any debate on the need for the committee, and, if a report resulted in termination of the committee, the citation for the report will give all the information needed to locate the full text of the report.

History of Congressional Committee Structure

During the first few Congresses, select committees were organized to study a particular problem or to bring in a bill and then were promptly discharged upon completion of their tasks.

In the House of Representatives a few committees were appointed on a regular basis and served for the duration of the Congressional session. These were not standing committees, however. For example, the Committee on Elections was first appointed on April 13, 1789,[1] during the 1st Congress, 1st Session, but it did not become a standing committee until November 13, 1794,[2] when a rule was adopted making the Committee on Elections and the Committee on Claims standing committees. A select Committee on Ways and Means was also appointed quite early in the first Congress, on July 24, 1789.[3] It remained a regular select committee until January 7, 1802,[4] when it was made a standing committee. By 1806 there were six standing committees in the House, in addition to the many short-lived select committees.[5] From this humble beginning, the House was to have over fifty standing and regular select committees by the end of the nineteenth century.

The Senate was slower in forming its first standing committees. On December 11, 1816,[6] eleven of the committees that were being regularly established as select committees were made into standing committees. The Senate Foreign Relations Committee was among these first standing committees. One author has estimated that as many as 250 select committees dealt with the various aspects of foreign relations prior to the establishment of the standing committee.[7] The small size of the Senate was a major reason for the late establishment of standing committees. In 1815, for example, there were only thirty-six members of the Senate, and meetings of the whole house were quite easy to arrange. By 1921, at the beginning of the 66th Congress, there were seventy-four standing committees in the Senate. There were only ninety-six members of the Senate, so each had to serve on a large number of committees. This overabundance of committees resulted in what was to be one of the many committee reorganizations in the history of the Senate. The 1921 reorganization of Senate committees resulted in a reduction from seventy-four to thirty-three committees.[8]

Scope of the Work

There are several types of Congressional committees.[9] Included in this compilation are standing committees, select and special committees, select and special joint committees, and statutory joint committees. Exceptions to this group are honorary, ceremonial, and housekeeping committees. Examples of these are the committees delegated to attend funerals, various celebrations, and those assigned to rearrange the seating or to attend to the ventilation of the halls of the respective bodies of Congress. Also excluded are political committees, committees of the whole, and conference committees. These committees serve political and procedural functions and are not comparable to the other types of committees. Subcommittees are also not listed since they are always subordinate to the main committees.

Because of the proliferation of select committees in the Senate before the establishment of the first standing committees, no committees are listed for the Senate before 1816.

Methodology

The committees that have existed since 1789 were determined by first consulting the list of committees found in the secondary sources already mentioned, after which a systematic search of the indexes of the Journals, 1789-1980, the Annals, 1789-1833, Congressional Globe, 1833-1873, and Congressional Record, 1873-1982 was conducted. The subject heading consulted was "committee," unless other evidence indicated that another heading might be appropriate. The Annals and Globe are generally not as well indexed as the Journals of the respective houses. All are less comprehensive during the early nineteenth century than are today's indexes; so often luck, rather than skill, resulted in finding the information sought.

The indexing of the House Journals for the first fifteen Congresses was discovered to be quite different, depending on which edition of the Journals was consulted. Two different editions were used: the Brookhaven Press microfiche edition and the Garland Press reprint edition. The pagination was not the same in these editions, and the microfiche edition index was not nearly as complete as was the index in the reprint. No distinction has been made between these two editions in the Congressional Committees because the text is the same in both, and the date would allow anyone checking these sources to find the same information in either.

Organization

Congressional Committees consists mainly of an alphabetical list of committees arranged by a key word in the title of the committee. The selection of the key word was based on an attempt to group similar committees under the same key word. For example, the many committees on Indians were filed under the key word of Indian or Indians.

Users can consult the main body of the work and find which committees have studied an issue such as slavery. The Subject Index may yield additional entries for the subject, as the names of the committees sometimes do not contain the word which is the main subject. Personal names can also be found quickly in the Subject Index. The Chronological List of Committees gives the scope of committees by Congress. The issues of concern for a given period become obvious when looking at the committees founded during that time.

The entry number assigned to each committee will expedite the use of the Subject Index. If the committee has been assigned a Superintendent of Documents classification number, the word from which the Cutter number of the classification number has been selected was usually used as the key word. Trial and error during the compilation sometimes resulted in finding a better word. If additional descriptors were added to the name of the committee to give it some meaning, these words were not used as key words. The key word is underscored, but the entry is not inverted from the key word.

The names of many of the nineteenth-century committees were overly long, and some judgment has been exercised to shorten them to something more manageable, while maintaining their meaning. Some committee names were not descriptive enough and have been augmented. For example, the Special Committee of Thirteen was changed to the Special Committee of Thirteen on the Disturbed Condition of the Country. The date of 1861 for this committee immediately gives a clue to its subject.

Each entry includes the date of formation of the committee and the resolution or Public Law creating it. Prior to the 1890s, resolution numbers were not regularly assigned to most resolutions, so the notation is only to the Congress and session. Often a committee appears for the first time upon adoption of the rules at the beginning of a session. This date is used as the beginning date of the committee in these cases. When no evidence of a committee can be found at the end of a session, it is assumed that the committee died at the end of the session, and that date is used as the committee's termination date, even though the committee may have ceased to be active before that date. When a committee issued a final report, the date of the report is given as the termination date. Often a committee is abolished by specific legislation such as the Congressional Reorganization Act of 1946 with an effective date of January 2, 1947. In such cases the effective date is used as the termination date. Sometimes the resolution establishing the committee gives a date by which time the work of the committee must be completed. If nothing is done to change that date, and the committee issues no final report, then the date specified in the enacting resolution is used as the termination date. Special and select committees are often extended for several successive Congresses by separate resolutions in each respective Congress. Only the resolution number setting up the committee for the first time is noted. Hinds points out that one Speaker of the House held that "a select committee expires at the end of a session of Congress; the appointment does not run through two sessions, as is the case with other committees, yet it has been uniformly held that the reference of any matter to a select committee that has expired has the effect to revive that committee, which is substantially the same as the creation of a new committee."[10]

Name changes of significance are considered as the termination of one committee and the establishment of another and are treated as such with a cross-reference in each entry to the other name.

Reports for investigating committees were searched in the indexes to the committee reports which are bound with the serial set volumes, in the CIS Serial Set Index, 1789-1969, the Documents Catalog, 1893-1940, and miscellaneous other sources. Some reports have no doubt been overlooked because the subject of the report is often far different from the apparent subject of the committee as suggested by its name. The footnotes for the reports include the serial set volume numbers for ease of use.

Each entry contains at least three elements: establishment, authority, and termination. If a committee has been assigned a Superintendent of Documents classification number, that is also included in the entry. If a resolution or Public Law was responsible for the abolition of a committee, an additional authority is included. Footnotes appear with each entry and have been abbreviated to prevent their dominating the entry. Each footnote is to a primary source easily found in any major library collection in the United States. This will allow the researcher to find easily the reason for establishment of the committee or any other attendant information of interest.

In the Chronological Index, committee names have been shortened from the key word. The Chronological Index is arranged by jurisdiction, i.e., House, Joint, and Senate and then by Congress, from the 1st through the 97th. If a committee existed at all during a Congress, the number of the Congress is included without regard to session. Exact dates are available in the main body of Congressional Committees.

Other Sources

The Congressional Directory can be used to identify committees that were in existence at the beginning of any given session of Congress, but it does not tell when the committee began, nor does it list committees that were created during the session and finished their work before the beginning of the next session. The first listing of committees in the Congressional Directory was in 1814.[11] The Checklist of United States Public Documents, 1789-1909 identifies those committees for which public documents existed in the Public Documents Room of the Government Printing Office at the time of its compilation.[12] It includes 164 entries for Congressional committees,[13] so it is far from complete even for the nineteenth century. John Andriot's Guide to U. S. Government Publications[14] is also useful, but it includes only those committees that have been assigned Superintendent of Documents classification numbers. Many other sources give partial lists of committees, but none is as complete as this compilation.

Notes

1. U. S., Congress, House, 1st Congress, 1st Session, Journal, 13. Hereinafter cited as H. J. (Cong.-Sess.): page.

2. H. J. (3-2): 229.

3. H. J. (1-1): 66.

4. H. J. (7-1): 40.

5. U. S., Congress, House, 9th Congress, 2nd Session, 1 December 1806, The Debates and Proceedings in the Congress of the United States, 111. Hereinafter cited as Annals (Cong.-Sess.): page.

6. U. S., Congress, Senate, 14th Congress, 2nd Session, Journal, 44. Hereinafter cited as S. J. (Cong.-Sess.): page.

7. James W. Gould, "The Origins of the Senate Committee on Foreign Relations," Western Political Quarterly 12 (September 1959): 670.

8. U. S., Congress, Senate, S. Res. 43, 67th Cong., Special sess., 18 April 1921, Congressional Record 67: 404-405. Hereinafter cited as vol. CR page.

9. Floyd Millard Riddick, The United States Congress: Organization and Procedure (Manassas, Va.: National Capital Publishers, 1949), pp. 146-199.

10. Asher Crosby Hinds, quoting Speaker Randall in Precedents of the House of Representatives of the United States, 11 vols. (Washington: Government Printing Office, 1907-1941), vol. 4, p. 870.

11. Perry M. Goldman and James S. Young, eds., The United States Congressional Directories 1789-1840. (New York: Columbia University Press, 1973), pp. 79-85.

12. Checklist of United States Public Documents, 1789-1900 (Washington: Government Printing Office, 1911), p. xii.

13. Ibid., pp. 1532-1652.

14. John Andriot, Guide to U. S. Government Publications, 2 vols., (McLean, Va.: Documents Index, 1982).

SAMPLE ENTRY

The following entry, typical for this work, is duplicated here to alert the user to both format and abbreviations.

14. Committee on Agriculture and Forestry (Senate)[1]

Sudocs: Y4. Ag8/2:[2]

Established: February 5, 1884,[3] when name of Agriculture Committee was changed (Entry 13).[4] 15 CR 879.[5]

Authority: Res. of the Senate[6] (48-1)[7]

Terminated: February 11, 1977,[8] when name was changed to Committee on Agriculture, Nutrition and Forestry (Entry 15).[9] 123 CR 3660.[10]

Authority: S. Res. 4 (95-1)[11]

1. Committee Name
2. Superintendent of Documents Classification Number
3. Date of Committee Establishment
4. Former Name of Committee, and Entry Number of that Committee
5. Congressional Record Citation to Establishment
6. Resolution of the Senate
7. 48th Congress, 1st Session
8. Date of Committee Termination
9. Name and Entry Number of Committee Replacing this One
10. Congressional Record Citation on Termination
11. Senate Resolution 4 (95th Congress, 1st Session)

ABBREVIATIONS

Am. St. Papers	American State Papers
Annals	Debates and Proceedings in the Congress of the United States, 1789-1833
Cong. Globe	Congressional Globe, 1833-1873
CR	Congressional Record, 1873-1982
Ex. J. of the Senate	Executive Journal of the Senate
H. J.	House Journal, 1789-1980
PL	Public Law
Res.	Resolution
S. J.	Senate Journal, 1789-1980
Stat.	U. S. Statutes at Large
Sudocs	Superintendent of Documents Classification Number
U. S. C.	U. S. Code

PART I

CONGRESSIONAL COMMITTEES

1. Select Committee on Alleged Abstraction of Books from the Library of the House (House)
   Established: February 14, 1861
     H. J. (36-2): 314.
   Authority: Res. of the House
     (36-2)
   Terminated: February 28, 1861
     H. rpt. 90 (36-2) 1105.

2. Select Committee on Alleged Abstraction of a Report from the Clerk's Office (House)
   Established: March 3, 1863
     H. J. (37-3): 617.
   Authority: Res. of the House
     (37-3)
   Terminated: March 3, 1863, at the end of the 37-3.

3. Select Committee on Securing a Greater Accountability of Public Moneys (House)
   Established: April 12, 1822
     H. J. (17-1): 452.
   Authority: Res. of the House
     (17-1)
   Terminated: May 8, 1822, at the end of the 17-1.

4. Committee on Accounts (House)
   Sudocs: Y4. Ac2:
   Established: December 27, 1803
     Annals (8-1): 790.
   Authority: Res. of the House
     (8-1)
   Terminated: January 2, 1947

60 Stat. 812.
Authority: PL 79-601

5. Select Committee on Admission to the Floor (House)
   Established: June 18, 1886
     17 CR 5909.
   Authority: Res. of the House
     (49-1)
   Terminated: January 27, 1887
     H. rpt. 3798 (49-2) 2500.

6. Committee on Aeronautical and Space Sciences (Senate)
   Sudocs: Y4. Ae8:
   Established: July 24, 1958
     104 CR 14857.
   Authority: S. Res. 327 (85-2)
   Terminated: February 11, 1977, when its functions were transferred to the Committee on Commerce, Science and Transportation (Entry 251).
     123 CR 3681.
   Authority: S. Res. 4 (95-1)

7. Committee on Aging (Senate)
   Sudocs: Y4. Ag4:
   Established: March 1, 1977, when it replaced the Special Committee on Aging (Entry 9).
     123 CR 3691.
   Authority: S. Res. 4 (95-1)
   Terminated: Still in existence at the end of the 97-2.

8. Permanent Select Committee on Aging (House)
   Sudocs: Y4. Ag4/2:

Established: October 8, 1974
120 CR 34469.
Authority: H. Res. 988 (93-2)
Terminated: Still in existence
at the end of the 97-2.

9. Special Committee on Aging
(Senate)
Sudocs: Y4. Ag4:
Established: February 13, 1961
107 CR 2104.
Authority: S. Res. 33 (87-1)
Terminated: November 15, 1978,
when it was made the Committee
on Aging (Entry 7).
123 CR 3691.
Authority: S. Res. 4 (95-1)

10. Select Committee on the
Memorial of the Agricultural Bank
of Mississippi (House)
Established: January 7, 1842
H. J. (27-2): 131.
Authority: Res. of the House
(27-2)
Terminated: April 9, 1842
H. rpt. 553 (27-2) 409.

11. Committee on Agriculture
(House)
Sudocs: Y4. Ag8/1:
Established: May 3, 1820
Annals (16-1): 2179.
Authority: Res. of the House
(16-1)
Terminated: Still in existence
at the end of the 97-2.

12. Committee on Agriculture -
1st (Senate)
Sudocs: Y4. Ag8/1:
Established: December 9, 1825
Annals (19-1): 6.
Authority: Res. of the Senate
(19-1)
Terminated: March 3, 1857, at
the end of the 34-3.

13. Committee on Agriculture -
2nd (Senate)
Sudocs: Y4. Ag8/2:
Established: March 6, 1863
S. J. (37-3): 451.
Authority: Res. of Senate (37-
Special)

Terminated: February 5, 1884,
when the name was changed to
the Committee on Agriculture
and Forestry (Entry 14).
15 CR 879.
Authority: Res. of the Senate
(48-1)

14. Committee on Agriculture and
Forestry (Senate)
Sudocs: Y4. Ag8/2:
Established: February 5, 1884,
when name of Agriculture Committee was changed (Entry 13).
15 CR 879.
Authority: Res. of the Senate
(48-1)
Terminated: February 11, 1977,
when name was changed to Committee on Agriculture, Nutrition and Forestry (Entry 15).
123 CR 3660.
Authority: S. Res. 4 (95-1)

15. Committee on Agriculture,
Nutrition and Forestry (Senate)
Sudocs: Y4. Ag8/3:
Established: February 4, 1977,
having been preceded by the
Committee on Agriculture and
Forestry and the Committee on
Nutrition and Human Needs (En-
tries 14, 984).
123 CR 3691.
Authority: S. Res. 4 (95-1)
Terminated: Still in existence at
the end of the 97-2.

16. Select Committee to Investi-
gate Air Accidents (House)
Established: March 6, 1941
87 CR 1940.
Authority: H. Res. 125 (77-1)
Terminated: January 7, 1943
H. rpt. 1 (78-1) 10760.

17. Special Committee on Investi-
gation of Air Mail and Ocean Mail
Contracts (Senate)
Sudocs: Y4. Ai7/2:
Established: February 25, 1933
76 CR 5008.
Authority: S. Res. 349 (72-2)
Terminated: June 30, 1936, at the
end of the 74-2.

18. Select Committee of Inquiry
into Operation of Air Services
(House)
  Sudocs: Y4. Ai7:
  Established: March 24, 1924
    65 CR 4817.
  Authority: H. Res. 192 (68-1)
  Terminated: 1925
    H. rpt. 1653 (68-2) 8391.

19. Committee to Investigate
Control of Aircraft for Seacoast
Defense (Joint)
  Established: March 4, 1929
    70 CR 5233.
  Authority: S. Con. Res. 11 (70-2)
  Terminated: March 3, 1931, at the
    end of the 71-3.

20. Select Committee on Admission
of Alabama to the Union (House)
  Established: December 7, 1818
    H. J. (15-2): 66.
  Authority: Res. of the House
    (15-2)
  Terminated: March 3, 1819, at the
    end of the 15-2.

21. Select Committee on the
Condition of Affairs in Alabama
(House)
  Established: December 21, 1874
    H. J. (43-2): 92.
  Authority: Res. of the House
    (43-2)
  Terminated: February 23, 1875
    H. rpt. 262 (43-2) 1661.

22. Select Committee on the Con-
stitution of the State of Alabama
(Senate)
  Established: December 6, 1819
    S. J. (16-1): 6.
  Authority: Res. of the Senate
    (16-1)
  Terminated: May 15, 1820, at the
    end of the 16-1.

23. Select Committee on Memorial
of the State of Alabama to Purchase
Certain Public Lands from Within
the State (Senate)
  Established: February 4, 1828
    S. J. (20-1): 133.
  Authority: Res. of the Senate
    (20-1)

Terminated: May 26, 1828, at the
    end of the 20-1.

24. Committee on Investigation of
Conditions in Alaska (Joint)
  Established: March 4, 1911
    46 CR 4290.
  Authority: S. Con. Res. 42 (61-3)
  Terminated: April 4, 1911, at
    beginning of 62-1.

25. Special Select Committee on
the Investigation of the Alaska
Railroad (Senate)
  Established: July 1, 1930
    72 CR 12165.
  Authority: S. Res. 298 (71-2)
  Terminated: December 4, 1933
    75 CR 14359.
  Authority: S. Res. 257 (72-1)

26. Select Committee on Alcohol
in the Arts (Joint)
  Sudocs: Y4. Al1/1:
  Established: June 3, 1896
    29 Stat. 195.
  Authority: PL 54-310
  Terminated: December 17, 1897
    S. rpt. 411 (55-2) 3621.

27. Committee on Alcoholic Liquor
Traffic (House)
  Sudocs: Y4. Al1/2:
  Established: August 18, 1893,
    when it replaced the Select
    Committee on Alcoholic Liquor
    Traffic (Entry 28).
      25 CR 478.
  Authority: Res. of the House
    (53-1)
  Terminated: December 5, 1927
    69 CR 14.
  Authority: H. Res. 7 (70-1)

28. Select Committee on Alco-
holic Liquor Traffic (House)
  Sudocs: Y4. Al1/2:
  Established: May 16, 1879
    9 CR 1394.
  Authority: Res. of the House
    (46-1)
  Terminated: August 18, 1893, when
    it was made the Committee on
    Alcoholic Liquor Traffic
    (Entry 27).
      25 CR 478.

Authority: Res. of the House
(53-1)

29. Select Committee on the Af-
fairs of the U.S. with the Dey and
Regency of Algiers (House)
  Established: February 9, 1808
    H. J. (10-1): 359.
  Authority: Res. of the House
    (10-1)
  Terminated: April 25, 1808
    Ibid. 643.

30. Select Committee to Investi-
gate the Alien Property Custo-
dian's Office (Senate)
  Established: July 3, 1926
    67 CR 12965.
  Authority: S. Res. 71 (69-1)
  Terminated: March 3, 1927, at the
    end of the 69-2.

31. Select Committee on the Reso-
lution to Amend the Constitution
(Senate)
  Established: June 2, 1834
    S. J. (23-1): 291.
  Authority: Res. of the Senate
    (23-1)
  Terminated: June 30, 1834, at the
    end of the 23-1.

32. Committee on Amending the
Constitution in Electing the Presi-
dent and Vice President (Joint)
  Established: January 30, 1854
    S. J. (33-1): 141.
  Authority: H. Jt. Res. (33-1)
  Terminated: August 7, 1854, at
    the end of the 33-1.

33. Select Committee on Amending
the Constitution on the Election of
the President and Vice President
(Senate)
  Established: March 15, 1830
    S. J. (21-1): 186.
  Authority: Res. of the Senate
    (21-1)
  Terminated: March 3, 1821, at the
    end of the 21-2.

34. Select Committee on Amendment
of Constitution on Appointment of
Members of Congress to Office
(House)

Established: January 11, 1837
  H. J. (25-2): 256.
Authority: Res. of the House
  (25-2)
Terminated: July 9, 1838, at the
  end of the 25-2.

35. Select Committee on Amend-
ments to the Constitution on the
Election of the President and Vice
President (House)
  Established: December 17, 1835
    H. J. (24-1): 72.
  Authority: Res. of the House
    (24-1)
  Terminated: February 28, 1837
    H. rpt. 296 (24-2) 306.

36. Select Committee on Certain
Amendments Proposed to the Consti-
tution by the Convention held in
Washington City (Senate)
  Established: February 27, 1861
    S. J. (36-2): 333.
  Authority: Senate Order (36-2)
  Terminated: February 28, 1861
    S. J. (36-2): 337.

37. Select Committee on Proposed
Amendments to the Constitution
(Senate)
  Established: November 23, 1820
    S. J. (16-2): 27.
  Authority: Res. of the Senate
    (16-2)
  Terminated: March 3, 1825, at the
    end of the 18-2.

38. Select Committee on the Amer-
ican Colonization Society (Senate)
  Established: February 29, 1820
    S. J. (16-1): 194.
  Authority: Res. of the Senate
    (16-1)
  Terminated: May 15, 1820, at the
    end of the 16-1.

39. Select Committee on the Memo-
rial of the American Colonization
Society (House)
  Established: January 29, 1827
    H. J. (19-2): 214.
  Authority: Res. of the House
    (19-2)
  Terminated: February 7, 1832
    H. rpt. 277 (22-1) 225.

40. Special Committee to Investigate American Merchant Marine (Senate)
   Sudocs: Y4. Am3/4:
   Established: February 25, 1938
      83 CR 2443.
   Authority: S. Res. 231 (75-3)
   Terminated: August 5, 1939, at
      the end of the 76-1.

41. Special Committee on Investigation of American Retail Federation (House)
   Sudocs: Y4. Am3/3:
   Established: April 24, 1935
      79 CR 6338.
   Authority: H. Res. 203 (74-1)
   Terminated: April 7, 1936
      H. rpt. 2373 (74-2) 9996.

42. Committee on American Shipbuilding (House)
   Sudocs: Y4. Am3/1:
   Established: December 19, 1883
      15 CR 190.
   Authority: Res. of House (48-1)
   Terminated: February 12, 1887
      H. rpt. 4043 (49-2) 2501.

43. Special Committee to Study Problems of American Small Business (Senate)
   Sudocs: Y4. Am3/5:
   Established: October 8, 1940
      86 CR 13372.
   Authority: S. Res. 298 (76-3)
   Terminated: February 20, 1950,
      when the Select Committee on
      Small Business was established
      (Entry 1313).
         96 CR 1944.
   Authority: S. Res. 58 (81-2)

44. Special Committee on Investigation of American Sugar Refining Company (House)
   Sudocs: Y4. Am3/2:
   Established: May 9, 1911
      47 CR 1147.
   Authority: H. Res. 157 (62-1)
   Terminated: April 20, 1912
      H. rpt. 331 (62-2) 6135.

45. Select Committee on Charges Against the Honorable Lucien Anderson (House)
   Established: January 18, 1865
      H. J. (38-2): 111.
   Authority: Res. of the House
      (38-2)
   Terminated: March 3, 1865
      H. rpt. 29 (38-2) 1235.

46. Special Committee to Study the Anthracite Emergency Program (House)
   Established: September 12, 1940
      86 CR 12040.
   Authority: H. Res. 564 (76-3)
   Terminated: January 3, 1941, at
      the end of the 76-3.
   (The committee was not authorized
      to hold hearings and no appro-
      priations were authorized for
      it.)

47. Select Committee on Apportionment of Representatives (House)
   Established: December 13, 1841
      H. J. (27-2): 40.
   Authority: Res. of the House
      (27-2)
   Terminated: January 22, 1842
      H. rpt. 43 (27-2) 407.

48. Select Committee to Bring in a Bill for the Apportionment of Representatives (House)
   Established: November 8, 1811
      H. J. (12-1): 20.
   Authority: Res. of the House
      (12-1)
   Terminated: November 20, 1811
      Ibid. 62.

49. Select Committee on Apportionment of Representatives Under the Fourth Census (House)
   Established: December 29, 1820
      H. J. (16-2): 96.
   Authority: Res. of the House
      (16-2)
   Terminated: March 3, 1821, at the
      end of the 16-2.

50. Select Committee on Apportionment of Representatives Under the Next Census (House)
   Established: December 11, 1826
      H. J. (19-2): 43.

Authority: Res. of the House
  (19-2)
Terminated: March 3, 1827, at the
  end of the 19-2.

51. Committee on Appropriations
(House)
  Sudocs: Y4. Ap6/1:
  Established: March 2, 1865
    Cong. Globe (38-1): 1317.
  Authority: Res. of the House
    (38-2)
  Terminated: Still in existence at
    the end of the 97-2.

52. Committee on Appropriations
(Senate)
  Sudocs: Y4. Ap6/2:
  Established: March 6, 1867
    S. J. (40-1): 8.
  Authority: Res. of the Senate
    (40-1)
  Terminated: Still in existence at
    the end of the 97-2.

53. Select Committee on Impeach-
ment of Robert W. Archibald
(Senate)
  Established: July 15, 1912
    48 CR 9054.
  Authority: Res. of the Senate
    (62-2)
  Terminated: January 13, 1913,
    upon conclusion of trial.
      S. doc. 1140 (62-3) 6356-7.

54. Select Committee on the Con-
dition of Affairs in Arkansas
(House)
  Established: May 27, 1874
    H. J. (43-1): 1042.
  Authority: Res. of the House
    (43-1)
  Terminated: February 6, 1875
    H. rpt. 127 (43-2) 1657.

55. Select Committee on the Con-
stitution of the State of Arkansas
(Senate)
  Established: March 14, 1835
    S. J. (24-1): 219.
  Authority: Res. of the Senate
    (24-1)
  Terminated: July 4, 1836, at the
    end of the 24-1.

56. Select Committee to Define
the Limits of the Territory of
Arkansas (House)
  Established: January 9, 1823
    H. J. (17-2): 113.
  Authority: Res. of the House
    (17-2)
  Terminated: March 3, 1823, at
    the end of the 17-2.

57. Select Committee on the Divi-
sion of the Missouri Territory and
Establishing a Territory on the
Arkansas (House)
  Established: December 16, 1818
    H. J. (15-2): 107.
  Authority: Res. of the House
    (15-2)
  Terminated: December 21, 1818
    Ibid. 119.

58. Select Committee on Memorial
of the Legislature of Arkansas
(Senate)
  Established: December 17, 1823
    S. J. (18-1): 47.
  Authority: Res. of the Senate
    (18-1)
  Terminated: March 23, 1824
    S. doc. 58 (18-1) 91.

59. Select Committee to Investi-
gate Armed Bodies of Men for Pri-
vate Purposes (Senate) (Pinkerton
Detective Force)
  Established: August 2, 1892
    23 CR 7015.
  Authority: Res. of the Senate
    (51-2)
  Terminated: February 10, 1893
    S. rpt. 1280 (52-2) 3072.

60. Committee on Armed Services
(House)
  Sudocs: Y4. Ar5/2:
  Established: January 2, 1947
    60 Stat. 812.
  Authority: PL 79-601
  Terminated: Still in existence at
    the end of the 97-2.

61. Committee on Armed Services
(Senate)
  Sudocs: Y4. Ar5/3:
  Established: January 2, 1947
    60 Stat. 812.

Authority: PL 79-601
Terminated: Still in existence at
the end of the 97-2.

62. Special Committee to Inves-
tigate Cost of Armor Plant (Joint)
Sudocs: Y4. Ar5:
Established: June 30, 1914
38 Stat. 414
Authority: PL 63-121
Terminated: February 24, 1915
H. doc. 1620 (63-3) 6889.

63. Select Committee on the Sub-
ject of a National Armory and
Foundry (Senate)
Established: March 21, 1862
S. J. (37-2): 328.
Authority: Senate Order (37-2)
Terminated: July 17, 1862, at the
end of the 37-2.

64. Select Committee on the
Establishment of a National Armory
(House)
Established: July 10, 1861
H. J. (37-1): 62.
Authority: Res. of the House
(37-1)
Terminated: July 4, 1864, at the
end of the 38-1.

65. Select Committee on Prohib-
iting the Exportation of Arms,
Ammunition, Canvas and Cordage
(House)
Established: February 27, 1809
H. J. (10-2): 469.
Authority: Res. of the House
(10-2)
Terminated: February 27, 1809
Ibid. 470.

66. Select Committee on a Message
Communicating Copies of Contracts
for Arms, Cannon, Shot, Shells,
etc. (House)
Established: January 7, 1824
H. J. (18-1): 122.
Authority: Res. of the House
(18-1)
Terminated: March 27, 1824, at
the end of the 18-1.

67. Select Committee to Inquire
into the Sale of Arms to French

Agents (Senate)
Established: February 29, 1872
Cong. Globe (42-2): 1290.
Authority: Res. of the Senate
(42-2)
Terminated: March 11, 1872
S. rpt. 183 (42-2) 1497.

68. Select Committee on a Bill
(S. 4) to Promote the Efficiency
of the Army (Senate)
Established: July 6, 1861
S. J. (37-1): 21.
Authority: Senate Order (37-1)
Terminated: August 6, 1861, at
the end of the 37-1.

69. Select Committee to Inquire
into the Manner of Making Contracts
for Supplying the Army (House)
Established: February 3, 1814
H. J. (13-2): 271.
Authority: Res. of the House
(13-2)
Terminated: April 13, 1814
Ibid. 588.

70. Select Committee to Inquire
What Unauthorized Advances of Pub-
lic Moneys Have Been Made to the
Commander-in-Chief of the Army
(House)
Established: February 3, 1809
H. J. (10-2): 356.
Authority: Res. of the House
(10-2)
Terminated: February 22, 1809
Ibid. 423.

71. Committee on the Reorganiza-
tion of the Army (Joint)
Established: June 18, 1878
20 Stat. 151.
Authority: PL of 45-2
Terminated: December 12, 1878
S. rpt. 555 (45-3) 1837.

72. Select Committee on the State
and Disposition of the Army (House)
Established: January 22, 1810
H. J. (11-2): 235.
Authority: Res. of the House
(11-2)
Terminated: April 27, 1810
Ibid. 606.

73. Select Committee on the Army Appropriations Inquiry (House)
  Established: December 10, 1819
    H. J. (16-1): 31.
  Authority: Res. of the House
    (16-1)
  Terminated: February 28, 1820
    Ibid. 253.

74. Select Committee on Rules and Regulations for the Army of the U.S. (House)
  Established: December 6, 1805
    H. J. (9-1): 32.
  Authority: Res. of the House
    (9-1)
  Terminated: April 21, 1806, at
    the end of the 9-1.

75. Select Committee on Bill to Regulate Army Pay (House)
  Established: December 16, 1844
    H. J. (28-2): 81.
  Authority: Res. of the House
    (28-2)
  Terminated: March 3, 1845, at the
    end of the 28-2.

76. Select Committee on the Memorial of the Artist of the United States (House)
  Established: May 31, 1858
    Cong. Globe (35-1): 2546.
  Authority: Res. of the House
    (35-1)
  Terminated: March 3, 1859
    H. rpt. 198 (35-2) 1018.

77. Select Committee on Alterations in the Several Acts for the Encouragement of Learning, and Promotion of the Useful Arts (House)
  Established: November 17, 1807
    H. J. (10-1): 71.
  Authority: Res. of the House
    (10-1)
  Terminated: March 7, 1808
    Ibid. 445.

78. Select Committee to Investigate Charges Against the Honorable J. M. Ashley (House)
  Established: December 4, 1862
    H. J. (37-2): 36.
  Authority: Res. of the House
    (37-3)

Terminated: February 28, 1863
    H. rpt. 47 (37-3) 1173.

79. Select Committee on Assassinations (House)
  Sudocs: Y4. As7:
  Established: February 2, 1977
    123 CR 3369.
  Authority: H. Res. 222 (95-1)
  Terminated: March 29, 1979
    H. rpt. 1828 (95-2) 13204-11.

80. Select Committee on Assault on the President's Secretary (House)
  Established: April 18, 1828
    H. J. (20-1): 588.
  Authority: Res. of the House
    (20-1)
  Terminated: May 16, 1828
    H. rpt. 260 (20-1) 179.

81. Select Committee on Establishing an Assay Office in the Gold Region (House)
  Established: January 4, 1831
    H. J. (21-2): 141.
  Authority: Res. of the House
    (21-2)
  Terminated: April 4, 1834
    H. rpt. 391 (23-1) 262.

82. Select Committee on the Propriety of Giving the Assent of Congress to an Act of the Legislature of Virginia (House)
  Established: April 8, 1816
    H. J. (14-1): 606.
  Authority: Res. of the House
    (14-1)
  Terminated: April 9, 1816
    Ibid. 613.

83. Select Committee on Astronautics and Space Exploration (House)
  Sudocs: Y4. As8:
  Established: March 5, 1958
    104 CR 3443.
  Authority: H. Res. 496 (85-2)
  Terminated: July 21, 1958, when
    the standing Committee on Science and Astronautics was
    established (Entry 1263).
    104 CR 14514.
  Authority: H. Res. 580 (85-2)

84. Committee on <u>Atomic</u> Energy
(Joint)
  Sudocs: Y4. At7/2:
  Established: August 1, 1946
    (Entry 85)
      60 Stat. 772.
  Authority: PL 79-585.
  Terminated: September 30, 1977
    (Entry 417)
      91 Stat. 884.
  Authority: PL 95-110

85. Special Committee on <u>Atomic</u>
Energy (Senate)
  Sudocs: Y4. At7:
  Established: October 22, 1945
    91 CR 9898.
  Authority: S. Res. 179 (79-1)
  Terminated: August 1, 1946, when
    the Joint Committee on Atomic
    Energy was established
    (Entry 84).
      60 Stat. 772.
  Authority: PL 79-585.

86. Select Committee on Estab-
lishing an Additional Executive
Office of <u>Attorney</u> General (Senate)
  Established: December 10, 1816
    S. J. (14-2): 47.
  Authority: Res. of the Senate
    (14-2)
  Terminated: March 3, 1817, at the
    end of the 14-2.

87. Select Committee on Investi-
gation of <u>Attorney</u> General (Senate)
  Sudocs: Y4. At8:
  Established: March 3, 1924
    65 CR 3410.
  Authority: S. Res. 157 (64-1)
  Terminated: March 4, 1925, at the
    end of the 64-2.

88. Select Committee on the
Office of <u>Attorney</u> General and
Creating an Additional Department
(House)
  Established: December 4, 1816
    H. J. (14-2): 25.
  Authority: Res. of the House
    (14-2)
  Terminated: March 3, 1817, at the
    end of the 14-2.

89. Select Committee on the Case
of Dorence <u>Atwater</u> (House)
  Established: June 26, 1866
    H. J. (39-1): 906.
  Authority: Res. of the House
    (39-1)
  Terminated: March 3, 1867, at the
    end of the 39-2.

90. Select Committee to Inves-
tigate the Charges Against John
<u>Bailey</u> (House)
  Established: January 8, 1883
    14 CR 970.
  Authority: Res. of the House
    (47-2)
  Terminated: March 3, 1883
    H. rpt. 2003 (47-2) 2160.

91. Select Committee to Inves-
tigate the Proposed Purchase of
<u>Ballot</u> Boxes (House)
  Established: December 21, 1890
    H. J. (51-1): 89.
  Authority: Res. of the House
    (51-1)
  Terminated: January 31, 1891
    H. rpt. 3446 (51-2) 2885.

92. Select Committee to Inves-
tigate Incorporation into the
U.S.S.R. the <u>Baltic</u> States (House)
  Sudocs: Y4. B21:
  Established: July 27, 1953
    99 CR 10037.
  Authority: H. Res. 346 (83-1)
  Terminated: March 4, 1954, when
    the name was changed to the
    Committee on Communist Aggres-
    sion (Entry 256).
      100 CR 2717.
  Authority: H. Res. 438 (83-2)

93. Select Committee on U. S.
<u>Bank</u> Affairs (House)
  Established: March 14, 1832
    H. J. (22-1): 494.
  Authority: Res. of the House
    (22-1)
  Terminated: June 25, 1834
    H. J. (23-1): 831.

94. Select Committee on the
Expediency of an Amendment to the
Constitution, in Relation to the

Circulation of Bank Notes, And
other Paper Currency (Senate)
  Established: February 27, 1840
    S. J. (26-1): 206.
  Authority: Res. of the Senate
    (26-1)
  Terminated: July 21, 1840, at the
    end of the 26-1.

95. Select Committee on the Memo-
rial of the Bank of the U. S.
(Senate)
  Established: January 9, 1832
    S. J. (22-1): 65.
  Authority: Res. of the Senate
    (22-1)
  Terminated: March 13, 1832
    Ibid. 183.

96. Select Committee on the Con-
duct and Management of the Bank of
the U. S. (House)
  Established: November 30, 1818
    H. J. (15-2): 51.
  Authority: Res. of the House
    (15-2)
  Terminated: January 16, 1819
    Ibid. 191.

97. Select Committee on the
Petition of the Bank of the U. S.
(House)
  Established: December 13, 1820
    H. J. (16-2): 68.
  Authority: Res. of the House
    (16-2)
  Terminated: March 7, 1822
    H. J. (17-1): 324.

98. Committee on Banking and
Currency (House)
  Sudocs: Y4. B22/1:
  Established: March 2, 1865
    Cong. Globe (38-2): 1317.
  Authority: Res. of the House
    (38-2)
  Terminated: January 3, 1975, when
    the name was changed to the
    Committee on Banking, Currency
    and Housing (Entry 101).
      120 CR 34470.
  Authority: H. Res. 988 (93-2)

99. Committee on Banking and
Currency (Joint)

Established: March 4, 1923
  42 Stat. 1481.
Authority: PL 67-503
Terminated: March 3, 1925, at the
  end of the 68-2.

100. Committee on Banking and
Currency (Senate)
  Sudocs: Y4. B22/3:
  Established: May 22, 1913
    50 CR 1698.
  Authority: S. Res. 66 (63-1)
  Terminated: October 26, 1970,
    when name was changed to Com-
    mittee on Banking, Housing and
    Urban Affairs (Entry 103).
      84 Stat. 1163.
  Authority: PL 91-510

101. Committee on Banking, Cur-
rency and Housing (House)
  Sudocs: Y4. B22/1:
  Established: January 3, 1975,
    when name of Committee on Bank-
    ing and Currency was changed to
    this (Entry 98).
      120 CR 34470.
  Authority: H. Res. 988 (93-2)
  Terminated: January 4, 1977, when
    name was changed to Committee
    on Banking, Finance, and Urban
    Affairs (Entry 102).
      123 CR 70.
  Authority: H. Res. 5 (95-1)

102. Committee on Banking, Finance
and Urban Affairs (House)
  Sudocs: Y4. B22/1:
  Established: January 4, 1977,
    when name of Committee on Bank-
    ing, Currency and Housing was
    changed to this (Entry 101).
      123 CR 70.
  Authority: H. Res. 5 (95-1)
  Terminated: Still in existence at
    the end of the 97-2.

103. Committee on Banking, Housing
and Urban Affairs (Senate)
  Sudocs: Y4. B22/3:
  Established: October 26, 1970,
    when name of Committee on Bank-
    ing and Currency was changed to
    this (Entry 100).
      84 Stat. 1163.
  Authority: PL 91-510

Terminated: Still in existence at
the end of the 97-2.

**104. Select Committee on Memorials
of Banking Institutions, and Insurance Companies in Charleston, South
Carolina and the Bank of the U. S.
(House)**
  Established: January 20, 1823
    H. J. (17-2): 143.
  Authority: Res. of the House
    (17-2)
  Terminated: February 27, 1823
    Ibid. 270.

105. Select Committee on a Bankrupt Law (House)
  Established: July 15, 1861
    H. J. (37-1): 81.
  Authority: Res. of the House
    (37-1)
  Terminated: May 17, 1866
    S. J. (39-1): 714.

106. Select Committee on Establishing a Uniform System of Bankruptcy (House)
  Established: January 1, 1812
    H. J. (12-2): 210.
  Authority: Res. of the House
    (12-1)
  Terminated: July 6, 1812, at the
    end of the 12-1.

107. Select Committee on Establishing an Uniform System of Bankruptcy (Senate)
  Established: December 8, 1826
    S. J. (19-2): 26.
  Authority: Res. of the Senate
    (19-2)
  Terminated: March 3, 1827, at the
    end of the 19-2.

**108. Select Committee on the Bills
to Establish a Uniform System of
Bankruptcy Throughout the United
States (Senate)**
  Established: June 8, 1840
    S. J. (26-1): 416.
  Authority: Res. of the Senate
    (26-1)
  Terminated: July 21, 1840, at the
    end of the 26-1.

**109. Special Committee to Investigate Bankruptcy and Receivership
Proceedings in U. S. Courts
(Senate)**
  Sudocs: Y4. B22/4:
  Established: June 13, 1933
    77 CR 5864.
  Authority: S. Res. 78 (73-1)
  Terminated: May 29, 1936
    S. rpt. 2125 (74-2) 9991.

**110. Select Committee on Employment of an Agent by Deposit Banks
(House)**
  Established: January 3, 1837
    H. J. (24-2): 165.
  Authority: Res. of the House
    (24-2)
  Terminated: March 1, 1837
    H. rpt. 193 (24-2) 307.

**111. Select Committee on Failed
National Banks (Senate)**
  Sudocs: Y4. B22/2:
  Established: June 2, 1892
    23 CR 4947.
  Authority: Res. of the Senate
    (52-1)
  Terminated: March 15, 1893, when
    name was changed to Committee
    on National Banks (Entry 113).
      25 CR 17.
  Authority: Res. of the Senate
    (53-1)

**112. Select Committee on National
Banks - 1st (Senate)**
  Established: May 24, 1866
    S. J. (39-1): 463.
  Authority: Res. of the Senate
    (39-1)
  Terminated: July 28, 1866, at the
    end of the 39-1.

**113. Select Committee on National
Banks - 2nd (Senate)**
  Sudocs: Y4. B22/2:
  Established: March 15, 1893, when
    Select Committee on Failed National Banks was changed to
    this (Entry 111).
      25 CR 17.
  Authority: Res. of the Senate
    (53-1)
  Terminated: April 18, 1921
    61 CR 404-05.

Authority: S. Res. 43 (67 -
Special)

114. Select Committee to Inquire
and Report in Regard to the Char-
tering of Transport Vessels for the
Banks Expedition (Senate)
    Established: December 22, 1862
        S. J. (37-3): 65.
    Authority: Res. of the Senate
        (37-3)
    Terminated: February 9, 1863
        S. rpt. 84 (37-3) 1151.

115. Select Committee on Banks in
the District of Columbia (House)
    Established: December 4, 1844
        H. J. (28-2): 33.
    Authority: Res. of the House
        (28-2)
    Terminated: February 25, 1845
        H. rpt. 182 (28-2) 468.

116. Select Committee on the Banks
of the District of Columbia
(Senate)
    Established: December 17, 1857
        S. J. (35-1): 45.
    Authority: Res. of the Senate
        (35-1)
    Terminated: June 14, 1858, at the
        end of the 35-1.

117. Select Committee on Incorpo-
rated Banks in the District of
Columbia (House)
    Established: February 19, 1816
        H. J. (14-1): 364.
    Authority: Res. of the House
        (14-1)
    Terminated: March 3, 1817, at the
        end of the 14-2.

118. Select Committee on the Banks
of the District of Columbia (House)
    Established: December 31, 1835
        H. J. (24-1): 126.
    Authority: Res. of the House
        (24-1)
    Terminated: June 20, 1836
        H. rpt. 800 (24-1) 295.

119. Select Committee on Liquidation of the Balances Due From Banks
in Which Deposits Have Been Made
(Senate)

Established: December 27, 1824
    S. J. (18-2): 55.
Authority: Res. of the Senate
    (18-2)
Terminated: March 3, 1825, at the
    end of the 18-2.

120. Select Committee on Charges
Against Honorable Thomas H. Bayley
(House)
    Established: July 21, 1854
        H. J. (33-1): 1178.
    Authority: Res. of the House
        (33-1)
    Terminated: March 3, 1855
        H. rpt. 142 (33-2) 808.

121. Select Committee to Investigate Loss of Original Papers of
Mark and Richard Bean (Senate)
    Established: January 23, 1854
        S. J. (33-1): 121.
    Authority: Res. of the Senate
        (33-1)
    Terminated: August 7, 1854, at
        the end of the 33-1.

122. Select Committee to Investi-
gate and Study Certain Benefits for
Surviving Dependents of Deceased
Members and Former Members of the
Armed Forces (House)
    Established: August 4, 1954
        100 CR 13353.
    Authority: H. Res. 549 (83-2)
    Terminated: January 15, 1956
        101 CR 1079.
    Authority: H. Res. 35 (84-1)

123. Select Committee to Investigate the Escape of Grover Cleveland
Bergdoll (House)
    Sudocs: Y4. B45/2:
    Established: April 18, 1921
        61 CR 415.
    Authority: H. Res. 12 (67-1)
    Terminated: August 18, 1921
        H. rpt. 354 (67-1) 7921.

124. Special Committee on Victor
L. Berger (House)
    Sudocs: Y4. B45:
    Established: May 19, 1919
        58 CR 9.
    Authority: H. Res. 6 (66-1)

Terminated: October 24, 1919
  H. rpt. 413 (66-1) 7595.

125. Select Committee on the Peti-
tion of the Berkshire Association
(House)
  Established: January 29, 1817
    H. J. (14-2): 304.
  Authority: Res. of the House
    (14-2)
  Terminated: February 21, 1817
    Ibid. 440.

126. Select Committee on the Peti-
tion of the Bible Society of Phila-
delphia (House)
  Established: February 24, 1816
    H. J. (14-1): 392.
  Authority: Res. of the House
    (14-1)
  Terminated: March 5, 1816
    Ibid. 439.

127. Committee on Arrangements for
the Bicentennial (Joint)
  Sudocs: Y4. B47:
  Established: September 5, 1975
    121 CR 27723.
  Authority: S. Con. Res. 44 (94-1)
  Terminated: October 1, 1976, at
    the end of the 94-2.

128. Select Committee on a Bien-
nial Register (House)
  Established: April 28, 1832
    H. J. (22-1): 668.
  Authority: Res. of the House
    (22-1)
  Terminated: June 26, 1834
    H. rpt. 549 (23-1) 263.

129. Select Committee on Introduc-
tion of Bills and Resolutions
(House)
  Established: February 10, 1909
    43 CR 2150.
  Authority: H. Res. 553 (60-2)
  Terminated: March 3, 1909, at the
    end of the 60-2.

130. Select Committee on Fixing
the Rate and Rule of Damage on
Bills of Exchange (House)
  Established: January 13, 1826
    H. J. (19-1): 146.

Authority: Res. of the House
  (19-1)
Terminated: March 22, 1826
  H. rpt. 135 (19-1) 142.

131. Select Committee on Charge
Against the Honorable F. P. Blair,
Jr. (House)
  Established: March 23, 1864
    H. J. (38-1): 421.
  Authority: Res. of the House
    (38-1)
  Terminated: April 29, 1864
    H. rpt. 61 (38-1) 1206.

132. Select Committee on Petition
of Blair and Rives (House)
  Established: December 10, 1838
    H. J. (25-3): 50.
  Authority: Res. of the House
    (25-3)
  Terminated: August 31, 1842, at
    the end of the 27-2.

133. Select Committee on an Asylum
for the Blind (House)
  Established: December 12, 1831
    H. J. (22-1): 25.
  Authority: Res. of the House
    (22-1)
  Terminated: December 28, 1831
    Ibid. 101.

134. Select Committee on Memorial
of the New England Asylum for the
Blind (House)
  Established: January 3, 1831
    H. J. (21-2): 129.
  Authority: Res. of the House
    (21-2)
  Terminated: February 5, 1831
    Ibid. 266.

135. Select Committee on Petition
for the Benefit of the Blind
(House)
  Established: May 4, 1846
    H. J. (29-1): 740.
  Authority: Res. of the House
    (29-1)
  Terminated: August 10, 1846, at
    the end of the 29-1.

136. Select Committee on Setting
Apart the Bonus of the National
Bank and the United States Share of

its Dividends for Internal Improve-
ments (House)
   Established: December 16, 1816
     H. J. (14-2): 73.
   Authority: Res. of the House
     (14-2)
   Terminated: December 23, 1816
     Ibid. 93.

137. Select Committee on the True
Boundary of the Chickasaw Indians,
Between the Tennessee and Missis-
sippi Rivers (House)
   Established: February 6, 1834
     H. J. (23-1): 285.
   Authority: Res. of the House
     (23-1)
   Terminated: May 6, 1834
     Ibid. 586.

138. Select Committee on the
Bounty Land Act of 1850 (House)
   Established: December 5, 1850
     H. J. (31-2): 30.
   Authority: Res. of the House
     (31-2)
   Terminated: August 31, 1852, at
     the end of the 31-2.

139. Select Committee on Allowing
a Commutation of Bounty Lands
(House)
   Established: December 11, 1816
     H. J. (14-2): 63.
   Authority: Res. of the House
     (14-2)
   Terminated: January 11, 1817
     Ibid. 185.

140. Select Committee on the
Boynton Investigation (House)
   Established: February 8, 1884
     15 CR 1005.
   Authority: Res. of the House
     (48-1)
   Terminated: July 7, 1884, at the
     end of the 48-1.

141. Special Committee to Inves-
tigate Attempts at Bribery, etc.
(Senate)
   Established: May 17, 1894
     S. J. (53-2): 197.
   Authority: Res. of the Senate
     (53-2)

   Terminated: August 2, 1894
     S. rpt. 606 (53-2) 3188.

142. Select Committee on British
Depredations of the Northern
Frontier (House)
   Established: January 25, 1832
     H. J. (22-1): 239.
   Authority: Res. of the House
     (22-1)
   Terminated: March 17, 1832
     Ibid. 506.

143. Select Committee on the
Charges Against the Honorable
James Brooks (House)
   Established: January 10, 1870
     Cong. Globe (41-3): 418.
   Authority: Res. of the House
     (41-3)
   Terminated: March 3, 1871, at the
     end of the 41-3.

144. Select Committee on the
Brownstown Treaty (House)
   Established: January 26, 1820
     H. J. (16-1): 173.
   Authority: Res. of the House
     (16-1)
   Terminated: May 12, 1820
     H. rpt. 98 (16-1) 40.

145. Select Committee to Inquire
into the Official Conduct of Peter
J. Bruin, one of the Judges of the
Superior Court of the Mississippi
Territory (House)
   Established: April 18, 1808
     H. J. (10-1): 589.
   Authority: Res. of the House
     (10-1)
   Terminated: April 21, 1808
     Ibid. 607.

146. Committee on the Budget
(House)
   Sudocs: Y4. B85/3:
   Established: July 12, 1974
     88 Stat. 300
   Authority: PL 93-344
   Terminated: Still in existence at
     the end of the 97-2.

147. Committee on the Budget
(Senate)
   Sudocs: Y4. B85/2:

Established: July 12, 1974
88 Stat. 300.
Authority: PL 93-344
Terminated: Still in existence at
the end of the 97-2.

148. Committee for Consideration
of a National Budget (Senate)
Sudocs: Y4. B86/2:
Established: July 14, 1919
58 CR 2549.
Authority: S. Res. 58 (66-1)
Terminated: April 13, 1920
S. rpt. 524 (66-2) 7649.

149. Select Committee on the
Budget (House)
Sudocs: Y4. B86/1:
Established: July 31, 1919
58 CR 3437 (66-1)
Authority: H. Res. 168 (66-1)
Terminated: October 11, 1919
H. rpt. 373 (66-1)

150. Select Committee on the
Budget (House)
Established: April 11, 1921
61 CR 84.
Authority: H. Res. 8 (67-1)
Terminated: April 25, 1921
H. rpt. 14 (67-1) 7920.

151. Special Committee on the
Budget (Senate)
Established: July 14, 1919
58 CR 2549.
Authority: S. Res. 58 (66-1)
Terminated: April 13, 1920
S. rpt. 524 (66-2) 7649.

152. Committee on Budget Control
(Joint)
Established: October 27, 1972
86 Stat. 1324.
Authority: PL 92-599
Terminated: April 18, 1973
H. rpt. 147 (93-1) 13022-4.

153. Select Committee on Cabinet
Officers on the Floor of the Senate
(Senate)
Established: December 7, 1880
11 CR 14.
Authority: Res. of the Senate
(46-3)

Terminated: August 8, 1882, at
the end of the 47-1.

154. Select Committee on Letter of
John C. Calhoun, Vice President,
Asking for an Investigation of His
Conduct During His Tenure as Secre-
tary of War (House)
Established: December 29, 1826
H. J. (19-2): 110.
Authority: Res. of the House
(19-2)
Terminated: February 13, 1827
H. rpt. 79 (19-2) 159.

155. Select Committee on the
Admission of California to the
Union (Senate)
Established: January 24, 1849
S. J. (30-2): 148.
Authority: Res. of the Senate
(30-2)
Terminated: September 30, 1850,
at the end of the 31-1.

156. Select Committee to Investigate Certain Language Inserted in
the Congressional Record by Representative Callaway of Texas (House)
Established: July 21, 1916
53 CR 11402.
Authority: H. Res. 315 (64-2)
Terminated: August 22, 1916
H. rpt. 1170 (64-1) 6910.

157. Special Committee on Campaign
Expenditures (Senate)
Established: June 17, 1924
65 CR 11139.
Authority: S. Res. 248 (68-1)
Terminated: February 12, 1925
S. rpt. 1100 (68-2) 8389.

158. Special Committee to Investigate Campaign Expenditures (House)
Sudocs: Y4. C15:
Established: May 29, 1928, as a
select committee
69 CR 10689.
Authority: H. Res. 232 (70-1)
Terminated: December 20, 1974, at
the end of the 93-2.

159. Special Committee to Investigate Campaign Expenditures (Senate)

Established: July 11, 1932
  75 CR 14990.
Authority: S. Res. 174 (72-1)
Terminated: May 31, 1957
  S. rpt. 395 (85-1) 11977.

160. Committee on Relations with
Canada (Senate)
  Sudocs: Y4. C16:
  Established: January 13, 1892,
    having been preceded by a
    select committee (Entry 161).
    23 CR 285.
  Authority: Res. of the Senate
    (52-1)
  Terminated: April 18, 1921
    61 CR 404-405.
  Authority: S. Res. 43 (67 -
    Special)

161. Select Committee on Relations
with Canada (Senate)
  Established: July 31, 1888
    19 CR 7062.
  Authority: Res. of the Senate
    (50-1)
  Terminated: January 13, 1892,
    when made a standing committee
    (Entry 160).
    23 CR 285.
  Authority: Res. of the Senate
    (52-1)

162. Select Committee on Amend-
ments in the Act for the Relief
of Canadian Volunteers (House)
  Established: April 12, 1816
    H. J. (14-1): 634.
  Authority: Res. of the House
    (14-1)
  Terminated: January 11, 1817
    H. J. (14-2): 185.

163. Select Committee on Assis-
tance to the State of Indiana in
Opening a Canal Around the Falls
of the Ohio (House)
  Established: December 15, 1824
    H. J. (18-2): 49.
  Authority: Res. of the House
    (18-2)
  Terminated: March 3, 1825, at
    the end of the 18-2.

164. Select Committee on the
Manufacture of Cannon and Small

Arms and the Munitions of War
(House)
  Established: November 12, 1811
    H. J. (12-1): 36.
  Authority: Res. of the House
    (12-1)
  Terminated: December 16, 1811
    Ibid. 139.

165. Select Committee on the
Expenditure of Monies Appropriated
for the Capitol (House)
  Established: January 19, 1811
    H. J. (11-3): 144.
  Authority: Res. of the House
    (11-3)
  Terminated: February 6, 1811
    Ibid. 226.

166. Committee on Sanitary Condi-
tion of the Capitol (House)
  Established: January 24, 1895
    27 CR 1308.
  Authority: Res. of the House
    (53-3)
  Terminated: March 2, 1895
    H. rpt. 1980 (53-3) 3346.

167. Select Committee to Celebrate
the Centennial of the Laying of the
Capitol Cornerstone (Joint)
  Sudocs: Y4. C17:
  Established: August 17, 1893
    S. J. (53-1): 21.
  Authority: H. Jt. Res. (53-1)
  Terminated: August 28, 1894, at
    the end of the 53-2.

168. Select Committee on Pur-
chasing Catlin's Collection of
Indian Scenes and Portraits
(Senate)
  Established: February 3, 1852
    S. J. (32-1): 173.
  Authority: Res. of the Senate
    (32-1)
  Terminated: June 23, 1852
    S. rpt. 271 (32-1) 631.

169. Select Committee on Petitions
of Citizens of Cedar Bluffs, Alabama (House)
  Established: February 20, 1849
    H. J. (30-2): 477.
  Authority: Res. of the House
    (30-2)

Terminated: March 3, 1849, at the
end of the 30-2.

170. Select Committee to Study
Censure Charges (Senate)
  Established: August 2, 1954
  100 CR 12989.
  Authority: Res. of the Senate
  (83-2)
  Terminated: December 2, 1954,
  when a motion to censure Senator McCarthy passed the Senate.
  100 CR 16392.
  Authority: S. Res. 301 (83-2)

171. Committee on the Census
(House)
  Sudocs: Y4. C33/1:
  Established: December 2, 1901,
  having been preceded by the
  Select Committee on the Twelfth
  Census (Entry 182).
    35 CR 47.
  Authority: Res. of the House
  (57-1)
  Terminated: January 2, 1947
  60 Stat. 812.
  Authority: PL 79-601

172. Committee on the Census
(Senate)
  Sudocs: Y4. C33/2:
  Established: December 12, 1887,
  having been preceded by a se-
  lect committee (Entry 180).
    19 CR 16.
  Authority: Res. of the Senate
  (50-1)
  Terminated: April 18, 1921
  61 CR 404-405.
  Authority: S. Res. 43 (67 -
  Special)

173. Select Committee on Deficien-
cies in the Returns of the Census
(House)
  Established: February 28, 1811
  H. J. (11-3): 355.
  Authority: Res. of the House
  (11-3)
  Terminated: March 1, 1811
  Ibid. 364.

174. Select Committee on the Third
Census (House)

Established: June 1, 1809
  H. J. (11-1): 66.
  Authority: Res. of the House
  (11-1)
  Terminated: June 28, 1809
  Ibid. 200.

175. Select Committee on the
Fifth Census (House)
  Established: December 3, 1828
  H. J. (20-2): 23.
  Authority: Res. of the House
  (20-2)
  Terminated: May 3, 1832
  H. rpt. 463 (22-1) 227.

176. Select Committee on Errors in
the Sixth Census (House)
  Established: December 10, 1844
  H. J. (28-2): 47.
  Authority: Res. of the House
  (28-2)
  Terminated: March 3, 1845, at the
  end of the 28-2.

177. Select Committee on the Sev-
enth Census (Senate)
  Established: December 14, 1848
  S. J. (30-2): 64.
  Authority: Res. of the Senate
  (30-2)
  Terminated: June 28, 1852
  S. rpt. 276 (32-1) 631.

178. Select Committee on the Ninth
Census (Senate)
  Established: January 29, 1869
  Cong. Globe (40-3): 715.
  Authority: Res. of the Senate
  (40-3)
  Terminated: March 3, 1869, at the
  end of the 40-3.

179. Select Committee on the Tenth
Census (House)
  Established: December 13, 1881
  13 CR 88.
  Authority: Res. of the House
  (47-1)
  Terminated: March 3, 1887, at the
  end of the 48-2.

180. Select Committee on the Tenth
Census (Senate)
  Established: April 4, 1878
  S. J. (45-2): 365.

Authority: Res. of the Senate
  (45-2)
Terminated: March 3, 1887, at the
  end of the 49-2. A standing
  committee created in next Congress (Entry 172).

181. Select Committee on the Elev-
enth Census (House)
  Established: December 21, 1887
  19 CR 153.
  Authority: Res. of the House
    (50-1)
  Terminated: March 3, 1893, at the
    end of the 52-2.

182. Select Committee on the
Twelfth Census (House)
  Established: January 27, 1898
  31 CR 6379.
  Authority: Res. of the House
    (55-2)
  Terminated: December 2, 1901,
    when the standing Committee
    on the Census was established
    (Entry 171).
      35 CR 47.
  Authority: Res. of the House
    (57-1)

183. Select Committee on the
Census Bill (House)
  Established: June 26, 1841
  H. J. (27-1): 282.
  Authority: Res. of the House
    (27-1)
  Terminated: July 29, 1841
    Ibid. 289.

184. Select Committee on the
Centennial Celebration and the
Proposed National Census of 1875
(House)
  Established: December 6, 1872
  H. J. (42-3): 43.
  Authority: Res. of the House
    (42-3)
  Terminated: August 15, 1876, at
    the end of the 44-1.

185. Select Committee on the
Centennial of the Constitution and
the Discovery of America (Senate)
  Established: July 31, 1886
  17 CR 7779.

Authority: Res. of the Senate
  (49-1)
Terminated: March 3, 1889, at the
  end of the 50-2.

186. Select Committee on the
Central Pacific Railroad (House)
  Established: January 12, 1874
  H. J. (43-1): 226.
  Authority: Res. of the House
    (43-1)
  Terminated: June 23, 1874, at the
    end of the 43-1.

187. Special Committee to Investi-
gate Centralization of Heavy Indus-
try in the United States (Senate)
  Sudocs: Y4. C33/3:
  Established: December 21, 1943
    89 CR 10956.
  Authority: S. Res. 190 (78-1)
  Terminated: December 19, 1944, at
    the end of the 78-2.

188. Select Committee on Declaring
the Assent of Congress to an Act of
the General Assembly of North Caro-
lina "Authorizing the State of Ten-
nessee to Perfect Titles to Lands,
Reserved by the Cession Act"
(House)
  Established: January 16, 1806
  H. J. (9-1): 137.
  Authority: Res. of the House
    (9-1)
  Terminated: January 28, 1806
    Ibid. 168.

189. Select Committee on Charges
Against a Member of the Committee
on Accounts (House)
  Established: February 18, 1859
  H. J. (35-2): 438.
  Authority: Res. of the House
    (35-2)
  Terminated: February 24, 1859
    H. rpt. 186 (35-2) 1018.

190. Select Committee on Charges
of Corruption Contained in the New
York Tribune (House)
  Established: June 30, 1862
  H. J. (37-2): 950.
  Authority: Order of the House
    (37-2)

Terminated: January 12, 1863
   H. J. (37-3): 181.

191. Select Committee on Charges
Preferred by George Kremer, a mem-
ber from Pennsylvania, Against the
Speaker of the House (House)
   Established: February 3, 1825
      H. J. (18-2): 198.
   Authority: Res. of the House
      (18-2)
   Terminated: February 9, 1825
      Ibid. 219.

192. Select Committee to Investi-
gate Charges Against the Conduct of
the Secretary of the Treasury on
Charges Preferred by Ninian Edwards
(House)
   Established: April 19, 1824
      H. J. (18-1): 433.
   Authority: Res. of the House
      (18-1)
   Terminated: June 21, 1824
      Finance 712 (18-1) Am. St.
      Papers, v. 13.

193. Select Committee on the Chem-
ist of the Agricultural Department
(House)
   Established: January 19, 1864
      H. J. (38-1): 162.
   Authority: Res. of the House
      (38-1)
   Terminated: March 21, 1864
      H. rpt. 35 (38-1) 1206.

194. Select Committee on the Memo-
rial of Certain Cherokee Claimants
(Senate)
   Established: May 30, 1848
      S. J. (30-1): 361.
   Authority: Res. of the Senate
      (30-1)
   Terminated: August 14, 1848, at
      the end of the 30-1.

195. Select Committee to Investi-
gate Complaints of the Cherokee
Nation of the Invasion of their
Territory by Intruders (Senate)
   Established: August 5, 1892
      23 CR 7063.
   Authority: Res. of the Senate
      (52-1)

Terminated: March 3, 1893, at the
   end of the 52-2.

196. Select Committee on the
Chesapeake and Delaware Canal
(House)
   Established: January 13, 1813
      H. J. (12-2): 171.
   Authority: Res. of the House
      (12-2)
   Terminated: January 26, 1813
      Ibid. 221.

197. Select Committee on the Pro-
posed Chesapeake and Ohio Canal
(House)
   Established: December 5, 1823
      H. J. (18-1): 26.
   Authority: Res. of the House
      (18-1)
   Terminated: May 27, 1824, at the
      end of the 18-1.

198. Committee on Chickamauga and
Chattanooga National Military Park,
Dedication (Joint)
   Sudocs: Y4. C43:
   Established: February 9, 1895
      27 CR 1974.
   Authority: H. Con. Res. (53-3)
   Terminated: March 26, 1896
      H. rpt. 967 (54-1) 3460.

199. Select Committee on Children,
Youth, and Families (House)
   Sudocs: Y4. C43:
   Established: September 29, 1982
      128 CR H7963.
   Authority: H. Res. 421 (97-2)
   Terminated: Still in existence at
      the end of the 97-2.

200. Special Committee to Investi-
gate Chinese Immigration (Joint)
   Sudocs: Y4. C44:
   Established: July 17, 1876
      4 CR 4672.
   Authority: House Res. (44-1)
   Terminated: February 27, 1877
      S. rpt. 689 (44-2) 1734.

201. Select Committee on Investi-
gation of Cilley's Death in a Duel
(House)
   Established: February 28, 1837
      H. J. (25-2): 507.

Authority: Res. of the House
  (25-2)
Terminated: May 10, 1838
  H. rpt. 825 (25-2) 336.

202. Select Committee on Altering
the Time for Holding the Circuit
Court in the District of North
Carolina (House)
  Established: January 23, 1806
    H. J. (9-1): 157.
  Authority: Res. of the House
    (9-1)
  Terminated: January 30, 1806
    Ibid. 175.

203. Committee on Civil Service
(House)
  Sudocs: Y4. C49/1:
  Established: January 14, 1924,
    when the Committee on Reform in
    the Civil Service was changed
    to this (Entry 206).
    H. J. (68-1): 161.
  Authority: Res. of the House
    (68-1)
  Terminated: January 2, 1947, when
    the Committee on Post Office
    and Civil Service was estab-
    lished (Entry 1088).
    60 Stat. 812.
  Authority: PL 79-601

204. Committee on the Civil Ser-
vice (Senate)
  Sudocs: Y4. C49/2:
  Established: April 18, 1921,
    having been preceded by the
    Committee on Civil Service and
    Retrenchment (Entry 212).
    61 CR 404-05.
  Authority: S. Res. 43 (67 -
    Special)
  Terminated: January 2, 1947, when
    it was replaced by the Commit-
    tee on Post Office and Civil
    Service (Entry 1089).
    60 Stat. 812.
  Authority: PL 79-601

205. Committee to Examine the
Several Branches in Civil Service
(Senate)
  Established: December 8, 1875
    4 CR 187.

Authority: Res. of the Senate
  (44-1)
Terminated: April 18, 1921
  61 CR 404-05.
Authority: S. Res. 43 (67 -
  Special)

206. Committee on Reform in the
Civil Service (House)
  Established: August 18, 1893
    H. J. (53-1): 13.
  Authority: Res. of the House
    (53-1)
  Terminated: January 14, 1924,
    when the name was changed to
    the Committee on Civil Service
    (Entry 203).
    H. J. (68-1): 161.
  Authority: Res. of the House
    (68-1)

207. Select Committee to Investi-
gate the Operations of the Civil
Service (Senate)
  Established: March 13, 1888
    19 CR 1995.
  Authority: Res. of the Senate
    (50-1)
  Terminated: March 3, 1889, at the
    end of the 50-2.

208. Select Committee on the Re-
organization of the Civil Service
(House)
  Established: December 5, 1871
    Cong. Globe (42-2): 22.
  Authority: Res. of the House
    (42-2)
  Terminated: March 3, 1875, at the
    end of the 43-2.

209. Select Committee on Civil
Service Reform (House)
  Established: October 22, 1877,
    having been preceded by a
    standing committee in the pre-
    vious session (Entry 216).
    6 CR 132.
  Authority: Res. of the House
    (45-1)
  Terminated: August 18, 1893, when
    it was made a standing commit-
    tee (Entry 206).
    H. J. (53-1): 13.
  Authority: Res. of the House
    (53-1)

210. Special Committee to Investigate the <u>Civil</u> Service System (Senate)
   Established: April 1, 1938
      83 CR 4513.
   Authority: S. Res. 198 (75-3)
   Terminated: January 3, 1941, at
      the end of the 76-3.

211. Select Committee on Investigation of Illegal Appointments in <u>Civil</u> Service (Senate)
   Sudocs: Y4. C49/3:
   Established: May 19, 1928
      69 CR 9143.
   Authority: S. Res. 154 (70-1)
   Terminated: March 3, 1929, at the
      end of the 70-2.

212. Committee on <u>Civil</u> Service and Retrenchment (<u>Senate</u>)
   Sudocs: Y4. C49/2:
   Established: December 4, 1873
      2 CR 56.
   Authority: Res. of the Senate
      (43-1)
   Terminated: April 18, 1921, when
      the name was changed to Com-
      mittee on <u>Civil</u> Service
      (Entry 204).
         61 CR 404-05.
   Authority: S. Res. 43 (67 -
      Special)

213. Select Committee to Investigate the Examining Division of the <u>Civil</u> Service Commission (Senate)
   Established: January 19, 1922
      62 CR 1386.
   Authority: S. Res. 199 (67-2)
   Terminated: July 25, 1922
      S. rpt. 836 (67-2) 7954.

214. Committee to Reorganize the <u>Civil</u> Service in the Departments (<u>Joint</u>)
   Established: February 1, 1869
      Cong. Globe (40-3): 775.
   Authority: S. Con. Res. (40-3)
   Terminated: March 3, 1869, at the
      end of the 40-3.

215. Special Committee to Investigate Administration and Operation of <u>Civil</u> Service Laws (Senate)
   Sudocs: Y4. C49/4:

Established: April 1, 1938
   83 CR 4513.
Authority: S. Res. 198 (75-3)
Terminated: January 25, 1945
   S. rpt. 24 (79-1) 10925.

216. Committee on <u>Civil</u> Service Reform (House)
   Sudocs: Y4. C49/1:
   Established: December 20, 1875
      4 CR 251.
   Authority: Res. of the House
      (44-1)
   Terminated: March 3, 1877, at the
      end of the 44-2. Followed by a
      select committee in subsequent
      sessions (Entry 209).

217. Select Committee on the <u>Civil</u> Service of the United States (House)
   Established: March 12, 1865
      Cong. Globe (39-1): 1342.
   Authority: Res. of the House
      (39-1)
   Terminated: March 3, 1867, at the
      end of the 39-2.

218. Select Committee on Super-intendence of <u>Civil</u> Works By Military (House)
   Established: February 13, 1854
      H. J. (33-1): 372.
   Authority: Res. of the House
      (33-1)
   Terminated: March 3, 1855, at the
      end of the 33-2.

219. Committee on <u>Claims</u> (House)
   Sudocs: Y4. C52/1:
   Established: November 14, 1794
      H. J. (3-1): 231.
   Authority: Res. of the House
      (3-1)
   Terminated: January 2, 1947, when
      its functions were transferred
      to the Committee on the Judi-
      ciary (Entry 731).
         60 Stat. 812.
   Authority: PL 79-601

220. Committee on <u>Claims</u> (Senate)
   Sudocs: Y4. C52/2:
   Established: December 10, 1816
      Annals (14-2): 30.

Authority: Res. of the Senate
(14-2)
Terminated: January 2, 1947
60 Stat. 812.
Authority: PL 79-601

221. Select Committee on the Deci-
sions of R. B. Lee, Commissioner
of Claims (House)
Established: December 6, 1816
H. J. (14-2): 37.
Authority: Res. of the House
(14-2)
Terminated: December 31, 1816
Ibid. 125.

222. Select Committee on Prosecu-
tion of Claims by Officers of the
House (House)
Established: March 9, 1840
H. J. (26-1): 550.
Authority: Res. of the House
(26-1)
Terminated: July 21, 1840, at the
end of the 26-1.

223. Select Committee to Investi-
gate Charges Against Honorable
Senator Powell Clayton (Senate)
Established: January 9, 1872
Cong. Globe (42-2): 318.
Authority: Res. of the Senate
(42-2)
Terminated: February 26, 1873
S. rpt. 512 (42-3) 1550.

224. Select Committee on Increas-
ing the Salary of the Clerk of the
House (House)
Established: March 15, 1816
H. J. (14-1): 496.
Authority: Res. of the House
(14-1)
Terminated: March 23, 1816
Ibid. 527.

225. Select Committee on Clothing
Destitute Soldiers (House)
Established: March 11, 1867
Cong. Globe (40-1): 61.
Authority: Res. of the House
(40-1)
Terminated: March 12, 1867
S. J. (40-1): 39.

226. Select Committee on Furnish-
ing the Army, Navy, and Indian
Department Clothing of Domestic
Manufacture (House)
Established: January 4, 1820
H. J. (16-1): 105.
Authority: Res. of the House
(16-1)
Terminated: May 15, 1820, at the
end of the 16-1.

227. Select Committee on Alter-
ation in the Laws Providing for
the Pay, Subsistence, and Clothing
of the Militia of the United
States, When Called into Actual
Service (House)
Established: January 25, 1808
H. J. (10-1): 295.
Authority: Res. of the House
(10-1)
Terminated: March 1, 1808
Ibid. 430.

228. Committee on Coast and Insu-
lar Survey (Senate)
Sudocs: Y4. C63:
Established: December 15, 1899
33 CR 441.
Authority: Adoption of the rules
(56-1)
Terminated: April 18, 1921
61 CR 404-05.
Authority: S. Res. 43 (67 -
Special)

229. Committee on Coast Defenses
(Senate)
Established: March 13, 1885
17 CR 37.
Authority: Res. of the Senate
(49-1)
Terminated: April 18, 1921
61 CR 404-05.
Authority: S. Res. 43 (67 -
Special)

230. Select Committee on Coast
Survey (House)
Established: February 19, 1842
H. J. (27-2): 414.
Authority: Res. of the House
(27-2)
Terminated: January 12, 1843
H. rpt. 43 (27-3) 426.

231. Committee on Coinage, Weights and Measures (House)
Sudocs: Y4. C66:
Established: January 21, 1864
Cong. Globe (38-1): 297.
Authority: Res. of the House (38-1)
Terminated: January 2, 1947
60 Stat. 812.
Authority: PL 79-601

232. Select Committee on Continuing in Force the Act Regulating Currency of Foreign Coins (House)
Established: January 13, 1820
H. J. (16-1): 132.
Authority: Res. of the House (16-1)
Terminated: February 5, 1823
H. rpt. 83 (17-2) 87.

233. Select Committee on Coins (House)
Established: December 15, 1831
H. J. (22-1): 57.
Authority: Res. of the House (22-1)
Terminated: March 26, 1836
H. J. (24-1): 566.

234. Select Committee on Coins (Senate)
Established: December 10, 1829
S. J. (21-1): 24.
Authority: Res. of the Senate (21-1)
Terminated: December 15, 1830
S. doc. 3 (21-2) 203.

235. Select Committee on Value of Certain Coins (House)
Established: December 20, 1847
H. J. (30-1): 121.
Authority: Res. of the House (30-1)
Terminated: August 14, 1848, at the end of the 30-1.

236. Select Committee on Coins, Weights, and Measures (Senate)
Established: May 18, 1866
S. J. (39-1): 444.
Authority: Res. of the Senate (39-1)
Terminated: July 16, 1866
S. J. (39-1): 656.

237. Select Committee on Foreign Coins and Regulating Weights and Measures (House)
Established: November 27, 1818
H. J. (15-2): 45.
Authority: Res. of the House (15-2)
Terminated: January 26, 1819
Ibid. 211.

238. Select Committee on the Occurrence Alluded to in the Letter of I. A. Coles (House)
Established: December 8, 1809
H. J. (11-2): 46.
Authority: Res. of the House (11-2)
Terminated: December 30, 1809
Ibid. 107.

239. Select Committee on Collins and other Mail Steamers (House)
Established: February 13, 1854
H. J. (33-1): 366.
Authority: Res. of the House (33-1)
Terminated: July 14, 1854
H. rpt. 281 (33-1) 744.

240. Select Committee on Colt's Patent (House)
Established: July 8, 1854
H. J. (33-1): 1113.
Authority: Res. of the House (33-1)
Terminated: February 23, 1855
H. rpt. 132 (33-2) 808.

241. Select Committee on the Establishment of a Military Post at the Mouth of the Columbia River (House)
Established: December 8, 1824
H. J. (18-2): 28.
Authority: Res. of the House (18-2)
Terminated: January 16, 1826
H. rpt. 35 (19-1) 141.

242. Select Committee on the Occupation of the Columbia River (Senate)
Established: February 7, 1838
S. J. (25-2): 209.
Authority: Res. of the Senate (25-2)

Terminated: July 9, 1838, at the end of the 25-2.

243. Select Committee on Settlements at the Mouth of the Columbia River (House)
Established: December 19, 1820
H. J. (16-2): 80
Authority: Res. of the House (16-2)
Terminated: March 3, 1829, at the end of the 20-2.

244. Select Committee on the Columbian Exposition (House)
Established: January 4, 1892
H. J. (52-1): 18.
Authority: Res. of the House (52-1)
Terminated: March 3, 1893, at the end of the 52-2.

245. Select Committee on Petition of the Columbian Institute (House)
Established: February 9, 1824
H. J. (18-1): 216.
Authority: Res. of the House (18-1)
Terminated: February 25, 1824
Ibid. 270.

246. Committee on Commerce (House)
Sudocs: Y4. C73/1:
Established: December 18, 1819, when the Committee on Commerce and Manufactures was divided into two committees (Entries 249, 812).
Annals (16-1): 709.
Authority: Res. of the House (16-1)
Terminated: January 28, 1892, when it was replaced by the Committee on Interstate and Foreign Commerce (Entry 707).
23 CR 653.
Authority: Res. of the House (52-1)

247. Committee on Commerce - 1st (Senate)
Sudocs: Y4. C73/2:
Established: December 12, 1825, when the Committee on Commerce and Manufactures was divided into two committees (Entries 250, 813).
Annals (19-1): 4.
Authority: Res. of the Senate (19-1)
Terminated: January 2, 1947, when its functions transferred to Committee on Interstate and Foreign Commerce (Entry 710).
60 Stat. 812.
Authority: PL 79-601

248. Committee on Commerce - 2nd (Senate)
Sudocs: Y4. C73/2:
Established: April 13, 1961, when it replaced the Committee on Interstate and Foreign Commerce (Entry 710).
107 CR 5708.
Authority: S. Res. 117 (87-1)
Terminated: February 11, 1977.
Approved February 4, 1977.
123 CR 3691.
Authority: S. Res. 4 (95-1) when its functions transferred to newly created Committee on Commerce, Science and Transportation (Entry 251).

249. Committee on Commerce and Manufactures (House)
Established: December 14, 1795
Annals (4-1): 143.
Authority: Res. of the House (4-1)
Terminated: December 18, 1819, when it was divided into two committees (Entries 246, 812).
Annals (16-1): 709.
Authority: Res. of the House (16-1)

250. Committee on Commerce and Manufactures (Senate)
Established: December 10, 1816
Annals (14-2): 30.
Authority: Res. of the Senate (14-2)
Terminated: December 12, 1825, when committee was divided into two committees--Committee on Commerce and Committee on Manufactures (Entries 247, 813).
Ibid. (19-1) 4.

Authority: Res. of the Senate
(19-1)

251. Committee on Commerce, Science and Transportation (Senate)
Sudocs: Y4. C73/7:
Established: February 11, 1977,
when the functions of the
Committee on Aeronautical and
Space Sciences and the Committee on Commerce were transferred to this committee
(Entries 6, 248).
123 CR 3691.
Authority: S. Res. 4 (95-1)
Terminated: Still in existence at
the end of the 97-2.

252. Select Committee on Committees (House)
Sudocs: Y4. C73/6:
Established: January 31, 1973
119 CR 2812.
Authority: H. Res. 132 (93-1)
Terminated: December 20, 1974, at
the end of the 93-2.

253. Select Committee on Committees (House)
Sudocs: Y4. C73/6:
Established: March 19, 1979
H. J. (96-1): 280.
Authority: H. Res. 118 (96-1)
Terminated: April 1, 1980
H. rpt. 866 (96-2) 13362.

254. Select Committee to Investigate Commodity Transaction (House)
Sudocs: Y4. C73/4:
Established: December 18, 1947
93 CR 11640.
Authority: H. Res. 404 (80-1)
Terminated: December 31, 1948
H. rpt. 2472 (80-2) 11213.

255. Select Committee on Claims
of the United States Against the
Commonwealth Bank of Boston (House)
Established: April 29, 1840
H. J. (26-1): 853.
Authority: Res. of the House
(26-1)
Terminated: July 21, 1840, at the
end of the 26-1.

256. Select Committee on Communist
Aggression (House)
Sudocs: Y4. C73/5:
Established: March 4, 1954, when
it replaced the Committee to
Investigate Incorporation into
the U.S.S.R. the Baltic States
(Entry 92).
100 CR 2717.
Authority: H. Res. 438 (83-2)
Terminated: December 31, 1954, at
the end of the 83-2.

257. Special Committee to Investigate Communist Propaganda in the
United States (House)
Sudocs: Y4. C73/3:
Established: May 22, 1930
72 CR 9397.
Authority: H. Res. 220 (71-2)
Terminated: January 17, 1931
H. rpt. 2290 (71-3) 9331.

258. Select Committee on Changing
the Mode of Compensating the Members of Congress (House)
Established: March 4, 1816
H. J. (14-1): 433.
Authority: Res. of the House
(14-1)
Terminated: March 6, 1816
Ibid. 445.

259. Select Committee on Compensation (Senate)
Established: June 26, 1866
S. J. (39-1): 574.
Authority: Res. of the Senate
(39-1)
Terminated: July 2, 1866
S. rpt. 127 (39-1) 1240.

260. Select Committee on the Resolution to Amend the Constitution on
Compensation of Congress (Senate)
Established: December 11, 1816
S. J. (14-2): 40.
Authority: Res. of the Senate
(14-2)
Terminated: March 3, 1817, at the
end of the 14-2.

261. Select Committee on Repealing
or Modifying a Law on Compensation
of Members of Congress (Senate)

Established: December 9, 1816
  S. J. (14-2): 37.
Authority: Res. of the Senate
  (14-2)
Terminated: February 6, 1817
  Ibid. 205.

262. Select Committee on the Com-
pensation of the Officers of the
Senate and House of Representatives
(House)
  Established: December 5, 1805
    H. J. (9-1): 30.
  Authority: Res. of the House
    (9-1)
  Terminated: January 24, 1806
    Ibid. 158.

263. Select Committee on Addi-
tional Compensation to the Officers
of Congress (House)
  Established: July 2, 1812
    H. J. (12-1): 847.
  Authority: Res. of the House
    (12-1)
  Terminated: July 6, 1812, at the
    end of the 12-1.

264. Select Committee on Compen-
sation to Witnesses in Criminal
Cases (House)
  Established: November 19, 1811
    H. J. (12-1): 63.
  Authority: Res. of the House
    (12-1)
  Terminated: July 6, 1812, at the
    end of the 12-1.

265. Select Committee in Relation
to the First Comptroller, William
Medill (Senate)
  Established: June 1, 1860
    S. J. (36-1): 545.
  Authority: Res. of the Senate
    (36-1)
  Terminated: June 12, 1860
    S. rpt. 270 (36-1) 1040.

266. Committee to Inquire Into the
Condition of the States Which
Formed the So-Called Confederate
States (Joint)
  Established: December 13, 1865
    S. J. (39-1): 37.
  Authority: H. J. Res. (39-1)

Terminated: June 8, 1866
  S. rpt. 112 (39-1) 1240.

267. Committee on Organization of
the Congress (Joint)
  Sudocs: Y4. C76/3:
  Established: December 15, 1944
    90 CR 9527.
  Authority: S. Con. Res. 23 (78-2)
  Terminated: May 31, 1946
    S. rpt. 1400 (79-2) 11016.

268. Select Committee on the Con-
dition of the Country (House)
  Established: December 4, 1860
    H. J. (36-2): 37.
  Authority: Res. of the House
    (36-2)
  Terminated: January 29, 1861
    H. rpt. 31 (36-2) 1104.

269. Special Committee on Official
Conduct (Senate)
  Sudocs: Y4. C76/8:
  Established: January 18, 1977
    123 CR 1363.
  Authority: S. Res. 36 (95-1)
  Terminated: March 10, 1977
    S. rpt. 49 (95-1).

270. Committee on Organization of
the Congress (Joint)
  Sudocs: Y4. C76/3:
  Established: March 9, 1965
    111 CR 4780.
  Authority: S. Con. Res. 2 (89-1)
  Terminated: July 28, 1966
    S. rpt. 1414 (89-2) 12712-2.

271. Special Committee on Organi-
zation of Congress (Senate)
  Sudocs: Y4. C76/6:
  Established: August 26, 1966
    112 CR 20759.
  Authority: S. Res. 293 (89-2)
  Terminated: October 14, 1968, at
    the end of the 90-2.

272. Select Committee on Selling
Congress Books by Members (House)
  Established: January 22, 1845
    H. J. (29-1): 290.
  Authority: Res. of the House
    (29-1)
  Terminated: August 10, 1846, at
    the end of the 29-1.

273. Select Committee to Inquire into Providing for an Earlier meeting of Congress than the Constitutional Period (House)
Established: March 29, 1814
   H. J. (13-2): 509.
Authority: Res. of the House
   (13-2)
Terminated: April 5, 1814
   Ibid. 536.

274. Select Committee on the Purchase of Congressional Annals and Debates (House)
Established: March 14, 1864
   H. J. (38-1): 384.
Authority: Res. of the House
   (38-1)
Terminated: March 18, 1864
   Ibid. 405.

275. Select Committee on Congressional Elections in Cincinnati (House)
Established: March 21, 1879
   9 CR 32.
Authority: Res. of the House
   (46-1)
Terminated: July 1, 1879, at the
   end of the 46-1.

276. Select Committee on Congressional Operations (House)
Sudocs: Y4. C76/9:
Established: March 28, 1977
   123 CR 9257.
Authority: H. Res. 420 (95-1)
Terminated: December 31, 1978
   U. S. Congress, Select Committee on Congressional Operations. Court Proceedings and Actions of Vital Interest to the Congress, part 6, Report Current to December 31, 1978. Committee Print, GPO, 1979. Y4. C76/9: C83/pt. 6.

277. Committee on Congressional Operations (Joint)
Sudocs: Y4. C76/7:
Established: October 26, 1970
   84 Stat. 1140.
Authority: PL 91-510
Terminated: February 11, 1977.
   Functions transferred to the

Committee on Rules and Administration (Entry 1252).
   123 CR 3660.
Authority: S. Res. 4 (95-1)

278. Select Committee to Investigate Alleged Inaccuracies in the Congressional Record (House)
Established: January 27, 1917
   64 CR 2127.
Authority: Res. of the House
   (64-2)
Terminated: March 3, 1917
   64 CR 4948.
Authority: H. Res. 473 (64-2)

279. Committee to Investigate Congressional Salaries (Joint)
Established: March 4, 1923
   42 Stat. 1560.
Authority: PL 67-543
Terminated: May 1, 1924
   S. rpt. 481 (68-1) 8221.

280. Select Committee on Reduction of Congressional Salaries (Senate)
Established: December 19, 1820
   S. J. (16-2): 72.
Authority: Res. of the Senate
   (16-2)
Terminated: March 3, 1821, at the
   end of the 16-2.

281. Select Committee on the Connecticut Asylum for the Deaf and Dumb (House)
Established: January 18, 1819
   H. J. (15-2): 193.
Authority: Res. of the House
   (15-2)
Terminated: February 22, 1819
   Ibid. 297.

282. Select Committee on Consular System (House)
Established: March 12, 1846
   H. J. (29-1): 516.
Authority: Res. of the House
   (29-1)
Terminated: March 3, 1847, at the
   end of the 29-2.

283. Select Committee on Alteration in Laws Concerning Consuls and Vice-Consuls (House)

Established: January 13, 1812
  H. J. (12-1): 256.
Authority: Res. of the House
  (12-1)
Terminated: June 11, 1812
  Ibid. 731.

284. Select Committee to Inves-
tigate the Disbursement of the
Contingent Fund (House)
  Established: July 15, 1868. Mem-
  bers from Accounts Committee.
    Cong. Globe (40-2): 4080.
  Authority: Res. of the House
    (40-2)
  Terminated: February 27, 1869
    H. rpt. 36 (40-3) 1388.

285. Select Committee on Importa-
tion of Contract Labor, Convicts,
and Paupers (House)
  Sudocs: Y4. C76/2:
  Established: July 12, 1888
    19 CR 6194.
  Authority: H. Misc. doc 516
    (50-1)
  Terminated: March 3, 1889, at the
    end of the 50-2.

286. Select Committee on Contribu-
tion Investigation (Senate)
  Sudocs: Y4. C76/4:
  Established: February 7, 1956
    102 CR 2168.
  Authority: S. Res. 205 (84-2)
  Terminated: March 29, 1956
    S. rpt. 1724 (84-2) 11887.

287. Select Committee on Altering
the Copper Coins of the U. S.
(House)
  Established: March 10, 1814
    H. J. (13-2): 421.
  Authority: Res. of the House
    (13-2)
  Terminated: April 25, 1816
    H. J. (14-1): 712.

288. Select Committee on Inter-
national Copyright (House)
  Established: December 16, 1843
    H. J. (28-1): 58.
  Authority: Res. of the House
    (28-1)

Terminated: June 17, 1844, at the
  end of the 28-1.

289. Select Committee on an Inter-
national Copyright Law (Senate)
  Established: January 22, 1846
    S. J. (29-1): 115.
  Authority: Res. of the Senate
    (29-1)
  Terminated: August 10, 1846, at
    the end of the 29-1.

290. Select Committee on Alleged
Private Meetings of Members of the
House with a View to a Corrupt Bar-
gain with the President (House)
  Established: February 16, 1867
    H. J. (39-2): 404.
  Authority: Res. of the House
    (39-2)
  Terminated: February 27, 1867
    H. rpt. 26 (39-2) 1305.

291. Select Committee to Investi-
gate Alleged Corrupt Combinations
of Members of Congress (House)
  Sudocs: Y4. C81/1:
  Established: January 19, 1857
    Cong. Globe (34-3): 378.
  Authority: Res. of the House
    (34-3)
  Terminated: February 19, 1857
    H. rpt. 243 (34-3) 914.

292. Select Committee on the
Charges of Corruption Contained
in Daily Times (Senate)
  Established: March 12, 1846
    S. J. (29-1): 191.
  Authority: Res. of the Senate
    (29-1)
  Terminated: March 16, 1846
    S. doc. 222 (29-1) 474.

293. Select Committee to Investi-
gate Alleged Corruptions in Govern-
ment (House)
  Sudocs: Y4. C81/2:
  Established: March 5, 1860
    H. J. (36-1): 450.
  Authority: Res. of the House
    (36-1)
  Terminated: June 16, 1860
    H. rpt. 648 (36-1) 1071

294. Select Committee to Investi-
gate Connection of Thomas Corwin
with Gardiner Claim (House)
  Established: August 23, 1852
    H. J. (32-1): 1065.
  Authority: Res. of the House
    (32-1)
  Terminated: December 7, 1852
    H. rpt. 1 (32-2) 687.

295. Select Committee to Investi-
gate the Cotton Situation in the
South (House)
  Established: October 24, 1914
    51 CR 16977.
  Authority: H. Res. 660 (63-3)
  Terminated: October 24, 1914, at
    the end of 63-3.

296. Select Committee on Altering
the Times of Holding Court in
Connecticut and Virginia (House)
  Established: January 30, 1812
    H. J. (12-1): 310.
  Authority: Res. of the House
    (12-1)
  Terminated: January 31, 1812
    Ibid. 315.

297. Select Committee on Altering
the Times of Holding Court in Maine
(House)
  Established: January 9, 1810
    H. J. (11-2): 142.
  Authority: Res. of the House
    (11-2)
  Terminated: February 5, 1813
    H. J. (12-2): 260.

298. Select Committee on Estab-
lishing a District Court in the
Mississippi Territory (House)
  Established: June 1, 1813
    H. J. (13-1): 30.
  Authority: Res. of the House
    (13-1)
  Terminated: August 2, 1813, at
    the end of the 13-1.

299. Special Committee on Court
Reorganization and Judicial Pro-
cedure (Senate)
  Sudocs: Y4. R29/2:
  Established: August 6, 1937
    S. J. (75-1): 491.
  Authority: S. Res. 164 (75-1)

Terminated: August 5, 1939, at
  the end of the 76-1.

300. Select Committee on Court-
houses (House)
  Established: January 25, 1855
    H. J. (33-2): 242.
  Authority: Res. of the House
    (33-2)
  Terminated: March 3, 1855
    Ibid. 537.

301. Select Committee on Courts in
Alabama (House)
  Established: January 5, 1847
    H. J. (29-2): 134.
  Authority: Res. of the House
    (29-2)
  Terminated: March 3, 1847, at the
    end of the 29-2.

302. Select Committee on The Act
Abridging the Jurisdiction of the
District Courts of Kentucky, Ten-
nessee and Ohio (House)
  Established: December 30, 1808
    H. J. (10-2): 200.
  Authority: Res. of the House
    (10-2)
  Terminated: January 11, 1809
    Ibid. 265.

303. Select Committee on Altering
the Times of Holding Courts in
Maryland (House)
  Established: March 13, 1810
    H. J. (11-2): 368.
  Authority: Res. of the House
    (11-2)
  Terminated: March 16, 1810
    Ibid. 382.

304. Select Committee on Altering
the Times of Holding Courts in New
Jersey (House)
  Established: March 7, 1810
    H. J. (11-2): 348.
  Authority: Res. of the House
    (11-2)
  Terminated: May 1, 1810, at the
    end of the 11-2.

305. Select Committee on Altering
the Terms for the District Courts
of New York, Vermont, and Connecticut (House)

Established: January 17, 1811
   H. J. (11-3): 132.
Authority: Res. of the House
   (11-3)
Terminated: March 3, 1811, at the
   end of the 11-3.

306. Select Committee on Alter-
ations in the Times of Holding
Courts in New York and Virginia
(House)
   Established: February 5, 1813
      H. J. (12-2): 261.
   Authority: Res. of the House
      (12-2)
   Terminated: February 9, 1813
      Ibid. 269.

307. Select Committee on Altering
the Times of Holding Courts in
North Carolina (House)
   Established: March 16, 1810
      H. J. (11-2): 390.
   Authority: Res. of the House
      (11-2)
   Terminated: January 10, 1811
      H. J. (12-1): 248.

308. Select Committee on Alter-
ations in the Several Acts Regu-
lating the Holding of Circuit
Courts in the United States (House)
   Established: December 3, 1807
      H. J. (10-1): 60.
   Authority: Res. of the House
      (10-1)
   Terminated: January 19, 1808
      Ibid. 277.

309. Select Committee on Whether
the Laws of the Several States
Shall be Rules of Proceedings on
Judgements and Executions in the
Courts of the United States, Except
Where Otherwise Provided (House)
   Established: February 11, 1809
      H. J. (10-2): 388.
   Authority: Res. of the House
      (10-2)
   Terminated: February 14, 1809
      Ibid. 397.

310. Select Committee on Altering
the Times and Places for Holding
Courts in Vermont (House)

Established: November 15, 1808
   H. J. (10-2): 38.
Authority: Res. of the House
   (10-2)
Terminated: January 23, 1809
   Ibid. 306.

311. Select Committee on Alter-
ations in the Courts in Vermont
(House)
   Established: November 21, 1812
      H. J. (12-2): 54.
   Authority: Res. of the House
      (12-2)
   Terminated: December 2, 1812
      Ibid. 77.

312. Select Committee on What
Amendments are Necessary in the
Laws Regulating the Courts of the
United States (House)
   Established: January 2, 1807
      H. J. (9-2): 100.
   Authority: Res. of the House
      (9-2)
   Terminated: March 3, 1807, at the
      end of the 9-2.

313. Select Committee on Judge
Cranch's Code of Laws (House)
   Established: November 23, 1818
      H. J. (15-2): 29.
   Authority: Res. of the House
      (15-2)
   Terminated: January 28, 1819
      Ibid. 216.

314. Select Committee to Investi-
gate the Credit Mobilier--Poland
Committee (House)
   Sudocs: Y4. C86:
   Established: December 2, 1872
      Cong. Globe (42-3): 11.
   Authority: Res. of the House
      (42-3)
   Terminated: February 18, 1873
      H. rpt. 77 (42-3) 1577.

315. Select Committee to Investi-
gate the Credit Mobilier--Wilson
Committee (House)
   Sudocs: Y4. C86:
   Established: January 6, 1873
      Cong. Globe (42-3): 357.
   Authority: Res. of the House
      (42-3)

Terminated: March 3, 1873
  H. rpt. 95 (42-3) 1577.

316. Select Committee on Certain
Treaties Made with the Creek and
Cherokee Indians (House)
  Established: December 17, 1821
    H. J. (17-1): 63.
  Authority: Res. of the House
    (17-1)
  Terminated: April 15, 1824
    H. J. (18-1): 420.

317. Special Committee to Investi-
gate Organized Crime in Interstate
Commerce (Senate)
  Sudocs: Y4. C86/2:
  Established: May 3, 1950
    96 CR 6246.
  Authority: S. Res. 202 (81-2)
  Terminated: August 31, 1951
    S. rpt. 725 (82-1) 11491.

318. Select Committee on Crime
(House)
  Sudocs: Y4. C86/3:
  Established: May 1, 1969
    115 CR 11101.
  Authority: H. Res. 17 (91-1)
  Terminated: June 30, 1973
    119 CR 5925.
  Authority: H. Res. 256 (93-1)

319. Select Committee to Inquire
into Abuses, Bribery, or Fraud in
the Prosecution of Crimes (Senate)
  Established: August 6, 1852
    S. J. (32-1): 572.
  Authority: Res. of the Senate
    (32-1)
  Terminated: March 22, 1853
    S. rpt. 1 (33 - Special) 688.

320. Select Committee on the
Revision and Amendment of the Laws
for the Punishment of Crimes
Against the United States (House)
  Established: December 2, 1806
    H. J. (9-2): 12.
  Authority: Res. of the House
    (9-2)
  Terminated: March 3, 1809, at the
    end of the 10-2.

321. Select Committee on Crop
Insurance (Senate)

Sudocs: Y4. C88:
Established: September 9, 1922
  62 CR 12321.
Authority: S. Res. 341 (67-2)
Terminated: March 3, 1923, at the
  end of the 67-4.

322. Committee on Relations with
Cuba (Senate)
  Sudocs: Y4. C89:
  Established: December 15, 1899
    33 CR 442.
  Authority: Res. of the Senate
    (56-1)
  Terminated: April 18, 1921
    61 CR 404-05.
  Authority: S. Res. 43 (67 -
    Special)

323. Select Committee on the
Conduct and Accounts of William
Cullom, Late Clerk of the House
(House)
  Established: December 18, 1857
    H. J. (35-1): 88.
  Authority: Res. of the House
    (35-1)
  Terminated: February 28, 1859
    H. rpt. 188 (35-2) 1020.

324. Select Committee on the
Cumberland Road (House)
  Established: January 3, 1815
    H. J. (13-3): 413.
  Authority: Res. of the House
    (13-3)
  Terminated: March 23, 1816
    H. J. (14-1): 527.

325. Select Committee on the
Cumberland Road (House)
  Established: December 4, 1822
    H. J. (17-2): 21.
  Authority: Res. of the House
    (17-2)
  Terminated: May 7, 1824
    H. rpt. 118 (18-1) 106.

326. Select Committee on a Report
of the Commissioners Appointed to
Lay out the Cumberland Road (House)
  Established: February 9, 1807
    H. J. (9-2): 257.
  Authority: Res. of the House
    (9-2)

Terminated: June 8, 1809
  H. J. (11-1): 95.

327. Select Committee on Currency
(House)
  Established: June 8, 1841
    H. J. (27-1): 52.
  Authority: Res. of the House
    (27-1)
  Terminated: July 21, 1841
    Ibid. 267.

328. Special Committee on Purchase
of Danish West Indian Islands
(House)
  Established: March 27, 1902
    35 CR 3337.
  Authority: Res. of the House
    (57-1)
  Terminated: July 1, 1902
    H. rpt. 2479 (57-1) 4407.

329. Select Committee on Asylum
for Instruction of the Deaf and
Dumb (House)
  Established: December 14, 1827
    H. J. (20-1): 54.
  Authority: Res. of the House
    (20-1)
  Terminated: April 12, 1830
    H. J. (21-1): 528.

330. Select Committee on Granting
Assistance to Certain Associations
for Teaching the Deaf and Dumb
(House)
  Established: December 20, 1824
    H. J. (18-2): 61.
  Authority: Res. of the House
    (18-2)
  Terminated: January 19, 1825
    H. rpt. 28 (18-2) 122.

331. Select Committee on the
Institution for the Deaf and Dumb
in Kentucky (House)
  Established: April 5, 1824
    H. J. (18-1): 359.
  Authority: Res. of the House
    (18-1)
  Terminated: December 22, 1825
    H. rpt. 7 (19-1) 141.

332. Select Committee on Memorials
of the New York and Pennsylvania

Associations for Teaching the Deaf
and Dumb (House)
  Established: March 10, 1826
    H. J. (19-1): 328.
  Authority: Res. of the House
    (19-1)
  Terminated: April 6, 1826
    H. rpt. 155 (19-1) 142.

333. Select Committee on Abolish-
ing Imprisonment for Debt (House)
  Established: February 2, 1821
    H. J. (16-2): 192.
  Authority: Res. of the House
    (16-2)
  Terminated: February 24, 1821
    H. rpt. 63 (16-2) 57.

334. Select Committee on Abolish-
ing Imprisonment for Debt (Senate)
  Established: January 21, 1823
    S. J. (17-2): 97.
  Authority: Res. of the Senate
    (17-2)
  Terminated: March 3, 1829, at the
    end of the 20-2.

335. Select Committee on Alter-
ations in the Act for the Relief of
Persons Imprisoned for Debt (House)
  Established: December 23, 1807
    H. J. (10-1): 187.
  Authority: Res. of the House
    (10-1)
  Terminated: January 15, 1808
    Ibid. 268.

336. Select Committee on Imprison-
ment for Debt (House)
  Established: December 12, 1831
    H. J. (22-1): 40.
  Authority: Res. of the House
    (22-1)
  Terminated: January 17, 1832
    H. rpt. 5 (22-2) 236.

337. Select Committee on the As-
sumption by the General Government
of the Debts of the States (Senate)
  Established: January 8, 1840
    S. J. (26-1): 84.
  Authority: Res. of the Senate
    (26-1)
  Terminated: July 21, 1840, at the
    end of the 26-1.

338. Committee on Defense Production (Joint)
Sudocs: Y4. D36:
Established: September 8, 1950
    64 Stat. 820.
Authority: PL 81-774
Terminated: February 11, 1977
    123 CR 3691.
Authority: S. Res. 4 (95-1)

339. Special Committee to Investigate the National Defense Program (Senate)
Established: March 1, 1941
    87 CR 1615.
Authority: S. Res. 71 (77-1)
Terminated: April 28, 1948
    S. rpt. 440 (80-2) 11205.

340. Select Committee on the Defenses of the Northwestern Frontier (House)
Established: April 26, 1864
    H. J. (38-1): 571.
Authority: Res. of the House
    (38-1)
Terminated: June 20, 1864
    H. rpt. 119 (38-1) 1207.

341. Select Committee on Dental Surgery (House)
Established: December 29, 1837
    H. J. (25-2): 160.
Authority: Res. of the House
    (25-2)
Terminated: July 9, 1838, at the end of the 25-2.

342. Select Committee on Direct Taxes and Forfeited Land (House)
Established: December 17, 1866
    H. J. (39-2): 91.
Authority: Res. of the House
    (39-2)
Terminated: March 3, 1867, at the end of the 39-2.

343. Committee to Investigate Dirigible Disasters (Joint)
Sudocs: Y4. D63:
Established: April 20, 1933
    77 CR 2054.
Authority: H. Con. Res. 15 (73-1)
Terminated: June 14, 1933
    S. doc. 75 (73-1) 9748.

344. Select Committee on the Removal of Political Disabilities (Senate)
Established: March 20, 1869
    Cong. Globe (41-1): 176.
Authority: Res. of the Senate
    (41-1)
Terminated: March 12, 1873
    S. J. (42-3): 609.
Authority: Res. of the Senate
    (42-3)

345. Select Committee on Establishing a Uniform Mode of Discipline for the Army (House)
Established: November 23, 1814
    H. J. (13-3): 222.
Authority: Res. of the House
    (13-3)
Terminated: December 24, 1814
    Ibid. 391.

346. Select Committee on the Disorder in the Senate of April 17, 1850 (Senate)
Established: April 17, 1850
    S. J. (31-1): 290.
Authority: Res. of the Senate
    (31-1)
Terminated: September 30, 1850, at the end of the 31-1.

347. Select Committee on Distilled Spirit Tax Bill (Senate)
Established: May 4, 1882
    13 CR 3627.
Authority: Res. of the Senate
    (47-1)
Terminated: August 8, 1882
    S. rpt. 878 (47-1) 2007.

348. Committee on the District of Columbia (House)
Sudocs: Y4. D63/1:
Established: January 27, 1808
    H. J. (10-1): 146.
Authority: Res. of the House
    (10-1)
Terminated: Still in existence at the end of the 97-2.

349. Committee on the District of Columbia (Senate)
Sudocs: Y4. D63/2:
Established: December 18, 1816
    Annals (14-2): 36.

Authority: Res. of the Senate
(14-2)
Terminated: February 11, 1977,
and its functions transferred
to the Committee on Governmental Affairs (Entry 587).
123 CR 3691.
Authority: S. Res. 4 (95-1)

350. Committee on Corporations
Organized in the District of
Columbia (Senate)
Established: March 19, 1896,
having previously been a
select committee (Entry 351).
28 CR 2960.
Authority: Res. of the Senate
(54-1)
Terminated: April 18, 1921
61 CR 405.
Authority: S. Res. 43 (67 -
Special)

351. Select Committee on Corporations Organized in the District of
Columbia (Senate)
Established: July 27, 1892
23 CR 6853.
Authority: Res. of the Senate
(52-1)
Terminated: March 19, 1896, when
it became a standing committee
(Entry 350).
28 CR 2960.
Authority: Res. of the Senate
(54-1)

352. Select Committee to Investi-
gate Charities and Reformatory In-
stitutions in District of Columbia
(Joint)
Sudocs: Y4. D63/3:
Established: June 11, 1896
29 Stat. 393.
Authority: District of Columbia
Appropriations Act of 1896
Terminated: March 28, 1898
S. rpt. 781 (55-2) 3565.

353. Select Committee to Investigate Public School System of District of Columbia (Senate)
Sudocs: Y4. D63/6:
Established: February 24, 1920
59 CR 3388.
Authority: S. Res. 310 (66-2)

Terminated: May 26, 1920
S. rpt. 635 (66-2) 7651.

354. Select Committee on a System
of Common Schools for the District
of Columbia (House)
Established: December 20, 1866
H. J. (39-2): 104.
Authority: Res. of the House
(39-2)
Terminated: November 10, 1868, at
the end of 40-2.

355. Select Committee on Charges
Against Members of the Board of Po-
lice Commissioners of the District
of Columbia (House)
Established: January 8, 1877
H. J. (44-2): 174.
Authority: Res. of the House
(44-2)
Terminated: March 3, 1877
H. rpt. 189 (44-2) 1770.

356. Select Committee on the Bill
to Prohibit the Issue and Circula-
tion of Bank Notes in the District
of Columbia (Senate)
Established: January 9, 1860
S. J. (36-1): 67.
Authority: Senate Order (36-1)
Terminated: January 17, 1860
S. rpt. 9 (36-1) 1039.

357. Select Committee to Frame a
Form of Government for the District
of Columbia (Joint)
Established: August 14, 1876
S. J. (44-1): 872.
Authority: Res. of the Senate
(44-1)
Terminated: January 11, 1877
S. rpt. 572 (44-2) 1732.

358. Select Committee to Inquire
into the Affairs of the District of
Columbia (Joint)
Established: February 5, 1874
S. J. (43-1): 218.
Authority: Con. Res. of the House
(43-1)
Terminated: June 16, 1874
S. rpt. 453 (43-1) 1590-2.

359. Committee on District of
Columbia Public Parks (Joint)

Established: June 30, 1906
 34 Stat. 788.
Authority: PL 59-385
Terminated: January 15, 1907
 S. rpt. 5011 (59-2) 5060.

360. Committee on Fiscal Relations
Between the District of Columbia
and the United States - 1st (Joint)
 Sudocs: Y4. D63/5:
 Established: March 3, 1915
 38 Stat. 894.
 Authority: PL 63-268
 Terminated: January 6, 1916
 H. doc. 495 (64-1) 7098.

361. Committee on Fiscal Relations
Between the District of Columbia
and the United States - 2nd (Joint)
 Sudocs: Y4. D63/5:
 Established: June 29, 1922
 42 Stat. 670.
 Authority: PL 67-256
 Terminated: February 24, 1923
 S. doc. 301 (67-4) 8166.

362. Special Committee to Investi-
gate District of Columbia Excise
Board (Senate)
 Sudocs: Y4. D63/4:
 Established: January 26, 1915
 52 CR 2302.
 Authority: S. Res. 522 (63-3)
 Terminated: March 4, 1915
 S. doc. 981 (63-3).

363. Select Committee on the
District of Columbia Gas and
Telephone Companies (House)
 Established: February 14, 1898
 31 CR 1702.
 Authority: H. Res. 148 (55-2)
 Terminated: March 3, 1899, at the
 end of the 55-3.

364. Select Committee to Investi-
gate Fiscal Relations Between Dis-
trict of Columbia and U. S. (House)
 Sudocs: Y4. D63/7:
 Established: July 3, 1930
 72 CR 12530.
 Authority: H. Res. 285 (71-2)
 Terminated: December 15, 1931
 H. rpt. 3 (72-1) 9491.

365. Special Committee on Examina-
tion and Disposition of Documents
(House)
 Established: March 14, 1900
 33 CR 2884.
 Authority: H. Res. 168 (56-1)
 Terminated: March 3, 1903, at the
 end of the 57-2.

366. Select Committee on Examina-
tion and Disposition of Documents
(Senate)
 Established: June 15, 1906
 40 CR 8335.
 Authority: Res. of the Senate
 (59-1)
 Terminated: March 22, 1909, when
 the Committee on Disposition of
 Useless Papers in the Executive
 Departments was established
 (Entry 1031).
 44 CR 121.
 Authority: Res. of the Senate
 (61-1)

367. Select Committee on a Report
of the Secretary of the Treasury on
Domestic Manufactures (House)
 Established: April 19, 1810
 H. J. (11-2): 560.
 Authority: Res. of the House
 (11-2)
 Terminated: April 26, 1810
 Ibid. 599.

368. Select Committee on Alleged
Corruption in the Contested Elec-
tion Case of Donnelly vs. Washburn
(House)
 Established: April 17, 1880
 10 CR 2502.
 Authority: Res. of the House
 (46-2)
 Terminated: March 3, 1881
 H. rpt. 395 (46-2) 1983.

369. Select Committee on the
Charges Against the Honorable
Ignatius Donnelly (House)
 Established: May 4, 1868
 Cong. Globe (40-2): 2359.
 Authority: Res. of the House
 (40-2)
 Terminated: June 1, 1868
 H. rpt. 48 (40-2) 1358.

370. Select Committee on Accounts and Conduct of the Late Doorkeeper (House)
   Established: January 18, 1858
      H. J. (35-1): 198.
   Authority: Res. of the House
      (35-1)
   Terminated: June 14, 1858, at the end of the 35-1.

371. Select Committee on Inspection of Imported Drugs (House)
   Established: April 6, 1848
      H. J. (30-1): 655.
   Authority: Res. of the House
      (30-1)
   Terminated: June 2, 1848
      H. rpt. 664 (30-1) 526.

372. Select Committee on Duelling (Senate)
   Established: February 25, 1831
      S. J. (21-2): 176.
   Authority: Res. of the Senate
      (21-2)
   Terminated: March 3, 1831, at the end of the 21-2.

373. Select Committee on Bill to Prohibit Duelling (House)
   Established: December 6, 1838
      H. J. (25-3): 41.
   Authority: Res. of the House
      (25-3)
   Terminated: March 3, 1839, at the end of the 25-3.

374. Select Committee on the Bill (H. R. 338) to Provide for the Payment of Outstanding Treasury Notes, to Authorize and Loan, and to Regulate and Fix the Duties on Imports (Senate)
   Established: January 23, 1861
      S. J. (36-2): 137.
   Authority: Senate Order (36-2)
   Terminated: February 1, 1861
      S. J. (36-2): 174.

375. Select Committee on an Act Authorizing the City Council of the City of Charleston, South Carolina, to Impose a Duty on Vessels (House)
   Established: December 16, 1805
      H. J. (9-1): 49.

Authority: Res. of the House
      (9-1)
   Terminated: January 8, 1806
      Ibid. 120.

376. Economic Committee (Joint)
   Sudocs: Y4. Ec7:
   Established: June 18, 1956, when the Joint Economic Report Committee was changed to this (Entry 377).
      70 Stat. 290.
   Authority: PL 84-591
   Terminated: Still in existence at the end of the 97-2.

377. Committee on Economic Report (Joint)
   Sudocs: Y4. Ec7:
   Established: February 20, 1946
      60 Stat. 25.
   Authority: PL 79-304
   Terminated: June 18, 1956, when the name was changed to Joint Economic Committee (Entry 376).
      70 Stat. 290.
   Authority: PL 84-591

378. Committee on Temporary National Economics (Joint)
   Sudocs: Y4. T24:
   Established: June 16, 1938
      52 Stat. 705.
   Authority: Public Res. 113 (75-3)
   Terminated: March 31, 1941
      S. doc. 35 (77-1) 10564.

379. Committee on the Economy (House)
   Established: February 23, 1932
      75 CR 4537.
   Authority: H. Res. 151 (72-1)
   Terminated: March 11, 1933
      H. rpt. 1 (73-1) 9774.

380. Select Committee on a Bureau of Education (House)
   Established: February 14, 1866
      Cong. Globe (39-1): 835.
   Authority: Res. of the House
      (39-1)
   Terminated: June 19, 1866
      S. J. (39-1): 866.

381. Committee on Education (House)

Sudocs: Y4. Ed8/2:
Established: December 19, 1883,
  when Committee on Education
  and Labor was divided into two
  Committees (Entry 384).
    15 CR 196.
Authority: Res. of the House
  (48-1)
Terminated: January 2, 1947
  60 Stat. 812.
Authority: PL 79-601

382. Committee on Education
(Senate)
  Sudocs: Y4. Ed8/3:
  Established: January 28, 1869
    Cong. Globe (40-3): 664.
  Authority: Res. of the Senate
    (40-3)
  Terminated: February 14, 1870,
    when the name was changed to
    the Committee on Education and
    Labor (Entry 386).
      Cong. Globe (41-2): 1251.
  Authority: Res. of the Senate
    (41-2)

383. Select Committee on Creating
a Fund for Education and Internal
Improvements by Increasing Duty on
Foreign and Imposing Duty on Domes-
tic Spirits (House)
  Established: February 8, 1826
    H. J. (19-1): 238.
  Authority: Res. of the House
    (19-1)
  Terminated: May 16, 1826
    Ibid. 602.

384. Committee on Education and
Labor - 1st (House)
  Established: July 19, 1867
    Cong. Globe (40-1): 739.
  Authority: Res. of the House
    (40-1)
  Terminated: December 19, 1883,
    when it was divided into a
    Committee on Education and a
    Committee on Labor (Entries
    381, 741).
      15 CR 196.
  Authority: Res. of the House
    (48-1)

385. Committee on Education and
Labor - 2nd (House)

Sudocs: Y4. Ed8/1:
Established: January 2, 1947
  60 Stat. 812.
Authority: PL 79-601
Terminated: Still in existence at
  the end of the 97-2.

386. Committee on Education and
Labor (Senate)
  Sudocs: Y4. Ed8/3:
  Established: February 14, 1870,
    when the Committee on Educa-
    tion was changed to this
    (Entry 382).
      Cong. Globe (41-2): 1251.
  Authority: Res. of the Senate
    (41-2)
  Terminated: January 2, 1947, when
    its functions were transferred
    to the Committee on Labor and
    Public Welfare (Entry 744).
      60 Stat. 812.
  Authority: PL 79-601

387. Select Committee on Amending
the Constitution in the Mode of
Electing the House, and President
and Vice President (House)
  Established: December 5, 1823
    H. J. (18-1): 29.
  Authority: Res. of the House
    (18-1)
  Terminated: May 22, 1826, at the
    end of the 19-1.

388. Select Committee on Amendment
to the Constitution on Electing
President and Vice President
(House)
  Established: January 18, 1854
    H. J. (33-1): 238.
  Authority: Res. of the House
    (33-1)
  Terminated: August 7, 1854, at
    the end of the 33-1.

389. Select Committee on Rules
to be Observed in the House in
Electing a President of the United
States (House)
  Established: January 14, 1825
    H. J. (18-2): 143.
  Authority: Res. of the House
    (18-2)
  Terminated: January 26, 1825
    H. rpt. 41 (18-2) 122.

390. Select Committee on Fixing an Uniform Mode of Electing Senators, Representatives, and Electors of the President (House)
   Established: December 14, 1813
      H. J. (13-2): 39.
   Authority: Res. of the House (13-2)
   Terminated: January 5, 1814
      Ibid. 99.

391. Select Committee on Alleged Frauds in the Late Presidential Election (House)
   Established: October 22, 1877
      6 CR 133.
   Authority: Res. of the House (45-1)
   Terminated: March 3, 1879
      H. rpt. 140 (45-3) 1866.

392. Select Committee on the Recent Election in Florida (House)
   Established: December 4, 1876
      H. J. (44-2): 22.
   Authority: Res. of the House (44-2)
   Terminated: January 31, 1877
      H. rpt. 143 (44-2) 1769.

393. Select Committee on the Recent Election in Louisiana (House)
   Established: December 4, 1876
      H. J. (44-2): 22.
   Authority: Res. of the House (44-2)
   Terminated: February 1, 1877
      H. rpt. 156 (44-2) 1769.

394. Select Committee on the Recent Election in South Carolina (House)
   Established: December 4, 1876
      H. J. (44-2): 22.
   Authority: Res. of the House (44-2)
   Terminated: February 21, 1877
      H. rpt. 175 (44-2) 1770.

395. Select Committee on Election Laws of the Several States (House)
   Established: December 23, 1825
      H. J. (19-1): 87.
   Authority: Res. of the House (19-1)

Terminated: May 16, 1826
   Ibid. 575.

396. Select Committee on What Officers in the Executive Departments Endeavored to Defeat Election of General Taylor, by Money, etc. (House)
   Established: May 6, 1850
      H. J. (31-1): 877.
   Authority: Res. of the House (31-1)
   Terminated: September 30, 1850, at the end of the 31-1.

397. Committee on Election of the President and Vice-President of the U. S. (House)
   Sudocs: Y4. E12/1:
   Established: August 18, 1893, having been preceded by a select committee (Entry 398).
      25 CR 478.
   Authority: Res. of the House (53-1)
   Terminated: January 2, 1947
      60 Stat. 812.
   Authority: PL 79-601

398. Select Committee on Election of President and Vice-President of the U. S. (House)
   Sudocs: Y4. E12/1:
   Established: December 13, 1881
      13 CR 114.
   Authority: Res. of the House (47-1)
   Terminated: August 18, 1893, when it was made a standing committee (Entry 397).
      25 CR 478.
   Authority: Res. of the House (53-1)

399. Committee on Election of President, Vice-President and Representatives (House)
   Sudocs: Y4. E12/1:
   Established: December 19, 1907
      42 CR 428.
   Authority: Res. of the House (60-1)
   Terminated: May 29, 1928, at the end of the 70-1.

400. Committee on Elections
(House)
   Sudocs: Y4. E12/2:
   Established: April 13, 1789
      Annals (1-1): 128.
   Authority: Res. of the House
      (1-1)
   Terminated: December 17, 1895,
      when the single committee was
      made into three (Entries 401-
      403).
         28 CR 216.
   Authority: Res. of the House
      (54-1)

401. Committee on Elections no. 1
(House)
   Established: December 17, 1895
      Replaced former Committee on
      Elections (Entry 400).
         28 CR 216.
   Authority: Res. of the House
      (54-1)
   Terminated: January 2, 1947
      60 Stat. 812.
   Authority: PL 79-601

402. Committee on Elections no. 2
(House)
   Established: December 17, 1895
      Replaced former Committee on
      Elections (Entry 400).
         28 CR 216.
   Authority: Res. of the House
      (54-1)
   Terminated: January 2, 1947
      60 Stat. 812.
   Authority: PL 79-601

403. Committee on Elections no. 3
(House)
   Established: December 17, 1895
      Replaced former Committee on
      Elections (Entry 400).
         28 CR 216.
   Authority: Res. of the House
      (54-1)
   Terminated: January 2, 1947
      60 Stat. 812.
   Authority: PL 79-601

404. Select Committee on Bill to
Secure Freedom of Elections (House)
   Established: March 5, 1837
      H. J. (25-2): 523.

Authority: Res. of the House
   (25-2)
Terminated: July 9, 1838, at the
   end of the 25-2.

405. Select Committee on Contested
Elections (House)
   Established: April 1, 1836
      H. J. (24-1): 613.
   Authority: Res. of the House
      (24-1)
   Terminated: July 4, 1836, at the
      end of the 24-1.

406. Select Committee on Contested
Elections of the House (House)
   Established: December 3, 1806
      H. J. (9-2): 23.
   Authority: Res. of the House
      (9-2)
   Terminated: December 9, 1806
      Ibid. 37.

407. Select Committee to Consider
the State of the Law Respecting the
Ascertaining And Declaration of the
Result of the Elections of the
President and Vice-President
(Senate)
   Established: October 23, 1877
      S. J. (45-1): 28.
   Authority: Res. of the Senate
      (45-1)
   Terminated: July 1, 1879, at the
      end of the 46-1.

408. Select Committee to Inquire
into Alleged Frauds and Violence in
the Elections of 1878 (Senate)
   Established: December 17, 1878
      S. J. (45-3): 69.
   Authority: Res. of the Senate
      (45-3)
   Terminated: March 3, 1881, at the
      end of the 46-3.

409. Select Committee on Counting
the Electoral Vote (House)
   Established: December 14, 1876
      H. J. (44-2): 78.
   Authority: Res. of the House
      (44-2)
   Terminated: January 18, 1877
      H. rpt. 108 (44-2) 1769.

410. Select Committee on Counting the Electoral Vote (Senate)
  Established: December 18, 1876
    S. J. (44-2): 55.
  Authority: Res. of the Senate (44-2)
  Terminated: March 3, 1877, at the end of the 44-2.

411. Select Committee on Charges Against Commodore Elliott (House)
  Established: February 14, 1839
    H. J. (25-3): 543.
  Authority: Res. of the House (25-3)
  Terminated: February 22, 1839
    H. rpt. 295 (25-3) 352.

412. Select Committee on Emancipation (House)
  Established: April 7, 1862
    H. J. (37-2): 509.
  Authority: Res. of the House (37-2)
  Terminated: March 3, 1865, at the end of the 38-2.

413. Select Committee on the Protection of the Emigrant Route and a Telegraphic Line from Missouri to California and Oregon (Senate)
  Established: January 20, 1853
    S. J. (32-2): 118.
  Authority: Res. of the Senate (32-2)
  Terminated: March 3, 1853, at the end of the 32-2.

414. Select Committee on Foreign Emigration (House)
  Established: December 15, 1863
    H. J. (38-1): 58.
  Authority: Res. of the House (38-1)
  Terminated: April 16, 1864
    H. rpt. 56 (38-1) 1206.

415. Select Committee to Investigate the Causes Which Have Led to the Emigration of Negroes from the Southern to the Northern States (Senate)
  Established: December 19, 1879
    S. J. (46-1): 79.
  Authority: Res. of the Senate (46-2)

Terminated: June 1, 1880
    S. rpt. 693 (46-2) 1899-1900.

416. Ad Hoc Committee on Energy (House)
  Sudocs: Y4. En2/2:
  Established: April 21, 1977
    123 CR 11556.
  Authority: H. Res. 508 (95-1)
  Terminated: October 15, 1978, at the end of the 95-2.

417. Committee on Energy and Natural Resources (Senate)
  Sudocs: Y4. En2:
  Established: February 11, 1977
    Absorbed Committee on Interior and Insular Affairs and later Joint Committee on Atomic Energy (Entries 693, 84).
    123 CR 3691.
  Authority: S. Res. 4 (95-1)
  Terminated: Still in existence at the end of the 97-2.

418. Select Committee on the Corps of Engineers (House)
  Established: December 10, 1810
    H. J. (11-3): 24.
  Authority: Res. of the House (11-3)
  Terminated: February 15, 1811
    Ibid. 264.

419. Special Committee to Inquire into the Official Conduct of Judge George Washington English (House)
  Established: March 4, 1925
    66 CR 5531.
  Authority: H. J. Res. 347 (68-2)
  Terminated: December 19, 1925
    H. doc. 145 (69-1) 8578.

420. Committee on Engraving (House)
  Established: March 16, 1844
    Cong. Globe (28-1): 393.
  Authority: Res. of the House (28-1)
  Terminated: March 3, 1861, at the end of the 36-2.

421. Select Committee on Engraving, Lithography, etc. (House)
  Established: January 12, 1844
    H. J. (28-1): 213.

Authority: Res. of the House
   (28-1)
Terminated: March 8, 1844
   H. rpt. 305 (28-1) 445.

422. Committee on Engrossed Bills
(Senate)
   Established: March 9, 1875
      4 CR 9.
   Authority: Res. of the Senate
      (44-1)
   Terminated: April 18, 1921
      61 CR 404-05.
   Authority: S. Res. 43 (67 -
      Special)

423. Committee on Enrolled Bills
(House)
   Established: August 14, 1876,
      having been preceded by a joint
      committee (Entry 424).
         4 CR 5567.
   Authority: Res. of the House
      (44-1)
   Terminated: January 2, 1947, when
      its functions were transferred
      to the Committee on House
      Administration (Entry 611).
         60 Stat. 812.
   Authority: PL 79-601

424. Committee on Enrolled Bills
(Joint)
   Established: July 27, 1789
      H. J. (1-1): 67.
   Authority: Res. of the House
      (1-1)
   Terminated: August 14, 1876, when
      each house formed separate com-
      mittees (Entries 423, 425).
         4 CR 5567.
   Authority: Res. of the House
      (44-1)

425. Committee on Enrolled Bills
(Senate)
   Established: March 9, 1875,
      having been preceded by a joint
      committee (Entry 424).
         4 CR 9.
   Authority: Res. of the Senate
      (44-1)
   Terminated: January 2, 1947, when
      its functions were transferred

to the Committee on Rules and
   Administration (Entry 1252).
      60 Stat. 812.
   Authority: PL 79-601.

426. Committee on Environment and
Public Works (Senate)
   Sudocs: Y4. P96/10:
   Established: February 11, 1977,
      when Committee on Public Works
      name was changed to this
      (Entry 1163).
         123 CR 3691.
   Authority: S. Res. 4 (95-1)
   Terminated: Still in existence at
      the end of the 97-2.

427. Committee on Epidemic Dis-
eases (Senate)
   Sudocs: Y4. Ep4/2:
   Established: December 12, 1887,
      having been preceded by a
      select committee (Entry 428).
         19 CR 16.
   Authority: Res. of the Senate
      (50-1)
   Terminated: March 19, 1896, when
      name was changed to Committee
      on Public Health and National
      Quarantine (Entry 1149).
         28 CR 2960.
   Authority: Res. of the Senate
      (54-1)

428. Select Committee on Epidemic
Diseases (Senate)
   Sudocs: Y4. Ep4/2:
   Established: December 4, 1878
      8 CR 31.
   Authority: Res. of the Senate
      (45-3)
   Terminated: December 12, 1887,
      when it was made a standing
      committee (Entry 427).
         19 CR 16.
   Authority: Res. of the Senate
      (50-1)

429. Select Committee on Origin,
Introduction and Prevention of
Epidemic Diseases (House)
   Sudocs: Y4. Ep4/1:
   Established: April 9, 1879
      9 CR 337 (46-1).
   Authority: Res. of the House
      (46-1)

Terminated: March 3, 1881, at the
end of the 46-3.

430. Select Committee on Equal
Educational Opportunity (Senate)
Sudocs: Y4. Eq2:
Established: February 19, 1970
116 CR 4134.
Authority: S. Res. 359 (91-2)
Terminated: January 6, 1973
119 CR 412.
Authority: Senate Order (93-1)

431. Select Committee on Granting
Lands to the Erie and Wabash Canal
(House)
Established: December 24, 1833
H. J. (23-1): 124.
Authority: Res. of the House
(23-1)
Terminated: March 6, 1834
Ibid. 389.

432. Select Committee on Ether
Discovery (House)
Sudocs: Y4. Et3/1:
Established: December 10, 1851
H. J. (32-1): 74.
Authority: Res. of the House
(32-1)
Terminated: August 31, 1852, at
the end of the 32-1.

433. Select Committee on Ether
Discovery (Senate)
Sudocs: Y4. Et3/2:
Established: January 5, 1853
Cong. Globe (32-2): 219.
Authority: Res. of the Senate
(32-1)
Terminated: February 19, 1853
S. rpt. 421 (32-2) 671.

434. Select Committee on Ethics
(House)
Sudocs: Y4. Et3/3:
Established: March 9, 1977
123 CR 6817.
Authority: H. Res. 383 (95-1)
Terminated: January 3, 1979
H. rpt. 1837 (95-2) 13203-3.

435. Select Committee on Ethics
(Senate)
Sudocs: Y4. Et3/4:

Established: February 11, 1977,
when it replaced the Select
Committee on Standards and
Conduct (Entry 1336).
123 CR 3691.
Authority: S. Res. 4 (95-1)
Terminated: Still in existence at
the end of the 97-2.

436. Select Committee on the
Assault on Honorable John Ewing
(House)
Established: February 28, 1835
H. J. (23-2): 489.
Authority: Res. of the House
(23-2)
Terminated: February 28, 1835
H. rpt. 135 (23-2) 276.

437. Select Committee on Thomas
Ewing, Secretary of Interior, in
Paying Certain Claims (House)
Established: April 22, 1850
H. J. (31-1): 821.
Authority: Res. of the House
(31-1)
Terminated: September 30, 1850,
at the end of the 31-1.

438. Special Committee to Investi-
gate Charges of Execution without
Trial in France (Senate)
Sudocs: Y4. Ex3:
Established: November 4, 1921
61 CR 7292.
Authority: S. Res. 166 (67-1)
Terminated: March 1, 1923
S. rpt. 1256 (67-4) 8156.

439. Special Committee to Investi-
gate Executive Agencies (House)
Sudocs: Y4. Ex3/4:
Established: February 10, 1943
89 CR 872.
Authority: H. Res. 102 (78-1)
Terminated: November 20, 1944
H. rpt. 1912 (78-2) 10848.

440. Select Committee on Investi-
gation of Executive Agencies of the
Government (House)
Established: April 29, 1936
80 CR 6386.
Authority: H. Res. 460 (74-2)
Terminated: January 6, 1937
H. rpt. 4 (75-1) 10086.

441. Select Committee on Investigation of Executive Agencies of Government (Senate)
  Sudocs: Y4. Ex3/3:
  Established: February 24, 1936
    80 CR 2674.
  Authority: S. Res. 217 (74-2)
  Terminated: January 16, 1938, at the end of the 75-3.

442. Select Committee on the Administration of Executive Departments (House)
  Established: January 10, 1837
    H. J. (24-2): 233.
  Authority: Res. of the House (24-2)
  Terminated: March 3, 1837
    H. rpt. 194 (24-2) 307.

443. Select Committee to Investigate the Affairs of the Several Executive Departments (House)
  Established: April 4, 1822
    H. J. (17-1): 427.
  Authority: Res. of the House (17-1)
  Terminated: May 7, 1822
    Ibid. 585.

444. Select Committee on Methods of Business of the Executive Departments (Senate)
  Established: March 3, 1887
    18 CR 2663.
  Authority: Res. of the Senate (49-2)
  Terminated: March 28, 1889
    S. rpt. 3 (51 - Special) 2619.

445. Committee on Organization, Conduct and Expenditures of the Executive Departments (Senate)
  Established: December 15, 1899
    33 CR 441.
  Authority: Res. of the Senate (56-1)
  Terminated: December 17, 1907, to be replaced by Select Committee on Expenditures in the State Department on July 1, 1908 (Entry 476).
    42 CR 384.
  Authority: Res. of the Senate (60-1)

446. Select Committee on Reorganization of the Executive Department (House)
  Established: December 7, 1825
    H. J. (19-1): 30.
  Authority: Res. of the House (19-1)
  Terminated: December 15, 1826
    H. rpt. 10 (19-2) 159.

447. Committee to Examine the Accounts for Repairs and Furnishing of the Executive Mansion (Joint)
  Established: March 11, 1867
    S. J. (40-1): 26.
  Authority: Con. Res. of House (40-1)
  Terminated: November 10, 1868, at the end of the 40-2.

448. Committee on Disposition of Executive Papers (House)
  Sudocs: Y4. Ex3/2:
  Established: February 16, 1889
    25 Stat. 672.
  Authority: PL 50-171
  Terminated: January 2, 1947, when its functions were transferred to the Committee on House Administration (Entry 611).
    60 Stat. 812.
  Authority: PL 79-601

449. Committee on Disposition of (Useless) Executive Papers - 1st (Joint)
  Established: February 16, 1889
    25 Stat. 672.
  Authority: PL 50-171
  Terminated: July 7, 1943
    57 Stat. 381.
  Authority: PL 78-115

450. Committee on Disposition of Executive Papers - 2nd (Joint)
  Established: July 7, 1943
    57 Stat. 383.
  Authority: PL 78-115
  Terminated: June 23, 1970
    84 Stat. 321.
  Authority: PL 91-287

451. Committee on Expenditures in Department of Agriculture (House)
  Sudocs: Y4. Ex7/1:

Established: December 20, 1889
  21 CR 336.
Authority: Res. of the House
  (51-1)
Terminated: December 5, 1927, and
  its functions transferred to
  the Committee on Expenditures
  in the Executive Departments
  (Entry 457).
    69 CR 14.
Authority: H. Res. 7 (70-1)

452. Committee on Expenditures in
the Agriculture Department (Senate)
  Established: March 22, 1909,
    having been preceded by a
    select committee (Entry 453).
      44 CR 121.
  Authority: Res. of the Senate
    (61-1)
  Terminated: April 18, 1921
    61 CR 404-05.
  Authority: S. Res. 43 (67 -
    Special)

453. Select Committee on Expendi-
tures in the Agriculture Department
(Senate)
  Established: December 17, 1907
    42 CR 384.
  Authority: Res. of the Senate
    (60-1)
  Terminated: March 22, 1909, when
    it was made a standing commit-
    tee (Entry 452).
      44 CR 121.
  Authority: Res. of the Senate
    (61-1)

454. Committee on Expenditures in
the Department of Commerce (Senate)
  Established: June 24, 1914,
    having been preceded by the
    Committee on Expenditures in
    the Department of Commerce and
    Labor (Entry 456).
      S. J. (63-2): 357.
  Authority: Res. of the Senate
    (63-2)
  Terminated: April 18, 1921
    61 CR 404-05.
  Authority: S. Res. 43 (67 -
    Special)

455. Committee on Expenditures
in Department of Commerce and

Labor (House)
  Sudocs: Y4. Ex7/2:
  Established: December 11, 1905
    40 CR 298.
  Authority: Res. of the House
    (59-1)
  Terminated: December 5, 1927, and
    its functions were transferred
    to the Committee on Expendi-
    tures in the Executive Depart-
    ments (Entry 457).
      69 CR 14.
  Authority: H. Res. 7 (70-1)

456. Committee on Expenditures in
the Department of Commerce and
Labor (Senate)
  Established: April 5, 1912
    S. J. (62-2): 259.
  Authority: Res. of the Senate
    (62-2)
  Terminated: June 24, 1914, when
    it was split into two commit-
    tees (Entries 454, 465).
      S. J. (63-2): 357.
  Authority: Res. of the Senate
    (63-2)

457. Committee on Expenditures in
the Executive Departments (House)
  Sudocs: Y4. Ex7/13:
  Established: December 5, 1927,
    consolidating the eleven
    separate committees then in
    existence.
      69 CR 14.
  Authority: H. Res. 7 (70-1)
  Terminated: July 3, 1952, when
    its functions were transferred
    to the Committee on Government
    Operations (Entry 580).
      98 CR 9217.
  Authority: H. Res. 647 (82-2)

458. Committee on Expenditures in
the Executive Departments (Senate)
  Sudocs: Y4. Ex7/14:
  Established: April 18, 1921, hav-
    ing been preceded by several
    committees on expenditures in
    the various departments.
      61 CR 404.
  Authority: S. Res. 43 (67 -
    Special)
  Terminated: March 3, 1952, when
    it became Government Operations

Committee (Entry 581).
    98 CR 1702.
Authority: S. Res. 280 (82-2)

459. Committee on Expenditures in
the Interior Department (House)
  Sudocs: Y4. Ex7/3:
  Established: March 16, 1860
    Cong. Globe (36-1): 1209.
  Authority: Res. of the House
    (36-1)
  Terminated: December 5, 1927, and
    its functions were transferred
    to the Committee on Expendi-
    tures in the Executive Depart-
    ments (Entry 457).
      69 CR 14.
  Authority: H. Res. 7 (70-1)

460. Committee on Expenditures in
the Interior Department (Senate)
  Established: March 22, 1909,
    having been preceded by a
    select committee (Entry 461).
      44 CR 121.
  Authority: Res. of the Senate
    (61-1)
  Terminated: April 18, 1921
    61 CR 404-05.
  Authority: S. Res. 43 (67 -
    Special)

461. Select Committee on Expendi-
tures in the Interior Department
(Senate)
  Established: December 17, 1907
    42 CR 384.
  Authority: Res. of the Senate
    (60-1)
  Terminated: March 22, 1909, when
    it was made a standing commit-
    tee (Entry 460).
      44 CR 121.
  Authority: Res. of the Senate
    (61-1)

462. Committee on Expenditures in
the Department of Justice (House)
  Sudocs: Y4. Ex7/4:
  Established: January 16, 1874
    1 CR 677.
  Authority: Res. of the House
    (43-1)
  Terminated: December 5, 1927,
    when its functions were trans-
    ferred to the Committee on

Expenditures in the Executive
Departments (Entry 457).
    69 CR 14.
Authority: H. Res. 7 (70-1)

463. Committee on Expenditures in
the Justice Department (Senate)
  Established: March 22, 1909,
    having been preceded by a
    select committee (Entry 464).
      44 CR 121.
  Authority: Res. of the Senate
    (61-1)
  Terminated: April 18, 1921
    61 CR 404-05.
  Authority: S. Res. 43 (67 -
    Special)

464. Select Committee on Expendi-
tures in the Justice Department
(Senate)
  Established: December 17, 1907
    42 CR 384.
  Authority: Res. of the Senate
    (60-1)
  Terminated: March 22, 1909, when
    it was made a standing commit-
    tee (Entry 463).
      44 CR 121.
  Authority: Res. of the Senate
    (61-1)

465. Committee on Expenditures in
the Department of Labor (Senate)
  Established: June 24, 1914, hav-
    ing been preceded by the Com-
    mittee on Expenditures in the
    Department of Commerce and
    Labor (Entry 456).
      S. J. (63-2): 357.
  Authority: Res. of the Senate
    (63-1)
  Terminated: April 18, 1921
    61 CR 404-05.
  Authority: S. Res. 43 (67 -
    Special)

466. Committee on Expenditures in
the Navy Department (House)
  Sudocs: Y4. Ex7/5:
  Established: March 30, 1816
    Annals (14-1): 1298.
  Authority: Res. of the House
    (14-1)
  Terminated: December 5, 1927, and
    its functions were transferred

to the Committee on Expenditures in the Executive Departments (Entry 457).
69 CR 14.
Authority: H. Res. 7 (70-1)

467. Committee on Expenditures in
the Navy Department (Senate)
Established: March 22, 1909, having been preceded by a select
committee (Entry 468).
44 CR 121.
Authority: Res. of the Senate
(61-1)
Terminated: April 18, 1921
61 CR 404-05.
Authority: S. Res. 43 (67 -
Special)

468. Select Committee on Expenditures in the Navy Department
(Senate)
Established: December 17, 1907
42 CR 384.
Authority: Res. of the Senate
(60-1)
Terminated: March 22, 1909, when
it was made a standing committee (Entry 467).
44 CR 121.
Authority: Res. of the Senate
(61-1)

469. Select Committee on Expen-
ditures in the 1930 Senatorial
Campaign (Senate)
Established: April 10, 1930
72 CR 6841.
Authority: S. Res. 215 (71-2)
Terminated: December 3, 1931
S. rpt. 20 (72-1) 9489.

470. Committee on Expenditures in
the Post-Office Department (House)
Sudocs: Y4. Ex7/6:
Established: March 30, 1816
Annals (14-1): 1298.
Authority: Res. of the House
(14-1)
Terminated: December 5, 1927, and
its functions were transferred
to the Committee on Expenditures in the Executive Departments (Entry 457).
69 CR 14.
Authority: H. Res. 7 (70-1)

471. Committee on Expenditures in
the Post-Office Department (Senate)
Established: December 22, 1909
44 CR 121.
Authority: Res. of the Senate
(61-1)
Terminated: April 18, 1921
61 CR 404-05.
Authority: S. Res. 43 (67 -
Special)

472. Committee on Expenditures in
Public Buildings (House)
Sudocs: Y4. Ex7/7:
Established: March 30, 1816
Annals (14-1): 1298.
Authority: Res. of the House
(14-1)
Terminated: December 5, 1927,
when its functions were trans-
ferred to the Committee on
Expenditures in the Executive
Departments (Entry 457).
69 CR 14.
Authority: H. Res. 7 (70-1)

473. Committee on Expenditures in
Senatorial Primary and General
Elections (Senate)
Sudocs: Y4. Ex7/12:
Established: May 19, 1926
67 CR 9678.
Authority: S. Res. 195 (69-1)
Terminated: May 3, 1929, at the
end of the 70-2.

474. Committee on Expenditures in
the State Department (House)
Sudocs: Y4. Ex7/8:
Established: March 30, 1816
Annals (14-1): 1298.
Authority: Res. of the House
(14-1)
Terminated: December 5, 1927, and
its functions were transferred
to the Committee on Expenditures in the Executive Departments (Entry 457).
69 CR 14.
Authority: H. Res. 7 (70-1)

475. Committee on Expenditures in
the State Department (Senate)
Established: March 22, 1909,
having been preceded by a

select committee (Entry 476).
  44 CR 121.
Authority: Res. of the Senate
  (61-1)
Terminated: April 18, 1921
  61 CR 404-05.
Authority: S. Res. 43 (67 -
  Special)

476. Select Committee on Expen-
ditures in the State Department
(Senate)
  Established: December 17, 1907,
  when it replaced the Committee
  on Organization, Conduct and
  Expenditures of Executive
  Departments (Entry 445).
    42 CR 384.
  Authority: Res. of the Senate
    (60-1)
  Terminated: March 22, 1909, when
  it was made a standing commit-
  tee (Entry 475).
    44 CR 121.
  Authority: Res. of the Senate
    (61-1)

477. Committee on Expenditures in
the Treasury Department (House)
  Sudocs: Y4. Ex7/9:
  Established: March 30, 1816
    Annals (14-1): 1298.
  Authority: Res. of the House
    (14-1)
  Terminated: December 5, 1927,
    and its functions trans-
    ferred to the Committee
    on Expenditures in the
    Executive Departments
    (Entry 457).
      69 CR 14.
  Authority: H. Res. 7 (70-1)

478. Committee on Expenditures in
the Treasury Department (Senate)
  Established: December 22, 1909,
    having been preceded by a
    select committee (Entry 479).
      44 CR 121.
  Authority: Res. of the Senate
    (61-1)
  Terminated: April 18, 1921
    61 CR 404-05.
  Authority: S. Res. 43 (67 -
    Special)

479. Select Committee on Expen-
ditures in the Treasury Depart-
ment (Senate)
  Established: December 17, 1907
    42 CR 384.
  Authority: Res. of the Senate
    (60-1)
  Terminated: December 22, 1909,
    when it was made a standing
    committee (Entry 478).
      44 CR 121.
  Authority: Res. of the Senate
    (61-1)

480. Committee on Expenditures in
the War Department (House)
  Sudocs: Y4. Ex7/10:
  Established: March 30, 1816
    Annals (14-1): 1298.
  Authority: Res. of the House
    (14-1)
  Terminated: December 5, 1927,
    and its functions transferred
    to the Committee on Expendi-
    tures in the Executive Depart-
    ments. Temporarily replaced by
    select committee during 66th
    Congress 1919-21 (Entries 457,
    482).
      69 CR 14.
  Authority: H. Res. 7 (70-1)

481. Committee on Expenditures in
the War Department (Senate)
  Established: December 22, 1909,
    having been preceded by a
    select committee (Entry 483).
      44 CR 121.
  Authority: Res. of the Senate
    (61-1)
  Terminated: April 18, 1921
    61 CR 404-05.
  Authority: S. Res. 43 (67 -
    Special)

482. Select Committee on Expendi-
tures in the War Department (House)
  Sudocs: Y4. Ex7/11:
  Established: June 4, 1919, as a
    temporary replacement of the
    standing committee (Entry 480).
      58 CR 647.
  Authority: H. Res. 78 (66-1)
  Terminated: March 3, 1921, at the
    end of the 66-3.

483. Select Committee on Expen-
ditures in the War Department
(Senate)
  Established: December 17, 1907
    42 CR 384.
  Authority: Res. of the Senate
    (60-1)
  Terminated: December 22, 1909,
    when it was made a standing
    committee (Entry 481).
    44 CR 121.
  Authority: Res. of the Senate
    (61-1)

484. Select Committee on Expen-
ditures, Navigation Laws, and
duties on Imports (House)
  Established: February 1, 1858
    H. J. (35-1): 260.
  Authority: Res. of the House
    (35-1)
  Terminated: June 14, 1858, at
    the end of the 35-1.

485. Select Committee on Export
Control (House)
  Sudocs: Y4. Ex7/15:
  Established: September 7, 1961
    107 CR 18594.
  Authority: H. Res. 403 (87-1)
  Terminated: May 31, 1962
    H. rpt. 1753 (87-2) 12430

486. Select Committee to Investi-
gate Bureaus and Agencies Dealing
with the Welfare of Ex-Servicemen
(Senate)
  Established: June 9, 1921
    61 CR 2303.
  Authority: S. Res. 59 (67-1)
  Terminated: February 17, 1923
    S. rpt. 1239 (67-4) 8156.

487. Special Committee to Investi-
gate Farm Labor Conditions in the
West (Senate)
  Sudocs: Y4. F22:
  Established: October 24, 1942
    88 CR 8655.
  Authority: S. Res. 299 (77-2)
  Terminated: December 16, 1942, at
    the end of the 77-2.

488. Select Committee on Fasting,
Prayer, and Humiliation (House)

Established: July 9, 1832
  H. J. (22-1): 1113.
Authority: Res. of the House
  (22-1)
Terminated: July 10, 1832
  Ibid. 1117.

489. Committee on Federal Aid
in Construction of Post Roads
(Joint)
  Sudocs: Y4. F31:
  Established: August 24, 1912
    37 Stat. 551.
  Authority: PL 62-336
  Terminated: November 25, 1914
    H. doc. 1510 (63-3) 6884.

490. Select Committee to Investi-
gate Federal Communications Com-
mission (House)
  Sudocs: Y4. F31/4:
  Established: January 19, 1943
    89 CR 248.
  Authority: H. Res. 21 (78-1)
  Terminated: January 2, 1945
    H. rpt. 2095 (78-2) 10848.

491. Special Committee on Federal
Penal and Reformatory Institutions
(House)
  Sudocs: Y4. F31/3:
  Established: May 29, 1928
    69 CR 10690.
  Authority: H. Res. 233 (70-1)
  Terminated: January 31, 1929
    H. rpt. 2303 (70-2) 8981.

492. Committee to Determine what
Employment may be Furnished Federal
Prisoners (Joint)
  Sudocs: Y4. F31/2:
  Established: March 2, 1923
    64 CR 5148.
  Authority: H. Con. Res. 53 (67-4)
  Terminated: December 3, 1923
    S. rpt. 1 (68-1) 8222.

493. Committee on the Federal
Reserve System (Joint)
  Established: March 4, 1923
    42 Stat. 1481.
  Authority: PL 67-503
  Terminated: March 3, 1925, at the
    end of the 68-2.

494. Select Committee on Assault
by A. P. Field on the Honorable
W. D. Kelley (House)
  Established: January 23, 1865
    H. J. (38-2): 135.
  Authority: Res. of the House
    (38-2)
  Terminated: February 7, 1865
    H. rpt. 10 (38-2) 1235.

495. Select Committee to Inquire
into an Error in the Publication
of the System of Field Services and
Police Adopted for the Army (House)
  Established: April 30, 1822
    H. J. (17-1): 520.
  Authority: Res. of the House
    (17-1)
  Terminated: May 6, 1822
    H. rpt. 108 (17-1) 71.

496. Select Committee on Fight
Between Mr. Wise and Mr. Stanly
(House)
  Established: September 9, 1841
    H. J. (27-1): 282.
  Authority: Res. of the House
    (27-1)
  Terminated: September 11, 1841
    Ibid. 513.

497. Select Committee on Fight in
the House Between Messrs. Bynum and
Rice Garland (House)
  Established: April 21, 1840
    H. J. (26-1): 814.
  Authority: Res. of the House
    (26-1)
  Terminated: April 27, 1840
    H. rpt. 488 (26-1) 371.

498. Committee on Finance (Senate)
  Sudocs: Y4. F49:
  Established: December 10, 1816
    Annals (14-2): 30.
  Authority: Res. of the Senate
    (14-2)
  Terminated: Still in existence at
    the end of the 97-2.

499. Select Committee on Finance
and Currency (House)
  Established: December 13, 1841
    H. J. (27-2): 40.
  Authority: Res. of the House
    (27-2)

Terminated: February 17, 1842
    H. rpt. 244 (27-2) 407.

500. Select Committee on Remission
of Fines and Forfeitures from the
Treasury Department (House)
  Established: December 18, 1812
    H. J. (12-2): 106.
  Authority: Res. of the House
    (12-2)
  Terminated: February 25, 1813
    Ibid. 365.

501. Select Committee on Purchase
of Fire Engines (Senate)
  Established: December 13, 1820
    S. J. (16-2): 61.
  Authority: Res. of the Senate
    (16-2)
  Terminated: March 3, 1821, at the
    end of the 16-2.

502. Special Committee on Fiscal
Affairs of the Government (Senate)
  Established: February 13, 1941
    87 CR 973.
  Authority: S. Res. 22 (77-1)
  Terminated: December 16, 1942, at
    the end of the 77-2.

503. Select Committee on the Em-
ployment of a Fiscal Agent (Senate)
  Established: June 3, 1841
    S. J. (27-1): 20.
  Authority: Res. of the Senate
    (27-1)
  Terminated: July 21, 1841
    Ibid. 51.

504. Select Committee on the
Fiscal Corporation of the U. S.
(Senate)
  Established: August 24, 1841
    S. J. (27-1): 213.
  Authority: Res. of the Senate
    (27-1)
  Terminated: February 21, 1842
    S. doc. 133 (27-2) 397.

505. Committee on Fisheries
(Senate)
  Sudocs: Y4. F53:
  Established: January 11, 1884
    15 CR 366.
  Authority: Res. of the Senate
    (48-1)

Terminated: April 18, 1921
   61 CR 404-05.
Authority: S. Res. 43 (67 -
   Special)

506. Select Committee on the
Character and Origin of Fishing
Bounties and Allowances (Senate)
   Established: March 30, 1840
      S. J. (26-1): 271.
   Authority: Res. of the Senate
      (26-1)
   Terminated: April 10, 1840
      S. doc. 368 (26-1) 359.

507. Select Committee on Altering
the Flag of the United States
(House)
   Established: December 12, 1816
      H. J. (14-2): 62.
   Authority: Res. of the House
      (14-2)
   Terminated: January 2, 1817
      Ibid. 130.

508. Select Committee on Deposit-
ing a Flag Carried at the Battle of
Wyoming at Lucerne County, Pennsyl-
vania (House)
   Established: December 29, 1837
      H. J. (25-2): 160.
   Authority: Res. of the House
      (25-2)
   Terminated: July 9, 1838, at the
      end of the 25-2.

509. Select Committee to Inquire
into the State, Condition, and
Distribution of Flags and Standards
Taken from the Enemy (House)
   Established: December 20, 1813
      H. J. (13-2): 48.
   Authority: Res. of the House
      (13-2)
   Terminated: February 4, 1814
      Ibid. 276.

510. Committee on Flood Control
(House)
   Sudocs: Y4. F65:
   Established: February 3, 1916
      53 CR 2067.
   Authority: H. Res. 122 (64-1)
   Terminated: January 2, 1947
      60 Stat. 812.
   Authority: PL 79-601

511. Select Committee on the
Petition of Sundry Inhabitatants
of Florida (House)
   Established: December 31, 1821
      H. J. (17-1): 101.
   Authority: Res. of the House
      (17-1)
   Terminated: May 8, 1822, at the
      end of the 17-1.

512. Select Committee on West
Florida (House)
   Established: December 10, 1810
      H. J. (11-3): 23.
   Authority: Res. of the House
      (11-3)
   Terminated: July 6, 1812, at the
      end of the 12-1.

513. Select Committee on the Divi-
sion of Florida and its Admission
Into the Union (Senate)
   Established: February 12, 1840
      S. J. (26-1): 173.
   Authority: Res. of the Senate
      (26-1)
   Terminated: July 1, 1840, at the
      end of the 26-1.

514. Select Committee to Investi-
gate Supplies and Shortages of
Food, Particularly Meat (House)
   Established: March 27, 1945
      91 CR 2863.
   Authority: H. Res. 195 (79-1)
   Terminated: June 29, 1945
      H. rpt. 842 (79-1) 10934.

515. Select Committee to Investi-
gate use of Chemicals in Food
Products (House)
   Sudocs: Y4. F73/2:
   Established: June 20, 1950
      96 CR 8936.
   Authority: H. Res. 323 (81-2)
   Terminated: July 5, 1952
      H. rpt. 2356 (82-2) 11578.

516. Special Committee to Investi-
gate Food Shortages (House)
   Sudocs: Y4. F73:
   Established: March 27, 1945
      91 CR 2863.
   Authority: H. Res. 195 (79-1)
   Terminated: June 29, 1945
      H. rpt. 842 (79-1) 10934.

517. Select Committee on the Ford Theater Disaster (Senate)
  Established: December 14, 1893
    26 CR 234.
  Authority: Res. of the Senate
    (53-2)
  Terminated: August 28, 1894, at
    the end of the 53-2, when it
    merged with the joint commit-
    tee (Entry 518).

518. Committee on the Ford's Theater Disaster (Joint)
  Established: August 18, 1894
    28 Stat. 392.
  Authority: Public Act Making
    Appropriations for Sundry
    Civil Expenses of Government
    (53-2) (Entry 517).
  Terminated: February 25, 1897
    S. rpt. 1548 (54-2) 3476.

519. Committee on Foreign Affairs (House)
  Sudocs: Y4. F76/1:
  Established: March 13, 1822,
    having been preceded by several
    select committees.
      H. J. (17-1): 351.
  Authority: Res. of the House
    (17-1)
  Terminated: March 19, 1975, when
    the name was changed to the
    Committee on International
    Relations (Entry 702).
      121 CR 7344.
  Authority: H. Res. 163 (94-1)

520. Committee on Foreign Affairs (House)
  Sudocs: Y4. F76/1:
  Established: February 5, 1979,
    when it replaced the Committee
    on International Relations
    (Entry 702).
      125 CR 1849.
  Authority: H. Res. 89 (96-1)
  Terminated: Still in existence at
    the end of the 97-2.

521. Select Committee on Foreign Aid (House)
  Sudocs: Y4. F76/5:
  Established: July 22, 1947
    93 CR 9761.
  Authority: H. Res. 296 (80-1)

Terminated: May 3, 1948
  H. rpt. 1845 (80-2) 11214.

522. Special Committee to Study Foreign Aid Program (Senate)
  Sudocs: Y4. F76/6:
  Established: July 11, 1956
    102 CR 12320.
  Authority: S. Res. 285 (84-2)
  Terminated: August 30, 1957, at
    the end of the 85-1.

523. Select Committee on Investi-gation of Depreciation of Foreign Currencies (Senate)
  Established: April 12, 1932
    75 CR 8007.
  Authority: S. Res. 156 (72-1)
  Terminated: March 3, 1933, at the
    end of the 72-2.

524. Committee on Foreign Economic Cooperation (Joint)
  Established: April 3, 1948
    62 Stat. 156.
  Authority: PL 80-472
  Terminated: March 3, 1950
    S. doc. 142 (81-2) 11401.

525. Committee on Foreign Rela-tions (Senate)
  Sudocs: Y4. F76/2:
  Established: December 10, 1816
    Annals (14-2): 30.
  Authority: Res. of the Senate
    (14-2)
  Terminated: Still in existence at
    the end of the 97-2.

526. Committee on Forest Reser-vations and Protection of Game (Senate)
  Sudocs: Y4. F76/3:
  Established: March 19, 1896,
    having been preceded by the
    Select Committee on Forest
    Reservations (Entry 527).
      28 CR 2960.
  Authority: Res. of the Senate
    (54-1)
  Terminated: April 18, 1921
    61 CR 404-05.
  Authority: S. Res. 43 (67 -
    Special)

527. Select Committee on Forest
Reservations (Senate)
  Sudocs: Y4. F76/3:
  Established: March 15, 1893,
    having been preceded by
    Select Committee on Forest
    Reservations in California
    (Entry 528).
      25 CR 17.
  Authority: Res. of the Senate
    (53-1)
  Terminated: March 19, 1896,
    when it was made a standing
    committee (Entry 526).
      28 CR 2960.
  Authority: Res. of the Senate
    (54-1)

528. Select Committee on Forest
Reservations in California (Senate)
  Established: July 28, 1892
    23 CR 6887.
  Authority: Res. of the Senate
    (52-1)
  Terminated: March 15, 1893,
    when name was changed to
    Select Committee on Forest
    Reservations (Entry 527).
      25 CR 17.
  Authority: Res. of the Senate
    (53-1)

529. Committee on Forestry (Joint)
  Sudocs: Y4. F76/4:
  Established: June 14, 1938
    83 CR 9146.
  Authority: S. Con. Res. 31 (75-3)
  Terminated: March 24, 1941
    H. rpt. 323 (77-1) 10553.

530. Select Committee on Forms of
Returns Necessary for Members of
the House (House)
  Established: March 23, 1840
    H. J. (26-1): 669.
  Authority: Res. of the House
    (26-1)
  Terminated: July 21, 1840, at the
    end of the 26-1.

531. Select Committee on Sale of
the Fort Snelling Reservation
(House)
  Established: January 2, 1858
    H. J. (35-1): 129.

  Authority: Res. of the House
    (35-1)
  Terminated: April 27, 1858
    H. rpt. 351 (35-1) 965.

532. Select Committee of Five on
the Fort Sumter Surrender (House)
  Sudocs: Y4. F58:
  Established: January 9, 1861
    Cong. Globe (36-2): 296.
  Authority: Res. of the House
    (36-2)
  Terminated: February 28, 1861
    H. rpt. 91 (36-2) 1105.

533. Select Committee on the Re-
pairs to Fortifications, and to the
Farther Protection of Our Ports,
and Towns, and Rivers (House)
  Established: December 2, 1806
    H. J. (9-2): 9.
  Authority: Res. of the House
    (9-2)
  Terminated: April 25, 1808, at
    the end of the 10-1.

534. Select Committee on Exchang-
ing, for Other Land, the Site of
the Fortification Near Portland
Harbor (House)
  Established: April 5, 1808
    H. J. (10-1): 542.
  Authority: Res. of the House
    (10-1)
  Terminated: April 9, 1808
    Ibid. 557.

535. Select Committee on National
Foundry (House)
  Established: January 2, 1835
    H. J. (23-2): 156.
  Authority: Res. of the House
    (23-2)
  Terminated: March 3, 1835
    H. rpt. 141 (23-2) 276.

536. Select Committee on National
Foundry (House)
  Established: January 10, 1837
    H. J. (25-2): 252.
  Authority: Res. of the House
    (25-2)
  Terminated: July 21, 1840, at the
    end of the 26-1.

537. Select Committee on the
National Foundry (House)
  Established: December 13, 1841
    H. J. (27-2): 40.
  Authority: Res. of the House
    (27-2)
  Terminated: February 23, 1843
    H. rpt. 229 (27-3) 427.

538. Select Committee on Petition
of the Old Fourth Regiment of the
United States (House)
  Established: February 17, 1837
    H. J. (25-2): 461.
  Authority: Res. of the House
    (25-2)
  Terminated: July 21, 1840, at the
    end of the 26-1.

539. Select Committee on Alleged
Abuses of the Franking Privilege
(House)
  Established: March 23, 1840
    H. J. (26-1): 661.
  Authority: Res. of the House
    (26-1)
  Terminated: July 21, 1840, at the
    end of the 26-1.

540. Select Committee on the Bill
to Abolish the Franking Privilege
(House)
  Established: February 17, 1860
    H. J. (36-1): 338.
  Authority: Res. of the House
    (36-1)
  Terminated: December 6, 1860
    H. rpt. 1 (36-2) 1104.

541. Select Committee on Violation
of Franking Privilege by Members of
the Post Office Department (House)
  Established: May 22, 1844
    H. J. (28-1): 952.
  Authority: Res. of the House
    (28-1)
  Terminated: June 15, 1844
    H. rpt. 576 (28-1) 447.

542. Select Committee on Alleged
Fraud in Contract to Supply
Emigrating Indians (House)
  Established: May 14, 1832
    H. J. (22-1): 740.
  Authority: Res. of the House
    (22-1)

  Terminated: July 5, 1832
    Ibid. 1088.

543. Select Committee on Frauds
and Depredations in Public Service
(House)
  Established: January 9, 1909
    43 CR 699.
  Authority: H. Res. 480 (60-2)
  Terminated: March 3, 1909
    H. rpt. 2320 (60-2) 5387.

544. Select Committee on the
Freedman's Bank (House)
  Established: January 5, 1876
    H. J. (44-1): 105.
  Authority: Res. of the House
    (44-1)
  Terminated: May 19, 1876
    H. rpt. 502 (44-1) 1710.

545. Select Committee to Investi-
gate Freedman's Savings and Trust
Company (Senate)
  Established: April 7, 1879
    9 CR 286.
  Authority: Res. of the Senate
    (46-1)
  Terminated: April 2, 1880
    S. rpt. 440 (46-2) 1895.

546. Select Committee on Freedmen
(House)
  Established: December 6, 1865
    Cong. Globe (39-1): 14.
  Authority: Res. of the House
    (39-1)
  Terminated: December 4, 1866,
    when it was made a standing
    committee (Entry 547).
      H. J. (39-2): 25.
  Authority: Res. of the House
    (39-2)

547. Committee on Freedmen's
Affairs (House)
  Established: December 4, 1866,
    having been preceded by a
    select committee (Entry 546).
      H. J. (39-2): 25.
  Authority: Res. of the House
    (39-2)
  Terminated: March 3, 1875, at the
    end of the 43-2.

548. Select Committee on Pub-
lication of the Results of the
Exploring Expedition of John C.
Fremont (Senate)
   Established: June 26, 1848
      S. J. (30-1): 496.
   Authority: Res. of the Senate
      (30-1)
   Terminated: August 9, 1848
      S. rpt. 226 (30-1) 512.

549. Select Committee on French
Spoliations (Senate)
   Established: December 20, 1826
      S. J. (19-2): 51.
   Authority: Res. of the Senate
      (19-2)
   Terminated: March 3, 1835, at the
      end of the 23-2.

550. Select Committee on French
Spoliation Claims (Senate)
   Established: January 5, 1858
      S. J. (35-1): 80.
   Authority: Res. of the Senate
      (35-1)
   Terminated: June 11, 1860
      S. J. (36-1): 610.

551. Select Committee on French
Spoliations Prior to 1800 (Senate)
   Established: December 18, 1845
      S. J. (29-1): 56.
   Authority: Res. of the Senate
      (29-1)
   Terminated: March 3, 1847, at the
      end of the 29-2.

552. Select Committee on French
Spoliations Prior to 1801 (Senate)
   Established: January 9, 1850
      S. J. (31-1): 66.
   Authority: Res. of the Senate
      (31-1)
   Terminated: August 7, 1854, at
      the end of the 33-1.

553. Special Committee to Investi-
gate Fuel Situation in the Middle
West (Senate)
   Sudocs: Y4. F95:
   Established: December 15, 1942
      88 CR 9545.
   Authority: S. Res. 319 (77-2)
   Terminated: October 5, 1943
      S. rpt. 443 (78-1) 10757.

554. Special Committee to Investi-
gate the Production of Fuels in
Areas West of the Mississippi River
(Senate)
   Established: December 15, 1942
      88 CR 9545.
   Authority: S. Res. 319 (77-2)
   Terminated: August 2, 1946, at
      the end of the 79-2.

555. Select Committee on Petitions
of the Legislatures of the Territo-
ries of Illinois and Mississippi
and on a Resolution Relating to
Fugitives from Justice (House)
   Established: January 31, 1815
      H. J. (13-3): 590.
   Authority: Res. of the House
      (13-3)
   Terminated: February 6, 1815
      Ibid. 615.

556. Select Committee on Appre-
hending Fugitives from Justice in
the Indiana Territory (House)
   Established: December 20, 1810
      H. J. (11-3): 59.
   Authority: Res. of the House
      (11-3)
   Terminated: January 3, 1811
      Ibid. 96.

557. Select Committee on Fugitive
Slaves (House)
   Established: January 15, 1819
      H. J. (15-2): 188.
   Authority: Res. of the House
      (15-2)
   Terminated: January 16, 1819
      Ibid. 191.

558. Select Committee to Inves-
tigate Educational and Training
Program Under GI Bill (House)
   Sudocs: Y4. Ed8/4:
   Established: August 28, 1950
      96 CR 13629.
   Authority: H. Res. 474 (81-2)
   Terminated: February 14, 1952
      H. rpt. 1375 (82-2) 11579.

559. Select Committee on G. W.
Crawford's Connection with the
Galphin Claim (House)
   Established: April 3, 1850
      H. J. (31-1): 741.

Authority: Res. of the House
(31-1)
Terminated: September 30, 1850,
at the end of the 31-1.

560. Special Committee to Investigate Gasoline and Fuel Oil Shortages (Senate)
Sudocs: Y4. G21:
Established: August 28, 1941
87 CR 7239.
Authority: S. Res. 156 (77-1)
Terminated: December 19, 1944,
at the end of the 78-2.

561. Select Committee to Repeal
so much of the Ordinance for the
Territorial Governments As Autho-
rized Governors to Prolong General
Assemblies (House)
Established: June 2, 1809
H. J. (11-1): 71.
Authority: Res. of the House
(11-1)
Terminated: June 28, 1809, at the
end of the 11-1.

562. Committee on the Geological
Survey (Senate)
Established: December 15, 1899,
having been preceded by a
select committee (Entry 563).
33 CR 441.
Authority: Res. of the Senate
(56-1)
Terminated: April 18, 1921
61 CR 404-05.
Authority: S. Res. 43 (67 -
Special)

563. Select Committee to Investigate the Operations of the
Geological Survey (Senate)
Established: July 28, 1892
S. J. (52-1): 407.
Authority: Res. of the Senate
(52-1)
Terminated: December 15, 1899,
when it became a standing
committee (Entry 562).
33 CR 441.
Authority: Res. of the Senate
(56-1)

564. Select Committee on the memorial of the Citizens of Georgetown,

D. C. for the Retrocession of that
Part of the District (Senate)
Established: April 10, 1838
S. J. (25-2): 349.
Authority: Res. of the Senate
(25-2)
Terminated: July 3, 1838
Ibid. 519.

565. Select Committee on Estab-
lishing Certain Post-Roads in
Georgia (House)
Established: April 20, 1808
H. J. (10-1): 603.
Authority: Res. of the House
(10-1)
Terminated: April 21, 1808
Ibid. 607.

566. Select Committee on Inter-
ference with the Rights of Georgia
(House)
Established: February 7, 1817
H. J. (14-2): 359.
Authority: Res. of the House
(14-2)
Terminated: February 11, 1817
Ibid. 380.

567. Select Committee on Georgia
and the Creek Indians (Senate)
Established: February 5, 1827
S. J. (19-2): 150.
Authority: Res. of the Senate
(19-2)
Terminated: March 3, 1827, at the
end of the 19-2.

568. Select Committee on Georgia
Memorial for Payment of Revolution-
ary Debt (House)
Established: December 20, 1838
H. J. (25-3): 117.
Authority: Res. of the House
(25-3)
Terminated: July 21, 1840, at the
end of the 26-1.

569. Select Committee on the
Petition of the State of Georgia
to Survey Lands in the Big Bend
of Tennessee (House)
Established: December 3, 1818
H. J. (15-2): 59.
Authority: Res. of the House
(15-2)

Terminated: December 14, 1818
  Ibid. 91.

570. Select Committee on Honor-
able J. R. Giddings of Abstracting
Papers from the Post Office Depart-
ment (House)
  Established: July 6, 1850
    H. J. (31-1): 1086.
  Authority: Res. of the House
    (31-1)
  Terminated: September 30, 1850,
    at the end of the 31-1.

571. Select Committee on the Con-
stitutionality of the Appointment
of Peter B. Porter, as a Commis-
sioner to Run the Line Under the
Treaty of Ghent (House)
  Established: February 9, 1816
    H. J. (14-1): 303.
  Authority: Res. of the House
    (14-1)
  Terminated: April 30, 1816, at
    the end of the 14-1.

572. Select Committee on the
Fifth Article of the Treaty of
Ghent (House)
  Established: February 8, 1822
    H. J. (17-1): 255.
  Authority: Res. of the House
    (17-1)
  Terminated: May 8, 1822, at the
    end of the 17-1.

573. Select Committee on the
Fifth, Sixth, and Seventh Articles
of the Treaty of Ghent (House)
  Established: December 28, 1820
    H. J. (16-2): 94.
  Authority: Res. of the House
    (16-2)
  Terminated: February 3, 1821
    Ibid. 189.

574. Select Committee to Investi-
gate the Preparation, Sale, and
Final Disposition of Government
Bonds and Other Securities (House)
  Established: March 24, 1924
    65 CR 4818.
  Authority: H. Res. 231 (68-1)
  Terminated: March 2, 1925
    H. rpt. 1635 (68-2) 8392.

575. Special Committee on Investi-
gation of Government Competition
with Private Enterprise (House)
  Established: May 31, 1932
    75 CR 11682.
  Authority: H. Res. 235 (72-1)
  Terminated: February 8, 1933
    H. rpt. 1985 (72-2) 9650.

576. Select Committee on Govern-
ment Contracts (House)
  Established: July 8, 1861
    H. J. (37-1): 45.
  Authority: Res. of the House
    (37-1)
  Terminated: March 3, 1863
    H. rpt. 50 (37-3) 1173.

577. Select Committee In Regard to
Interest of Government Employees in
Banking Institutions Having Con-
tracts of Dealing in Stocks (House)
  Established: December 22, 1862
    H. J. (37-3): 117.
  Authority: Res. of the House
    (37-3)
  Terminated: March 3, 1863
    H. rpt. 64 (37-3) 1173.

578. Select Committee on Reduction
of Government Expenditures (House)
  Established: July 13, 1861
    H. J. (37-1): 78.
  Authority: Res. of the House
    (37-1)
  Terminated: March 3, 1863, at the
    end of the 37-3.

579. Special Committee on Investi-
gation of Government Hospital for
Insane (House)
  Sudocs: Y4. G74:
  Established: April 21, 1906
    40 CR 5660.
  Authority: H. Res. 277 (59-1)
  Terminated: February 18, 1907
    H. rpt. 7644 (59-2) 5066-67.

580. Committee on Government
Operations (House)
  Sudocs: Y4. G74/7:
  Established: July 3, 1952, when
    it replaced the Committee on
    Expenditures in the Executive
    Departments (Entry 457).
    98 CR 9217.

Authority: H. Res. 647 (82-2)
Terminated: Still in existence at
the end of the 97-2.

581. Committee on Government
Operations (Senate)
  Sudocs: Y4. G74/6:
  Established: March 3, 1952, when
    it replaced the Committee on
    Expenditures in the Executive
    Departments (Entry 458).
      S. J. (82-2): 127.
  Authority: S. Res. 280 (82-2)
  Terminated: February 11, 1977,
    when the Committee on Govern-
    mental Affairs was established
    (Entry 587).
      123 CR 3691.
  Authority: S. Res. 4 (95-1)

582. Select Committee on Govern-
ment Organization (House)
  Sudocs: Y4. G74/3:
  Established: January 14, 1937
    81 CR 243.
  Authority: H. Res. 60 (75-1)
  Terminated: January 3, 1941, at
    the end of the 76-3.

583. Committee on Government
Organization (Joint)
  Sudocs: Y4. G74/4:
  Established: February 3, 1937
    50 Stat. 7.
  Authority: H. J. Res. 81 (75-1)
  Terminated: August 21, 1937, at
    the end of the 75-1.

584. Select Committee on Govern-
ment Organization (Senate)
  Sudocs: Y4. G74/5:
  Established: January 29, 1937
    81 CR 551.
  Authority: S. Res. 69 (75-1)
  Terminated: January 3, 1941, at
    the end of the 76-3.

585. Select Committee on Inves-
tigation of Government Printing
Office (Senate)
  Sudocs: Y4. G74/2:
  Established: January 30, 1888
    19 CR 816.
  Authority: Res. of the House
    (50-1)

Terminated: August 23, 1888
  H. rpt. 3300 (50-1) 2608.

586. Select Committee on Govern-
ment Research (House)
  Sudocs: Y4. G74/8:
  Established: September 11, 1963
    109 CR 16754.
  Authority: H. Res. 504 (88-1)
  Terminated: January 3, 1965
    H. rpt. 1941 (88-2) 12621-5.

587. Committee on Governmental
Affairs (Senate)
  Sudocs: Y4. G74/9:
  Established: February 11, 1977,
    when it replaced several com-
    mittees (Entries 349, 581).
      123 CR 3691.
  Authority: S. Res. 4 (95-1)
  Terminated: Still in existence at
    the end of the 97-2.

588. Select Committee on Protec-
tion for Grain Growing Interest
(House)
  Established: January 7, 1842
    H. J. (27-2): 133.
  Authority: Res. of the House
    (27-2)
  Terminated: August 31, 1842, at
    the end of the 27-2.

589. Select Committee on
Alleged Assault on Honorable
Amos P. Granager (House)
  Established: August 18, 1856
    H. J. (34-1): 1527.
  Authority: Res. of the House
    (34-1)
  Terminated: August 26, 1856
    H. rpt. (34-2) 870.

590. Select Committee to Inves-
tigate the Official Conduct of
Gideon Granger, Post-Master
General (House)
  Established: March 21, 1806
    H. J. (9-1): 347.
  Authority: Res. of the House
    (9-1)
  Terminated: April 21, 1806
    Ibid. 487.

591. Select Committee on the Memorial of Duff Green (Senate)

Established: December 14, 1837
    S. J. (25-2): 47.
Authority: Res. of the Senate
    (25-2)
Terminated: July 9, 1838, at the
    end of the 25-2.

592. Select Committee on Guano
Trade (House)
    Established: June 10, 1854
        H. J. (33-1): 977.
    Authority: Res. of the House
        (33-1)
    Terminated: August 7, 1854

593. Select Committee on Printing
the Charts and Survey of the Coast
of the Gulf of Mexico (House)
    Established: May 12, 1842
        H. J. (27-2): 805.
    Authority: Res. of the House
        (27-2)
    Terminated: July 4, 1842
        Ibid. 1048.

594. Select Committee on Building
Gun Ships (House)
    Established: December 4, 1805
        H. J. (9-1): 23.
    Authority: Res. of the House
        (9-1)
    Terminated: April 25, 1808, at
        the end of the 10-1.

595. Committee on Haiti and Santo
Domingo (Senate)
    Sudocs: Y4. H12:
    Established: July 27, 1921
        61 CR 4333.
    Authority: S. Res. 112 (67-1)
    Terminated: June 26, 1922
        S. rpt. 794 (67-2) 7954.

596. Select Committee on a Monument to Nathan Hale (House)
    Established: January 6, 1836
        H. J. (24-1): 146.
    Authority: Res. of the House
        (24-1)
    Terminated: May 24, 1842
        H. rpt. 783 (27-2) 410.

597. Select Committee on Harpers
Ferry Invasion (Senate)
    Sudocs: Y4. H23:

Established: July 25, 1861
    Cong. Globe (37-1): 253.
Authority: Res. of the Senate
    (37-1)
Terminated: April 18, 1862
    S. rpt. 37 (37-2) 1125.

598. Select Committee to Inquire
into the Facts of the Recent Invasion and Seizure of the United
States Armory at Harpers Ferry
(Senate)
    Established: December 15, 1859
        S. J. (36-1): 12.
    Authority: Res. of the Senate
        (36-1)
    Terminated: June 15, 1860
        S. rpt. 278 (36-1) 1040.

599. Select Committee on Harriman
Geographic Code System (Joint)
    Sudocs: Y4. H23/2:
    Established: March 4, 1927
        68 CR 5917.
    Authority: Public Res. 70 (69-2)
    Terminated: February 7, 1929
        H. rpt. 2419 (70-2) 8980.

600. Select Committee on General
Harrison's Accounts (House)
    Established: December 31, 1816
        H. J. (14-2): 126.
    Authority: Res. of the House
        (14-2)
    Terminated: January 23, 1817
        Ibid. 268.

601. Select Committee Appointed to
Investigate the Memorial of Davis
Hatch (Senate)
    Sudocs: Y4. H28:
    Established: June 8, 1870
        Cong. Globe (41-2): 4201.
    Authority: Res. of the Senate
        (41-2)
    Terminated: June 25, 1870
        S. rpt. 234 (41-2) 1409.

602. Committee on Hawaii (Joint)
    Sudocs: Y4. H31:
    Established: August 21, 1937
        81 CR 9625.
    Authority: S. Con. Res. 18 (75-1)
    Terminated: February 15, 1938
        S. doc. 151 (75-3) 10247.

603. Select Committee to Investigate Charges by Mr. Heflin (House)
 Established: October 4, 1917
  H. J. (65-1): 400.
 Authority: H. Res. 165 (65-1)
 Terminated: October 6, 1917
  H. rpt. 201 (65-1) 7254.

604. Select Committee to Investigate a Certain Letter Written by Senator Heflin on Intermarriages in New York (Senate)
 Established: February 7, 1930
  72 CR 3241.
 Authority: Motion of the Senate (71-2)
 Terminated: March 3, 1931, at the end of the 71-3.

605. Select Committee on Agency for Inspection and Manufacture of Water-Rotted Hemp (House)
 Established: February 14, 1842
  H. J. (27-2): 396.
 Authority: Res. of the House (27-2)
 Terminated: April 7, 1842
  H. rpt. 551 (27-2) 408.

606. Select Committee on Charges Against Hornor, Doorkeeper (House)
 Established: April 18, 1850
  H. J. (31-1): 808.
 Authority: Res. of the House (31-1)
 Terminated: September 30, 1850, at the end of the 31-1.

607. Special Committee on the Cause of the Omission of the Clause Relating to the Hot Springs of Arkansas in the Sundry Civil Appropriation Bill (Senate)
 Established: December 3, 1878
  S. J. (45-3): 26.
 Authority: Res. of the Senate (45-3)
 Terminated: February 19, 1879
  S. rpt. 784 (45-3) 1838.

608. Select Committee on the Memorial of Certain Settlers on the Houmas Lands (Senate)
 Established: January 4, 1860
  S. J. (36-1): 59.
 Authority: Senate Order (36-1)

Terminated: March 23, 1860
  S. rpt. 150 (36-1) 1039.

609. Select Committee on the Number and Compensation of the Employees of the House (House)
 Established: August 3, 1854
  H. J. (33-1): 1295.
 Authority: Res. of the House (33-1)
 Terminated: August 7, 1854, at the end of the 33-1.

610. Select Committee on Charges Against the Clerk of the House (House)
 Established: May 18, 1876
  H. J. (44-1): 975.
 Authority: Res. of the House (44-1)
 Terminated: June 27, 1876
  H. J. (44-1): 1168-69.

611. Committee on House Administration (House)
 Sudocs: Y4. H31/3:
 Established: January 2, 1947, when several committees were abolished and their functions were transferred to this committee.
  60 Stat. 812.
 Authority: PL 79-601
 Terminated: Still in existence at the end of the 97-2.

612. Select Committee on the House Beauty Shop (House)
 Established: December 6, 1967
  113 CR 35143.
 Authority: H. Res. 1000 (90-1)
 Terminated: January 2, 1971, at the end of the 91-2.

613. Special Committee to Investigate the Appointment and Payment of House Employees (House)
 Established: February 23, 1901
  34 CR 2909.
 Authority: H. Res. 429 (56-2)
 Terminated: March 3, 1903, at the end of the 57-2.

614. Select Committee on Distribution of Rooms in the House Office Building (House)

Established: December 21, 1907
42 CR 465.
Authority: Res. of the House
(60-1)
Terminated: February 23, 1909
H. rpt. 2277 (60-2) 5386.

615. Select Committee on the House
Recording Studio (House)
Established: June 27, 1956
70 Stat. 356.
Authority: PL 84-624
Terminated: Still in existence at
the end of the 97-2.

616. Select Committee Pursuant to
House Resolution 1 - on the Seating
of Adam Clayton Powell (House)
Sudocs: Y4. 81/5:
Established: January 10, 1967
113 CR 27.
Authority: H. Res. 1 (90-1)
Terminated: February 23, 1967
H. rpt. 27 (90-1) 12755-2.

617. Select Committee on the House
Restaurant (House)
Sudocs: Y4. H81/6:
Established: July 10, 1969
115 CR 19081.
Authority: H. Res. 472 (91-1)
Terminated: December 20, 1974, at
the end of the 93-2.

618. Special Committee to Inves-
tigate Management and Control of
House Restaurant (House)
Sudocs: Y4. H81/2:
Established: April 25, 1934
78 CR 7360.
Authority: H. Res. 236 (73-2)
Terminated: June 8, 1934
H. rpt. 1920 (73-2) 9782.

619. Committee on Housing (Joint)
Sudocs: Y4. H81/4:
Established: July 25, 1947
93 CR 10187.
Authority: H. Con. Res. 104
(80-1)
Terminated: March 15, 1948
H. rpt. 1564 (80-2) 11210.

620. Select Committee to Conduct
the Trial of Samuel Houston (House)

Established: April 17, 1832
H. J. (22-1): 601.
Authority: Res. of the House
(22-1)
Terminated: April 17, 1832
H. rpt. 447 (22-1) 226.

621. Committee on Human Resources
(Senate)
Sudocs: Y4. H88:
Established: February 11, 1977,
when the name of the Committee
on Labor and Public Welfare was
changed to this (Entry 744).
123 CR 3691.
Authority: S. Res. 4 (95-1)
Terminated: March 7, 1979, when
name was changed to Committee
on Labor and Human Resources
(Entry 743).
125 CR 4243.
Authority: S. Res. 30 (96-1)

622. Select Committee on the
Message of the House of Represen-
tatives in Relation to the Impeach-
ment of West H. Humphreys (Senate)
Established: May 8, 1862
S. J. (37-2): 457.
Authority: Senate Order (37-2)
Terminated: May 9, 1862
Ibid. 465.

623. Select Committee on Illegal
Traffic of Negroes in and Through
the District of Columbia (House)
Established: March 1, 1816
H. J. (14-1): 424.
Authority: Res. of the House
(14-1)
Terminated: April 30, 1816
Ibid. 760.

624. Select Committee on the Con-
stitution of the State of Illinois
(House)
Established: November 19, 1818
H. J. (15-2): 22.
Authority: Res. of the House
(15-2)
Terminated: November 20, 1818
Ibid. 25.

625. Select Committee on an
Illinois Canal Between Lake Michigan and the Illinois River (House)

Established: January 3, 1825
  H. J. (18-2): 96.
Authority: Res. of the House
  (18-2)
Terminated: February 1, 1825
  H. rpt. 53 (18-2) 122.

626. Select Committee on Amendments to the Act to Extend the Right of Suffrage in the Illinois Territory (House)
  Established: February 4, 1813
    H. J. (12-2): 259.
  Authority: Res. of the House
    (12-2)
  Terminated: February 15, 1813
    Ibid. 299.

627. Select Committee on Certain Resolutions of the Legislature of the Illinois Territory (House)
  Established: January 25, 1813
    H. J. (12-2): 210.
  Authority: Res. of the House
    (12-2)
  Terminated: February 6, 1813
    Ibid. 263.

628. Committee on Immigration (Senate)
  Sudocs: Y4. Im6/2:
  Established: December 12, 1889
    21 CR 157.
  Authority: Res. of the Senate
    (51-1)
  Terminated: January 2, 1947,
    and functions were transferred
    to Judiciary Committee (Entry
    732).
      60 Stat. 812.
  Authority: PL 79-601

629. Committee on Immigration and Nationality Policy (Joint)
  Established: June 27, 1952
    66 Stat. 274.
  Authority: PL 82-414
  Terminated: October 26, 1970
    84 Stat. 1189.
  Authority: PL 91-510

630. Committee on Immigration and Naturalization (House)
  Sudocs: Y4. Im6/1:

Established: August 21, 1893,
  having been preceded by a
  select committee (Entry 632).
    25 CR 555.
Authority: Res. of the House
  (53-1)
Terminated: January 2, 1947
  60 Stat. 812.
Authority: PL 79-601

631. Committee on Immigration and Naturalization (Senate)
  Sudocs: Y4. Im6/1:
  Established: August 18, 1893,
    having been preceded by a
    select committee (Entry 633).
      25 CR 478.
  Authority: Res. of the Senate
    (53-1)
  Terminated: January 2, 1947
    60 Stat. 812.
  Authority: PL 79-601

632. Select Committee on Immigration and Naturalization (House)
  Established: December 20, 1889
    H. J. (51-1): 74.
  Authority: Res. of the House
    (51-1)
  Terminated: August 21, 1893,
    when it was made a standing
    committee (Entry 630).
      25 CR 555.
  Authority: Res. of the House
    (53-1)

633. Select Committee on Immigration and Naturalization (Senate)
  Sudocs: Y4. Im6/1:
  Established: December 20, 1889
    21 CR 336.
  Authority: Res. of the Senate
    (51-1)
  Terminated: August 18, 1893,
    when it was made a standing
    committee (Entry 631).
      25 CR 478.
  Authority: Res. of the Senate
    (53-1)

634. Select Committee to Consider and Report on the Message of the House Respecting the Impeachment of the President (Senate)
  Established: February 25, 1868
    Cong. Globe (40-2): 1407.

Authority: Res. of the Senate
(40-2)
Terminated: February 26, 1868
S. J. (40-2): 222.

635. Select Committee to Investi-
gate in Regard to Alleged Improper
Influences on the Impeachment Trial
(Senate)
Established: May 27, 1868
Cong. Globe (40-2): 2598.
Authority: Res. of the Senate
(40-2)
Terminated: November 10, 1868,
at the end of the 40-2.

636. Select Committee on Impress-
ments (House)
Established: January 18, 1812
H. J. (12-1): 276.
Authority: Res. of the House
(12-1)
Terminated: July 6, 1812, at the
end of the 12-1.

637. Select Committee on the
Official Conduct of Harry Inaes,
District Judge of the District of
Kentucky (House)
Established: March 31, 1808
H. J. (10-1): 535.
Authority: Res. of the House
(10-1)
Terminated: April 19, 1808
Ibid. 591.

638. Select Committee on Incendi-
ary Publications (Senate)
Established: December 26, 1835
S. J. (24-1): 46.
Authority: Res. of the Senate
(24-1)
Terminated: February 4, 1836
S. doc. 118 (24-1) 280.

639. Committee on Indian Affairs
(House)
Sudocs: Y4. In2/1:
Established: December 15, 1821,
having been preceded by a
select committee (Entry 642).
H. J. (17-1): 57.
Authority: Res. of the House
(17-1)

Terminated: January 2, 1947
60 Stat. 812.
Authority: PL 79-601

640. Committee on Indian Affairs
(Senate)
Sudocs: Y4. In2/2:
Established: January 3, 1820
Annals (16-1): 51.
Authority: Res. of the Senate
(16-1)
Terminated: January 2, 1947
60 Stat. 812.
Authority: PL 79-601

641. Select Committee on Indian
Affairs (House)
Established: November 12, 1811
H. J. (12-1): 36.
Authority: Res. of the House
(12-1)
Terminated: May 29, 1812
Ibid. 757.

642. Select Committee on Indian
Affairs (House)
Established: December 3, 1817
H. J. (15-1): 19.
Authority: Res. of the House
(15-1)
Terminated: December 15, 1821,
when it was made a standing
committee (Entry 639).
H. J. (17-1): 57.
Authority: Res. of the House
(17-1)

643. Select Committee on Indian
Affairs (House)
Established: January 17, 1865
H. J. (38-2): 107.
Authority: Res. of the House
(38-2)
Terminated: March 3, 1865, at the
end of the 38-2.

644. Temporary Select Committee on
Indian Affairs (Senate)
Sudocs: Y4. In2/11:
Established: February 11, 1977
123 CR 3691.
Authority: S. Res. 4 (95-1)
Terminated: Still in existence at
the end of the 97-2.

645. Committee on the Transfer of
the Indian Bureau (Joint)
  Sudocs: Y4. In2/3:
  Established: June 18, 1878
    20 Stat. 152.
  Authority: PL of (45-2)
  Terminated: January 31, 1879
    S. rpt. 693 (45-3) 1837.

646. Select Committee to Investi-
gate Indian Conditions of America
(House)
  Established: March 13, 1944
    90 CR 2531.
  Authority: H. Res. 166 (78-2)
  Terminated: December 23, 1944
    H. rpt. 2091 (78-2) 10848.

647. Select Committee on Investi-
gation of Indian Contracts (Senate)
  Established: June 25, 1910
    45 CR 9063.
  Authority: S. Res. 281 (61-2)
  Terminated: March 3, 1911, at the
    end of the 61-3.

648. Select Committee on Charges
of Corruption Against the Indian
Department by Mr. Clingman (House)
  Established: August 12, 1848
    H. J. (30-1): 1272.
  Authority: Res. of the House
    (30-1)
  Terminated: August 14, 1848, at
    the end of the 30-1.

649. Select Committee on Indian
Depredation Claims (House)
  Established: December 21, 1887
    19 CR 153.
  Authority: Res. of the House
    (50-1)
  Terminated: March 3, 1891, at the
    end of the 51-2.

650. Committee on Indian Depreda-
tions (Senate)
  Sudocs: Y4. In2/4:
  Established: April 5, 1893,
    having been preceded by a
    select committee (Entry 651).
      25 CR 90.
  Authority: Res. of the Senate
    (53-1)
  Terminated: April 18, 1921
    61 CR 404-05.

Authority: S. Res. 43 (67 -
  Special)

651. Select Committee on Indian
Depredations (Senate)
  Established: December 12, 1889
    S. J. (51-1): 39.
  Authority: Res. of the Senate
    (51-1)
  Terminated: April 5, 1893,
    when it was made a standing
    committee (Entry 650).
      25 CR 90.
  Authority: Res. of the Senate
    (53-1)

652. Select Committee to Investi-
gate Trespasses Upon Indian Lands
(Senate)
  Established: December 18, 1905
    40 CR 538.
  Authority: Res. of the Senate
    (59-1)
  Terminated: April 18, 1921
    61 CR 404-05.
  Authority: S. Res. 43 (67 -
    Special)

653. Select Committee on Indian
Schools and Yellowstone Park
(House)
  Established: March 3, 1885
    23 Stat. 417.
  Authority: PL 48-343
  Terminated: March 16, 1886
    H. rpt. 1076 (49-1) 2438.

654. Special Committee to Inves-
tigate Conditions in the Indian
Service (House)
  Sudocs: Y4. In2/9:
  Established: March 2, 1917
    39 Stat. 993.
  Authority: PL 64-369
  Terminated: March 3, 1919
    H. rpt. 1168 (65-3) 7455.

655. Select Committee to Examine
into the Circumstances Connected
with the Removal of the Northern
Cheyennes from the Sioux Reservation to the Indian Territory
(Senate)
  Established: February 12, 1879
    8 CR 1219.

Authority: Res. of the Senate
(45-3)
Terminated: May 31, 1880
S. rpt. 670 (46-2) 1898.

656. Select Committee to Investigate Affairs of Five Civilized Tribes in Indian Territory (Senate)
Established: June 30, 1906
40 CR 9787.
Authority: Res. of the Senate
(59-1)
Terminated: March 3, 1907, at the end of the 59-2.

657. Select Committee to Investigate Matters Connected with Affairs in Indian Territory (Senate)
Sudocs: Y4. In2/5:
Established: June 30, 1906
40 CR 9787.
Authority: Res. of the Senate
(59-1)
Terminated: January 16, 1907
S. rpt. 5013 (59-2) 5062-5063.

658. Select Committee on the Extinguishment of Indian Title to Certain Lands (Senate)
Established: March 4, 1818
S. J. (15-1): 209.
Authority: Res. of the Senate
(15-1)
Terminated: March 20, 1818
Ibid. 260.

659. Select Committee on Continuing in force the Act Relating to the Indian Trade (House)
Established: April 11, 1816
H. J. (14-1): 622.
Authority: Res. of the House
(14-1)
Terminated: April 30, 1816, at the end of the 14-1.

660. Select Committee on Indian Traders (Senate)
Established: June 3, 1886
17 CR 5183.
Authority: Res. of the Senate
(49-1)
Terminated: March 2, 1889
S. rpt. 2710 (50-2) 2624.

661. Select Committee on Alteration in the Act to Regulate Trade with the Indian Tribes (House)
Established: December 19, 1805
H. J. (9-1): 73.
Authority: Res. of the House
(9-1)
Terminated: July 6, 1812, at the end of the 12-1.

662. Special Committee on Conditions of Indian Tribes (Joint)
Sudocs: Y4. In2/6:
Established: March 3, 1865
Cong. Globe (38-2): 1339.
Authority: Res. of the Senate
(38-2)
Terminated: January 26, 1867
S. rpt. 156 (39-2) 1279.

663. Select Committee on the Condition of the Indian Tribes (House)
Established: December 4, 1816
H. J. (14-2): 25.
Authority: Res. of the House
(14-2)
Terminated: February 4, 1817
Ibid. 339.

664. Select Committee on the Abstraction of Indian Trust Bonds (House)
Established: December 24, 1860
H. J. (36-2): 116.
Authority: Res. of the House
(36-2)
Terminated: February 12, 1861
H. rpt. 78 (36-2) 1105.

665. Select Committee on the Petition of Sundry Inhabitants of Knox County, Indiana (House)
Established: January 24, 1817
H. J. (14-1): 276.
Authority: Res. of the House
(14-2)
Terminated: March 1, 1817
Ibid. 496.

666. Select Committee on Admitting Indiana into the Union (Senate)
Established: December 2, 1816
S. J. (14-2): 5.
Authority: Res. of the Senate
(14-2)

Terminated: December 16, 1816
  Ibid. 52.

667. Select Committee on Amending
the Ordinance of the Northwest
Territory, so far as Relates to the
Duties of the Supreme or Superior
Judges of the Indiana Territory
(House)
  Established: November 20, 1807
  H. J. (10-1): 78.
  Authority: Res. of the House
  (10-1)
  Terminated: December 23, 1807
  Ibid. 187.

668. Select Committee on Amend-
ments to the Act Dividing the
Indiana Territory (House)
  Established: May 27, 1812
  H. J. (12-1): 717.
  Authority: Res. of the House
  (12-1)
  Terminated: May 28, 1812
  Ibid. 719.

669. Select Committee Extending
the Right of Suffrage in the
Indiana Territory (House)
  Established: January 13, 1808
  H. J. (10-1): 259.
  Authority: Res. of the House
  (10-1)
  Terminated: December 5, 1809
  H. J. (11-2): 32.

670. Select Committee on Dividing
the Indiana Territory (House)
  Established: December 13, 1808
  H. J. (10-2): 110.
  Authority: Res. of the House
  (10-2)
  Terminated: December 20, 1808
  Ibid. 205.

671. Select Committee on a Letter
from William H. Harrison, Governor
of the Indiana Territory (House)
  Established: January 21, 1807
  H. J. (9-2): 173.
  Authority: Res. of the House
  (9-2)
  Terminated: February 12, 1807
  Ibid. 267.

672. Select Committee on the Pro-
test of the Legislative Council of
the Indiana Territory (House)
  Established: February 5, 1814
  H. J. (13-2): 285.
  Authority: Res. of the House
  (13-2)
  Terminated: February 11, 1814
  Ibid. 323.

673. Select Committee on the
Western Limits of the Indiana
Territory (House)
  Established: December 18, 1815
  H. J. (14-1): 67.
  Authority: Res. of the House
  (14-1)
  Terminated: April 30, 1816, at
  the end of the 14-1.

674. Select Committee on Modifi-
cations in the Act to Divide the
Indiana Territory, and Providing
for the Government of the Michigan
Territory (House)
  Established: November 24, 1812
  H. J. (12-2): 63.
  Authority: Res. of the House
  (12-2)
  Terminated: February 25, 1813
  Ibid. 354.

675. Select Committee on the
Petition of the Legislature of the
Indiana Territory for a State
Government (House)
  Established: December 28, 1815
  H. J. (14-1): 100.
  Authority: Res. of the House
  (14-1)
  Terminated: January 5, 1816
  Ibid. 128.

676. Committee on Five Civilized
Tribes of Indians (Senate)
  Established: March 22, 1909,
  having been preceded by a
  select committee (Entry 677).
  44 CR 121.
  Authority: Res. of the Senate
  (61-1)
  Terminated: April 18, 1921
  61 CR 404-05.
  Authority: S. Res. 43 (67 -
  Special)

677. Select Committee on the
Five Civilized Tribes of Indians
(Senate)
  Established: December 21, 1887
    19 CR 126.
  Authority: Res. of the Senate
    (50-1)
  Terminated: March 22, 1909, when
    it was made a standing commit-
    tee (Entry 676).
    44 CR 121.
  Authority: Res. of the Senate
    (61-1)

678. Select Committee on Expendi-
tures for Wild Indians by Butler
and Lewis (House)
  Established: July 24, 1846
    H. J. (29-1): 1137.
  Authority: Res. of the House
    (29-1)
  Terminated: February 8, 1847
    H. doc. 76 (29-2) 500.

679. Select Committee on Indus-
trial Arts and Expositions (House)
  Sudocs: Y4. In2/7:
  Established: December 10, 1901
    35 CR 245.
  Authority: Res. of the House
    (57-1)
  Terminated: December 5, 1927
    69 CR 12-13.
  Authority: H. Res. 7 (70-1)

680. Select Committee on Indus-
trial Expositions (Senate)
  Sudocs: Y4. In2/8:
  Established: December 15, 1899,
    having been preceded by the
    Select Committee on Inter-
    national Expositions (Entry
    701).
    33 CR 421.
  Authority: Res. of the Senate
    (56-1)
  Terminated: April 18, 1921
    61 CR 404-05.
  Authority: S. Res. 43 (67 -
    Special)

681. Select Committee on Relief
for Infirm and Superannuated
Officers and Soldiers (House)
  Established: November 28, 1808
    H. J. (10-2): 71.

Authority: Res. of the House
  (10-2)
Terminated: December 20, 1808
  Ibid. 160.

682. Select Committee on Extending
the Power of Granting Injunctions
to Judges of the District Courts
of the United States (House)
  Established: December 22, 1806
    H. J. (9-2): 70.
  Authority: Res. of the House
    (9-2)
  Terminated: January 5, 1807
    Ibid. 108.

683. Select Committee on House
Bill to Grant Land to the States
for the Indigent Insane (Senate)
  Established: August 18, 1852
    S. J. (32-1): 613.
  Authority: Res. of the Senate
    (32-1)
  Terminated: August 31, 1852, at
    the end of the 32-1.

684. Select Committee on Granting
Land to the States for the Relief
of Indigent Insane (Senate)
  Established: February 4, 1852
    S. J. (32-1): 179.
  Authority: Res. of the Senate
    (32-1)
  Terminated: August 31, 1852, at
    the end of the 32-1.

685. Committee on Insular Affairs
(House)
  Sudocs: Y4. In7/1:
  Established: December 8, 1899
    33 CR 160.
  Authority: Res. of the House
    (56-1)
  Terminated: January 2, 1947
    60 Stat. 812.
  Authority: PL 76-601

686. Select Committee to Inquire
into the Condition of Affairs in
Late Insurrectionary States (Joint)
  Sudocs: Y4. In7/2:
  Established: April 10, 1871
    Cong. Globe (42-1): 560.
  Authority: Con. Res. of the
    Senate (42-1)

Terminated: February 19, 1872
   S. rpt. 41 (42-2) 1484-1493.

687. Permanent Select Committee
on Intelligence (House)
   Sudocs: Y4. In8/18:
   Established: July 14, 1977,
   having been preceded by the
   Select Committee on Intelli-
   gence (Entry 688).
      123 CR 22949.
   Authority: H. Res. 658 (95-1)
   Terminated: Still in existence
   at the end of the 97-2.

688. Select Committee on Intelli-
gence (House)
   Sudocs: Y4. In8/18:
   Established: February 19, 1975
      121 CR 3618.
   Authority: H. Res. 138 (94-1)
   Terminated: July 14, 1977, when
   the Permanent Select Committee
   on Intelligence was established
   (Entry 687).
      123 CR 22949.
   Authority: H. Res. 658 (95-1)

689. Select Committee on Intelli-
gence Activities (Senate)
   Sudocs: Y4. In8/19:
   Established: May 19, 1976, having
   been preceded by the Select
   Committee to Study Governmental
   Operations with Respect to
   Intelligence Activities (Entry
   690).
      122 CR 14657.
   Authority: S. Res. 400 (94-2)
   Terminated: Still in existence
   at the end of the 97-2.

690. Select Committee to Study
Governmental Operations with
Respect to Intelligence Activities
(Senate)
   Sudocs: Y4. In8/17:
   Established: July 27, 1975
      121 CR 1431.
   Authority: S. Res. 21 (94-1)
   Terminated: May 19, 1976, when
   the Select Committee on Intel-
   ligence Activities was estab-
   lished (Entry 689).
      122 CR 14657.
   Authority: S. Res. 400 (94-2)

691. Select Committee on Certain
Alleged Interference by the
Executive with the Action of the
House (Hoard Committee) (House)
   Established: March 6, 1860
      H. J. (36-1): 465.
   Authority: Res. of the House
   (36-1)
   Terminated: June 25, 1860, at
   the end of the 36-1.

692. Committee on Interior and
Insular Affairs (House)
   Sudocs: Y4. In8/14:
   Established: February 2, 1951,
   when the Committee on Public
   Lands was changed to this
   (Entry 1150).
      97 CR 884.
   Authority: H. Res. 100 (82-1)
   Terminated: Still in existence
   at the end of the 97-2.

693. Committee on Interior and
Insular Affairs (Senate)
   Sudocs: Y4. In8/13:
   Established: January 28, 1948,
   when the name of the Committee
   on Public Lands was changed to
   this (Entry 1152).
      94 CR 604.
   Authority: S. Res. 179 (80-2)
   Terminated: February 11, 1977,
   when its functions were trans-
   ferred to the Committee on
   Energy and Natural Resources
   (Entry 417).
      123 CR 3691.
   Authority: S. Res. 4 (95-1)

694. Committee to Investigate the
Interior Department and Forestry
Service (Joint)
   Sudocs: Y4. In8/8:
   Established: January 19, 1910
      36 Stat. 871.
   Authority: Public Res. 9 (61-2)
   Terminated: March 4, 1911
      S. doc. 719 (61-3) 5892-5903.

695. Select Committee on Bill S.
282 to Reorganize the Clerical
Force in the Department of Interior
(Senate)

Established: April 24, 1866
  S. J. (39-1): 368.
Authority: Res. of the Senate
  (39-1)
Terminated: May 25, 1866
  Ibid. 465.

696. Select Committee on Internal
Improvements (House)
  Sudocs: Y4. In8/7:
  Established: December 10, 1829
    H. J. (21-1): 31.
  Authority: Res. of the House
    (21-1)
  Terminated: March 2, 1833, at the
    end of the 22-2.

697. Select Committee on Investi-
gation of Internal Revenue Bureau
(Senate)
  Sudocs: Y4. In8/10:
  Established: March 12, 1924
    65 CR 4023.
  Authority: S. Res. 168 (68-1)
  Terminated: February 6, 1926
    S. rpt. 27 (69-1) 8529.

698. Select Committee on Internal
Revenue Frauds (House)
  Sudocs: Y4. In8/2:
  Established: December 4, 1866
    Cong. Globe (39-2): 12.
  Authority: Res. of the House
    (39-2)
  Terminated: February 25, 1867
    H. rpt. 24 (39-2) 1305.

699. Committee on Internal Revenue
Taxation (Joint)
  Sudocs: Y4. In8/11:
  Established: February 26, 1926
    44 Stat. 127.
  Authority: Revenue Act of 1926
    (69-1)
  Terminated: October 4, 1976,
    when the name was changed to
    Joint Committee on Taxation
    (Entry 1379).
      90 Stat. 1835.
  Authority: PL 94-455

700. Committee on Internal Secu-
rity (House)
  Sudocs: Y4. In8/15:
  Established: February 18, 1969,
    having been preceded by

Committee on Un-American
  Activities (Entry 1419).
    115 CR 3746.
  Authority: H. Res. 89 (91-1)
  Terminated: January 14, 1975
    121 CR 22.
  Authority: H. Res. 5 (94-1)

701. Select Committee on Inter-
national Expositions (Senate)
  Established: December 30, 1895
    28 CR 421.
  Authority: Res. of the Senate
    (54-1)
  Terminated: December 15, 1899,
    when name was changed to
    Select Committee on Industrial
    Expositions (Entry 680).
      33 CR 442.
  Authority: Res. of the Senate
    (56-1)

702. Committee on International
Relations (House)
  Sudocs: Y4. In8/16:
  Established: March 19, 1975,
    when it replaced the Commit-
    tee on Foreign Affairs (Entry
    519).
      121 CR 7344.
  Authority: H. Res. 163 (94-1)
  Terminated: February 5, 1979,
    when the name was changed back
    to the Committee on Foreign
    Affairs (Entry 520).
      125 CR 1849.
  Authority: H. Res. 89 (96-1)

703. Committee on Interoceanic
Canal (Senate)
  Sudocs: Y4. In8/1:
  Established: December 15, 1899
    33 CR 441.
  Authority: Res. of the Senate
    (56-1)
  Terminated: January 2, 1947, when
    functions were transferred to
    Committee on Interstate and
    Foreign Commerce (Entry 710).
      60 Stat. 812.
  Authority: PL 79-601

704. Committee on Interstate
Commerce (Senate)
  Sudocs: Y4. In8/3:

Established: December 12, 1887,
having been preceded by a
select committee (Entry 706).
19 CR 16.
Authority: Res. of the Senate
(50-1)
Terminated: January 2, 1947, when
the name was changed to Committee on Interstate and Foreign
Commerce (Entry 710).
60 Stat. 812.
Authority: PL 79-601

705. Subcommittee on Interstate
Commerce (Joint)
Sudocs: Y4. In8/9:
Established: July 20, 1916
39 Stat. 387.
Authority: S. J. Res. 60 (64-1)
Terminated: March 3, 1919
S. doc. 445 (65-3) 7469.

706. Select Committee to Investi-
gate Interstate Commerce (Senate)
Established: March 17, 1885
S. J. (48-2): 516.
Authority: Res. of the Senate
(48-2)
Terminated: January 18, 1886
(Entry 704)
S. rpt. 46 (49-1) 2356-2357.

707. Committee on Interstate and
Foreign Commerce - 1st (House)
Sudocs: Y4. In8/4:
Established: January 28, 1892,
when it replaced Committee on
Commerce (Entry 246).
23 CR 656.
Authority: Res. of the House
(52-1)
Terminated: January 3, 1975,
when the name was changed to
Committee on Commerce and
Health (see note Entry 708).
120 CR 34470.
Authority: H. Res. 988 (93-2)

708. Committee on Interstate and
Foreign Commerce - 2nd (House)
Sudocs: Y4. In8/4:
Established: January 14, 1975,
when it replaced the Committee
on Commerce and Health which

existed only in name (Entry
707).
121 CR 32.
Authority: H. Res. 5 (94-1)
Terminated: Still in existence at
the end of the 97-2.

709. Committee on Interstate and
Foreign Commerce (Joint)
Established: July 20, 1916
39 Stat. 387.
Authority: Pub. Res. 25 (64-1)
Terminated: March 3, 1919, at
the end of the 65-3.

710. Committee on Interstate and
Foreign Commerce (Senate)
Sudocs: Y4. In8/3:
Established: January 2, 1947,
when it replaced the Interstate
Commerce Committee (Entry 704).
60 Stat. 812.
Authority: PL 79-601
Terminated: April 13, 1961, when
the name changed to Commerce
Committee (Entry 248).
107 CR 5708.
Authority: S. Res. 117 (87-1)

711. Select Committee on Inter-
state Migration of Destitute
Citizens (House)
Sudocs: Y4. In8/12:
Established: January 19, 1939
84 CR 536.
Authority: H. Res. 63 (76-1)
Terminated: April 3, 1947
H. rpt. 369 (77-1) 10559.

712. Committee on Invalid Pensions
(House)
Sudocs: Y4. In8/5:
Established: January 10, 1831
H. J. (21-2): 167.
Authority: Res. of the House
(21-2)
Terminated: January 2, 1947, when
functions were transferred to
Committee on Veterans Affairs
(Entry 1437).
60 Stat. 812.
Authority: PL 79-601

713. Select Committee on the
Invasion of our Territory by the

Troops of Spain (House)
  Established: December 2, 1806
    H. J. (9-2): 9.
  Authority: Res. of the House
    (9-2)
  Terminated: December 18, 1806
    Ibid. 63.

714. Committee on Investigation
and Retrenchment (Senate)
  Sudocs: Y4. In8/6:
  Established: December 14, 1871
    Cong. Globe (42-2): 132.
  Authority: Res. of the Senate
    (42-2)
  Terminated: March 3, 1873, at
    the end of the 42-3.

715. Select Committee on the Memo-
rials of the Manufacturers of Iron
(Senate)
  Established: January 27, 1831
    S. J. (21-2): 113.
  Authority: Res. of the Senate
    (21-2)
  Terminated: March 3, 1831, at the
    end of the 21-2.

716. Committee on Irrigation and
Reclamation (House)
  Sudocs: Y4. Ir7/2:
  Established: January 18, 1924,
    when the name of the Committee
    on Irrigation of Arid Lands was
    changed to this (Entry 717).
      65 CR 1143.
  Authority: H. Res. 146 (68-1)
  Terminated: January 2, 1947
    60 Stat. 812.
  Authority: PL 79-601

717. Committee on Irrigation of
Arid Lands (House)
  Sudocs: Y4. Ir7/2:
  Established: August 18, 1893,
    having been preceded by a
    select committee (Entry 720).
      25 CR 478.
  Authority: Res. of the House
    (53-1)
  Terminated: January 18, 1924,
    when the name was changed to
    the Committee on Irrigation and
    Reclamation (Entry 716).
      65 CR 1143.
  Authority: H. Res. 146 (68-1)

718. Committee on Irrigation and
Reclamation (Senate)
  Sudocs: Y4. Ir7/1:
  Established: December 16, 1891,
    having been preceded by a
    select committee (Entry 719).
      23 CR 73.
  Authority: Res. of the Senate
    (52-1)
  Terminated: January 2, 1947
    60 Stat. 812.
  Authority: PL 79-601

719. Select Committee on Irriga-
tion and Reclamation of Arid
Lands (Senate)
  Sudocs: Y4. Ir7/1:
  Established: February 14, 1889
    20 CR 1881.
  Authority: Res. of the Senate
    (50-2)
  Terminated: December 16, 1891,
    when made a standing committee
    (Entry 718).
      23 CR 73.
  Authority: Res. of the Senate
    (52-1)

720. Select Committee on Irriga-
tion of Arid Lands (House)
  Established: December 20, 1889
    H. J. (51-1): 74.
  Authority: Res. of the House
    (51-1)
  Terminated: August 18, 1893,
    when the standing committee
    was established (Entry 717).
      25 CR 478.
  Authority: Res. of the House
    (53-1)

721. Select Committee on Petition
of Citizens of Jackson County, Il-
linois, on Inundated Lands (House)
  Established: March 9, 1842
    H. J. (27-2): 514.
  Authority: Res. of the House
    (27-2)
  Terminated: April 12, 1842
    Ibid. 693.

722. Select Committee on a Memorial of James Jay (House)
  Established: March 2, 1808
    H. J. (10-1): 431.

Authority: Res. of the House
(10-1)
Terminated: April 20, 1808
Ibid. 604.

723. Select Committee on Memo-
rial of John Jay on Copyright
Law (House)
Established: April 13, 1848
H. J. (30-1): 677.
Authority: Res. of the House
(30-1)
Terminated: August 14, 1848,
at the end of the 30-1.

724. Select Committee on the
Accounts of Colonel James Johnson
(House)
Established: December 26, 1820
H. J. (16-2): 91.
Authority: Res. of the House
(16-2)
Terminated: March 1, 1821
Ibid. 296.

725. Select Committee on Distribu-
tion of Journals and Laws (House)
Established: December 17, 1832
H. J. (22-2): 70.
Authority: Res. of the House
(22-2)
Terminated: February 25, 1833
H. rpt. 107 (22-2) 236.

726. Select Committee on Continu-
ing in Force the Act Extending
Jurisdiction, in Certain Cases, to
State Judges and State Courts
(House)
Established: February 23, 1808
H. J. (10-1): 399.
Authority: Res. of the House
(10-1)
Terminated: March 1, 1808
Ibid. 429.

727. Select Committee on Disqual-
ifying Certain Judges from Holding
Other Offices (House)
Established: December 3, 1812
H. J. (12-2): 81.
Authority: Res. of the House
(12-2)
Terminated: December 15, 1812
Ibid. 98.

728. Select Committee on Extending
Jurisdiction to Superior Judges of
Territorial Courts (House)
Established: December 8, 1812
H. J. (12-2): 89.
Authority: Res. of the House
(12-2)
Terminated: January 29, 1813
Ibid. 235.

729. Select Committee Compelling
Judges to Reside within Their
Districts (House)
Established: November 16, 1812
H. J. (12-2): 38.
Authority: Res. of the House
(12-2)
Terminated: November 20, 1812
Ibid. 47.

730. Select Committee on Alter-
ations in the Judicial System
(House)
Established: February 24, 1812
H. J. (12-1): 406.
Authority: Res. of the House
(12-1)
Terminated: March 4, 1812
Ibid. 447.

731. Committee on the Judiciary
(House)
Sudocs: Y4. J89/1:
Established: June 3, 1813
Annals (13-1): 132.
Authority: Res. of the House
(13-1)
Terminated: Still in existence at
the end of the 97-2.

732. Committee on the Judiciary
(Senate)
Sudocs: Y4. J89/2:
Established: December 10, 1816
Annals (14-2): 30.
Authority: Res. of the Senate
(14-2)
Terminated: Still in existence at
the end of the 97-2.

733. Select Committee on Extending
Jurisdiction over White Persons
Residing Within the Indian Lines
(House)
Established: January 18, 1813
H. J. (12-2): 183.

Authority: Res. of the House
(12-2)
Terminated: March 3, 1813, at
the end of the 12-2.

734. Select Committee on Compensa-
tion to Jurors Serving in Federal
Courts (House)
Established: December 18, 1805
H. J. (9-1): 67.
Authority: Res. of the House
(9-1)
Terminated: January 28, 1806
Ibid. 169.

735. Select Committee on Securing
the Right to an Impartial Jury
(House)
Established: June 1, 1809
H. J. (11-1): 67.
Authority: Res. of the House
(11-1)
Terminated: June 28, 1809
Ibid. 200.

736. Special Committee Investi-
gating Election Fraud in the
Kansas Territory (House)
Sudocs: Y4. K13:
Established: March 20, 1856
Cong. Globe (34-1): 692.
Authority: Res. of the House
(34-1)
Terminated: 1856
H. rpt. 200 (34-1) 869.

737. Select Committee on Kansas
(Lecompton) Constitution (House)
Established: February 8, 1858
H. J. (35-1): 349.
Authority: Res. of the House
(35-1)
Terminated: June 14, 1858, at the
end of the 35-1.

738. Select Committee to Conduct
Investigation of Facts, Evidence
and Circumstances of Katyn Forest
Massacre (House)
Sudocs: Y4. K15:
Established: September 18, 1951
97 CR 11554.
Authority: H. Res. 390 (82-1)
Terminated: December 22, 1952
H. rpt. 2505 (82-2) 11578.

739. Select Committee on the
Nomination of Amos Kendall (Senate)
Established: March 10, 1830
S. J. (21-1): 423.
Authority: Res. of the Senate
(21-1)
Terminated: April 27, 1830
Ex. J. of the Senate (21-1):
96.

740. Select Committee on Certain
Surveys in Kentucky and Tennessee
(House)
Established: January 15, 1859
H. J. (35-2): 199.
Authority: Res. of the House
(35-2)
Terminated: March 3, 1859, at the
end of the 35-2.

741. Committee on Labor (House)
Sudocs: Y4. L11:
Established: December 19, 1883,
when the Committee on Education and Labor was divided
into two separate committees
(Entry 384).
15 CR 196.
Authority: Res. of the House
(48-1)
Terminated: January 2, 1947,
when it was renamed the Committee on Education and Labor
(Entry 385).
60 Stat. 812.
Authority: PL 79-601

742. Select Committee on the
Depression of Labor (House)
Established: April 11, 1879
9 CR 397.
Authority: Res. of the House
(46-1)
Terminated: March 19, 1880
H. rpt. 572 (46-2) 1935.

743. Committee on Labor and Human
Resources (Senate)
Sudocs: Y4. L11/4:
Established: March 7, 1979, when
the name of the Committee on
Human Resources was changed to
this (Entry 621).
125 CR 4243.
Authority: S. Res. 30 (96-1)

Terminated: Still in existence at
the end of the 97-2.

744. Committee on Labor and Public
Welfare (Senate)
  Sudocs: Y4. L11/2:
  Established: January 2, 1947
    60 Stat. 812.
  Authority: PL 79-601
  Terminated: February 11, 1977,
    when name was changed to
    Committee on Human Resources
    (Entry 621).
      123 CR 3691.
  Authority: S. Res. 4 (95-1)

745. Committee on Labor Management
Relations (Joint)
  Sudocs: Y4. L11/3:
  Established: June 23, 1947
    61 Stat. 160, title IV.
  Authority: PL 80-101
  Terminated: April 11, 1949
    Senate rpt. 374 (81-1) 11292.

746. Select Committee on Improper
Activities in the Labor or Manage-
ment Field (Senate)
  Established: January 30, 1957
    103 CR 1265.
  Authority: Senate Res. 74 (85-1)
  Terminated: March 31, 1960
    S. rpt. 1139 (86-2) 12241.

747. Select Committee on Labor
Troubles (House)
  Established: April 12, 1886
    17 CR 3395.
  Authority: Res. of the House
    (49-1)
  Terminated: March 3, 1887
    H. rpt. 4174 (49-2) 2502.

748. Select Committee on the Reso-
lution Respecting the Marquis de
La Fayette (Senate)
  Established: January 21, 1824
    S. J. (18-1): 121.
  Authority: Res. of the Senate
    (18-1)
  Terminated: May 27, 1824, at the
    end of the 18-1.

749. Select Committee on Services
and Sacrifices of General Lafayette
(House)

Established: December 8, 1824
  H. J. (18-2): 28.
Authority: Res. of the House
  (18-2)
Terminated: December 21, 1824
  Ibid. 66.

750. Select Committee on William
Lambert's Letters on the First
Meridian (House)
  Established: April 5, 1810
    H. J. (11-2): 501.
  Authority: Res. of the House
    (11-2)
  Terminated: January 20, 1813
    H. J. (12-2): 194.

751. Special Committee on Survey
of Land and Water Policies of
United States (Senate)
  Sudocs: Y4. L22:
  Established: January 25, 1935
    79 CR 989.
  Authority: S. Res. 58 (74-1)
  Terminated: June 20, 1936, at the
    end of the 74-2.

752. Select Committee on Reports
for Land Commissioners (Senate)
  Established: February 6, 1820
    S. J. (16-2): 169.
  Authority: Res. of the Senate
    (16-2)
  Terminated: March 3, 1821, at the
    end of the 16-2.

753. Select Committee on the Dis-
tribution of Land Laws (House)
  Established: January 30, 1811
    H. J. (11-3): 181.
  Authority: Res. of the House
    (11-3)
  Terminated: February 4, 1811
    Ibid. 209.

754. Select Committee on a More
Rigid and Strict Accounting of
Receivers of Land Offices (House)
  Established: May 8, 1826
    H. J. (19-1): 527.
  Authority: Res. of the House
    (19-1)
  Terminated: May 22, 1826, at the
    end of the 19-1.

755. Select Committee on Reports of the Secretary of the Treasury on the Examination of the Land Offices (House)
   Established: February 21, 1822
      H. J. (17-1): 284.
   Authority: Res. of the House (17-1)
   Terminated: March 29, 1822
      Ibid. 410.

756. Select Committee on Making Further Provision in Lands for the Officers and Soldiers of the Virginia Line of the Revolutionary Army (House)
   Established: March 17, 1812
      H. J. (12-1): 508.
   Authority: Res. of the House (12-1)
   Terminated: April 2, 1812
      Ibid. 555.

757. Select Committee on Claim of Three Percent to Ohio, Indiana, Illinois and Missouri, on Lands Sold (House)
   Established: January 2, 1847
      H. J. (29-2): 118.
   Authority: Res. of the House (29-2)
   Terminated: February 24, 1847
      H. rpt. 79 (29-2) 501.

758. Select Committee to Investigate Charges Against Representative John W. Langley (House)
   Established: December 9, 1925
      67 CR 568.
   Authority: H. Res. 41 (69-1)
   Terminated: December 22, 1925
      H. rpt. 30 (69-1) 8535.

759. Select Committee to Study Law Enforcement Undercover Activities of Components of the Department of Justice (Senate)
   Sudocs: Y4. L41:
   Established: March 24, 1982
      128 CR S2824.
   Authority: S. Res. 350 (97-2)
   Terminated: December 15, 1982
      S. rpt. 97-682.

760. Select Committee on Memorial for Impeachment of Judge P. K.

Lawrence of Louisiana (House)
   Established: January 7, 1839
      H. J. (25-3): 222.
   Authority: Res. of the House (25-3)
   Terminated: February 11, 1839
      H. rpt. 272 (25-3) 351.

761. Select Committee on Pike Street Highway, Lawrenceville, Pennsylvania (House)
   Established: March 14, 1842
      H. J. (27-2): 531.
   Authority: Res. of the House (27-2)
   Terminated: August 31, 1842, at the end of the 27-2.

762. Committee on Revision of Laws (House)
   Sudocs: Y4. L44/2:
   Established: July 25, 1868, to replace the Committee on Revisal and Unfinished Business (Entry 1214).
      Cong. Globe (40-2): 4495.
   Authority: Res. of the House (40-2)
   Terminated: January 2, 1947
      60 Stat. 812.
   Authority: PL 79-601

763. Committee on Revision of the Laws (Senate)
   Established: March 8, 1869
      S. J. (41-1): 16.
   Authority: Res. of the Senate (41-1)
   Terminated: January 14, 1928
      69 CR 1474.
   Authority: Senate Order (70-1)

764. Special Committee on Revision and Codification of the Laws (Joint)
   Sudocs: Y4. L44/1:
   Established: March 2, 1907
      34 Stat. 1423.
   Authority: Pub. Res. 19 (59-2)
   Terminated: March 15, 1910
      H. doc. 783 (61-2) 5830.

765. Select Committee on the Stereotyping of U. S. Laws (House)
   Established: December 8, 1828
      H. J. (20-2): 35.

Authority: Res. of the House
   (20-2)
Terminated: January 16, 1829
   H. rpt. 47 (20-2) 190.

766. Committee to Prepare a
Code of Laws for the District
of Columbia (Joint)
   Established: February 5, 1828
      S. J. (20-2): 109.
   Authority: H. Jt. Res. (20-2)
   Terminated: February 12, 1828
      Ibid. 121.

767. Committee on a Code of Laws
for the District of Columbia (Joint)
   Established: May 22, 1832
      S. J. (22-1): 293.
   Authority: H. Jt. Res. (22-1)
   Terminated: February 14, 1833
      H. rpt. 96 (22-2) 236.

768. Select Committee on Publica-
tion of Laws in Newspapers (House)
   Established: February 15, 1820
      H. J. (16-1): 219.
   Authority: Res. of the House
      (16-1)
   Terminated: March 20, 1820
      Ibid. 320.

769. Select Committee on Duff
Green's Memorial to Stereotype
Laws of the U. S. (House)
   Established: December 13, 1837
      H. J. (25-2): 69.
   Authority: Res. of the House
      (25-2)
   Terminated: January 4, 1838
      H. rpt. 286 (25-2) 333.

770. Select Committee on An Index
to the Laws of the United States
(House)
   Established: December 24, 1810
      H. J. (11-3): 72.
   Authority: Res. of the House
      (11-3)
   Terminated: December 28, 1810
      Ibid. 81.

771. Select Committee on Purchas-
ing the Tenth volume of Laws of the
U. S. (House)
   Established: March 27, 1846
      H. J. (29-1): 595.

Authority: Res. of the House
   (29-1)
Terminated: August 10, 1846, at
   the end of the 29-1.

772. Select Committee on Causing
the Laws to be Published in the
Several Territories (House)
   Established: November 3, 1814
      H. J. (13-3): 155.
   Authority: Res. of the House
      (13-3)
   Terminated: November 11, 1814
      Ibid. 179.

773. Select Committee to Provide
for the Leasing of Lead Mines in
Missouri (House)
   Established: February 7, 1815
      H. J. (13-3): 618.
   Authority: Res. of the House
      (13-3)
   Terminated: February 11, 1815
      Ibid. 647.

774. Select Committee on Leaven-
worth Soldiers' Home Investigation
(House)
   Established: June 9, 1896
      28 CR 6364.
   Authority: Res. of the House
      (54-1)
   Terminated: February 24, 1897
      H. rpt. 3035 (54-2) 3557.

775. Select Committee on the
Accounts of John P. Leedom, Late
Sergeant at Arms (House)
   Established: December 9, 1889
      H. J. (51-1): 14.
   Authority: Res. of the House
      (51-1)
   Terminated: January 18, 1890
      H. misdoc. 73 (51-1) 2760.

776. Select Committee on Making
Five Franc Pieces and South Amer-
ican Dollars Legal Tender (House)
   Established: December 22, 1830
      H. J. (21-1): 93.
   Authority: Res. of the House
      (21-2)
   Terminated: February 22, 1831
      Ibid. 341.

777. Committee on the Legislative
Budget (Joint)
  Sudocs: Y4. L52:
  Established: January 2, 1947
    60 Stat. 832.
  Authority: PL 79-601
  Terminated: January 3, 1971
    84 Stat. 1172.
  Authority: PL 91-510

778. Select Committee on a Letter
and Two Printed Books in the
German Language Addressed to the
Speaker (House)
  Established: December 12, 1805
    H. J. (9-1): 45.
  Authority: Res. of the House
    (9-1)
  Terminated: March 6, 1806
    Ibid. 304.

779. Select Committee on Compensa-
tion to Lewis and Clark (House)
  Established: January 2, 1807
    H. J. (9-2): 104.
  Authority: Res. of the House
    (9-2)
  Terminated: January 23, 1807
    Ibid. 191.

780. Select Committee to Inquire
What Prosecutions Have Been
Commenced for Libel (House)
  Established: May 25, 1809
    H. J. (11-1): 29.
  Authority: Res. of the House
    (11-1)
  Terminated: July 6, 1812, at the
    end of the 12-1.

781. Committee on the Library
(House)
  Sudocs: Y4. L61/1:
  Established: February 27, 1806
    H. J. (9-1): 291.
  Authority: Jt. Res. of the Senate
    (9-1)
  Terminated: January 2, 1947
    60 Stat. 812.
  Authority: PL 79-601

782. Committee on the Library
(Joint)
  Sudocs: Y4. L61/2:
  Established: February 27, 1806
    H. J. (9-1): 291.

Authority: Jt. Res. of the Senate
    (9-1)
  Terminated: January 2, 1947
    60 Stat. 812.
  Authority: PL 79-601

783. Committee on the Library
(Senate)
  Sudocs: Y4. L61/3:
  Established: February 26, 1806
    H. J. (9-1): 287.
  Authority: Jt. Res. of the Senate
    (9-1)
  Terminated: January 2, 1947
    60 Stat. 812.
  Authority: PL 79-601

784. Special Committee on Library
Building (House)
  Established: February 15, 1888
    19 CR 1231.
  Authority: Res. of the House
    (50-1)
  Terminated: January 19, 1889
    H. rpt. 3795 (50-2) 2673.

785. Select Committee on Library
Investigation (House)
  Established: September 4, 1888
    19 CR 8261.
  Authority: Res. of the House
    (50-1)
  Terminated: March 3, 1889, at the
    end of the 50-2.

786. Select Committee on Addi-
tional Accommodations for the
Library of Congress (Senate)
  Established: March 3, 1881
    11 CR 2429.
  Authority: Res. of the Senate
    (47-1)
  Terminated: April 18, 1921
    61 CR 404-05.
  Authority: S. Res. 43 (67 -
    Special)

787. Select Committee on Investi-
gation of Charges Made by George L.
Lilley (House)
  Sudocs: Y4. L62:
  Established: March 6, 1908
    42 CR 2973.
  Authority: H. Res. 288 (60-1)
  Terminated: May 12, 1908
    H. rpt. 1727 (60-1) 5227-5228.

788. Select Committee on the Death
of President Lincoln (House)
  Established: December 11, 1865
    Cong. Globe (39-1): 21.
  Authority: Res. of the House
    (39-1)
  Terminated: February 16, 1866
    S. J. (39-1): 280.

789. Select Committee on Live Oaks
in Florida (House)
  Established: March 20, 1832
    H. J. (22-1): 521.
  Authority: Res. of the House
    (22-1)
  Terminated: July 16, 1832, at the
    end of the 22-1.

790. Select Committee on Loans
From Deposit Banks to Members of
Congress and Public Officers, to
Speculate in Public Lands (House)
  Established: June 20, 1836
    H. J. (24-1): 1055.
  Authority: Res. of the House
    (24-1)
  Terminated: July 2, 1836
    H. rpt. 846 (24-1) 295.

791. Select Committee on Lobby
Investigation (House)
  Sudocs: Y4. L78:
  Established: July 9, 1913
    50 CR 2353.
  Authority: H. Res. 198 (63-1)
  Terminated: December 9, 1913
    H. rpt. 113 (63-2) 6564.

792. Select Committee on Lobbying
Activities (House)
  Sudocs: Y4. L78/3:
  Established: August 12, 1949
    95 CR 11385.
  Authority: H. Res. 298 (81-1)
  Terminated: December 26, 1950
    H. rpt. 3232 (81-2) 11385.

793. Special Committee to Investi-
gate Lobbying Activities (Senate)
  Sudocs: Y4. L78/2:
  Established: July 11, 1935
    79 CR 11005.
  Authority: S. Res. 165 (74-1)
  Terminated: June 16, 1938, at the
    end of the 75-3.

794. Committee to Investigate
Election of William Lorimer
(Senate)
  Sudocs: Y4. L89:
  Established: June 7, 1911
    47 CR 1734.
  Authority: S. Res. 60 (62-1)
  Terminated: May 20, 1912
    S. rpt. 769 (62-2) 6126.

795. Select Committee on Aliens
in the State of Louisiana (House)
  Established: February 16, 1824
    H. J. (18-1): 238.
  Authority: Res. of the House
    (18-1)
  Terminated: March 8, 1824
    Ibid. 298.

796. Select Committee on the
Constitution of the Territory of
Orleans (alias State of Louisiana)
(House)
  Established: March 5, 1812
    H. J. (12-1): 406.
  Authority: Res. of the House
    (12-1)
  Terminated: March 16, 1812
    Ibid. 447.

797. Select Committee to Inquire
Into Certain Matters Touching the
Late Presidential Election in
Louisiana (Senate)
  Established: June 5, 1878
    S. J. (45-2): 619.
  Authority: Res. of the Senate
    (45-2)
  Terminated: March 1, 1879
    S. rpt. 867 (45-3) 1838.

798. Select Committee to Investi-
gate the Condition of Affairs in
Louisiana (House)
  Established: January 15, 1872
    Cong. Globe (42-2): 397.
  Authority: Res. of the House
    (42-2)
  Terminated: May 30, 1872
    H. rpt. 92 (42-2) 1543.

799. Select Committee on the Cen-
tennial of the Louisiana Purchase
(House)
  Established: March 21, 1900
    33 CR 3129.

Authority: Res. of the House
(56-1)
Terminated: March 3, 1901, at the
end of the 56-2.

800. Select Committee on Reim-
bursement of Loyal States (House)
Established: December 11, 1865
Cong. Globe (39-1): 18.
Authority: Res. of the House
(39-1)
Terminated: March 3, 1867, at the
end of the 39-2.

801. Select Committee on Loyalty
of Government Employees (House)
Established: July 9, 1861
Cong. Globe (37-1): 26.
Authority: Res. of the House
(37-1)
Terminated: August 6, 1861, at
the end of the 37-1.

802. Select Committee to Study
Censure Charges Against Senator
McCarthy (Senate)
Established: August 2, 1954
100 CR 12989.
Authority: Senate Order (83-2)
Terminated: November 8, 1954
S. rpt. 2508 (83-2) 11732.

803. Select Committee to Inquire
into Allowing Madison County,
Mississippi, a Representative in
the General Assembly (House)
Established: May 27, 1809
H. J. (11-1): 39.
Authority: Res. of the House
(11-1)
Terminated: May 31, 1809
Ibid. 62.

804. Select Committee on Publica-
tion of Madison's Writings (House)
Established: January 13, 1846
H. J. (29-1): 243.
Authority: Res. of the House
(29-1)
Terminated: March 9, 1846
H. rpt. 410 (29-1) 489.

805. Select Committee on Mr.
Magruder's Letters (House)
Established: September 22, 1814
H. J. (13-3): 18.

Authority: Res. of the House
(13-3)
Terminated: January 19, 1815
Ibid. 537.

806. Select Committee on Permanent Arrangement with Railroads
for Carrying the Mail (House)
Established: May 4, 1848
H. J. (30-1): 787.
Authority: Res. of the House
(30-1)
Terminated: August 14, 1848, at
the end of the 30-1.

807. Special Committee to Inves-
tigate Facts on Mail Cover on
Senators (Senate)
Established: December 1, 1954
100 CR 16344.
Authority: S. Res. 332 (83-2)
Terminated: December 3, 1954
S. rpt. 2510 (83-2) 11732.

808. Committee on Second Class
Mail Matter (Joint)
Established: June 26, 1906
34 Stat. 477.
Authority: PL 59-297
Terminated: January 28, 1907
S. rpt. 5630 (59-2) 5060.

809. Committee on Second Class
Mail Matter and Compensation for
Railway Mail Service (Joint)
Established: August 24, 1912
37 Stat. 546.
Authority: PL 62-336
Terminated: December 8, 1914
H. doc. 1257 (63-3) 6888.

810. Select Committee on Petitions
from Various Parts of the Country
in Opposition to the Practice of
Opening the Mail on Sunday (House)
Established: January 6, 1817
H. J. (14-2): 140.
Authority: Res. of the House
(14-2)
Terminated: March 1, 1817
Ibid. 496.

811. Select Committee on the
Election of the Honorable S. R.
Mallory to a Seat in the Senate,

Contested by the Honorable D. L.
Yullee (Senate)
  Established: December 1, 1851
    S. J. (32-1): 6.
  Authority: Res. of the Senate
    (32-1)
  Terminated: August 21, 1852
    S. rpt. 349 (32-1) 631.

812. Committee on Manufactures
(House)
  Sudocs: Y4. M31/1:
  Established: December 19, 1819,
    when the Committee on Commerce
    and Manufactures was divided
    into two committees (Entries
    246, 249).
      Annals (16-1): 709.
  Authority: Res. of the House
    (16-1)
  Terminated: April 5, 1911
    47 CR 80.
  Authority: H. Res. 11 (62-1)

813. Committee on Manufactures--
1st (Senate)
  Sudocs: Y4. M31/2:
  Established: December 12, 1825,
    when the Committee on Commerce
    and Manufactures was divided
    into two committees (Entries
    247, 250).
      Annals (19-1): 4.
  Authority: Res. of the Senate
    (19-1)
  Terminated: March 3, 1855, at the
    end of the 33-2.

814. Committee on Manufactures--
2nd (Senate)
  Sudocs: Y4. M31/2:
  Established: February 10, 1864
    S. J. (38-1): 143.
  Authority: Res. of the Senate
    (38-1)
  Terminated: January 2, 1947
    60 Stat. 812.
  Authority: PL 79-601

815. Select Committee on Printing
Maps of Boundary Between Texas and
the United States (House)
  Established: March 25, 1842
    H. J. (27-2): 594.
  Authority: Res. of the House
    (27-2)

Terminated: August 30, 1842
  Ibid. 1456.

816. Select Committee on Disposal
of Maps of Exploring Expeditions
(House)
  Established: January 17, 1845
    H. J. (28-2): 225.
  Authority: Res. of the House
    (28-2)
  Terminated: February 25, 1845
    H. rpt. 160 (28-2) 468.

817. Select Committee on Pay
of Officers of the Marine Corps
(House)
  Established: May 5, 1846
    H. J. (29-1): 755.
  Authority: Res. of the House
    (29-1)
  Terminated: August 10, 1846, at
    the end of the 29-1.

818. Select Committee on the
Marine Corps Pay Bill (House)
  Established: February 16, 1807
    H. J. (9-2): 278.
  Authority: Res. of the House
    (9-2)
  Terminated: February 19, 1807
    Ibid. 294.

819. Select Committee on Adopt-
ing any Legislative Provision
Respecting the Extent of Maritime
Precincts, and a Maritime League
(House)
  Established: June 14, 1809
    H. J. (11-1): 119.
  Authority: Res. of the House
    (11-1)
  Terminated: June 28, 1809, at the
    end of the 11-1.

820. Select Committee to Investi-
gate Impeachment Charges Against
H. Snowden Marshall (House)
  Established: April 5, 1916
    53 CR 5541.
  Authority: H. Res. 193 (64-1)
  Terminated: April 14, 1916
    H. rpt. 544 (64-1) 6908.

821. Select Committee on Further
Security Required of Marshalls
(House)

Established: December 31, 1805
H. J. (9-1): 109.
Authority: Res. of the House
(9-1)
Terminated: January 8, 1806
Ibid. 121.

822. Select Committee to report a
Summary Mode of Proceeding Against
Marshalls in Certain Cases (House)
Established: May 31, 1809
H. J. (11-1): 62.
Authority: Res. of the House
(11-1)
Terminated: June 6, 1809
Ibid. 78.

823. Select Committee on Claim of
State of Maryland (House)
Established: January 24, 1832
H. J. (22-1): 234.
Authority: Res. of the House
(22-1)
Terminated: July 16, 1832, at the
end of the 22-1.

824. Select Committee on Massachu-
setts Resolutions (House)
Established: December 22, 1843
H. J. (28-1): 97.
Authority: Res. of the House
(28-1)
Terminated: April 4, 1844
H. rpt. 404 (28-1) 446.

825. Select Committee on Charges
Against O. B. Matteson (House)
Established: February 25, 1858
H. J. (35-1): 425.
Authority: Res. of the House
(35-1)
Terminated: March 22, 1858
H. rpt. 179 (35-1) 964.

826. Select Committee on Transpor-
tation and Sale of Meat Products
(Senate)
Sudocs: Y4. M46:
Established: May 16, 1888
19 CR 4216.
Authority: Res. of the House
(50-1)
Terminated: April 18, 1921
61 CR 404-405.
Authority: S. Res. 43 (67 -
Special)

827. Committee on Eradication of
the Mediterranean Fruitfly (Joint)
Established: August 19, 1940
86 CR 10529.
Authority: S. Con. Res. 40 (76-3)
Terminated: October 27, 1941
S. rpt. 777 (77-1) 10546.

828. Select Committee to Inves-
tigate Alleged Charges Against
Members of Congress (House)
Sudocs: Y4. M51:
Established: March 12, 1924
65 CR 4041.
Authority: H. Res. 217 (68-1)
Terminated: May 15, 1924
H. rpt. 759 (68-1) 8232.

829. Special Committee to Preserve
Memorabilia of the Senate (Senate)
Established: July 28, 1958
104 CR 15248.
Authority: S. Res. 318 (85-2)
Terminated: April 2, 1959
105 CR 2063.
Authority: S. Res. 72 (86-1)

830. Committee on Memorials
(House)
Established: January 3, 1929
70 CR 1081.
Authority: H. Res. 272 (70-2)
Terminated: January 2, 1947
60 Stat. 812.
Authority: PL 79-601

831. Select Committee on the
Memphis Convention (Senate)
Established: February 3, 1846
S. J. (29-1): 131.
Authority: Res. of the Senate
(29-1)
Terminated: June 26, 1846
S. doc. 410 (29-1) 477.

832. Select Committee on Memphis
Navy Yard (House)
Established: January 4, 1855
H. J. (33-2): 143.
Authority: Res. of the House
(33-2)
Terminated: February 1, 1855
H. rpt. 61 (33-2) 808.

833. Select Committee on the
Memphis Riot (House)

Established: May 14, 1866
  Cong. Globe (39-1): 2572.
Authority: Res. of the House
  (39-1)
Terminated: July 25, 1866
  H. rpt. 101 (39-1) 1274.

834. Committee on Merchant Marine
and Fisheries (House)
  Sudocs: Y4. M53:
  Established: December 21, 1887
    19 CR 146.
  Authority: Res. of the House
    (50-1)
  Terminated: Still in existence at
    the end of the 97-2.
  Committee was named Merchant
    Marine, Radio, and Fisheries
    from 1932-1935.

835. Special Committee on Investi-
gation of American Merchant Marine
(Senate)
  Established: February 25, 1938
    83 CR 2443.
  Authority: S. Res. 231 (75-3)
  Terminated: January 31, 1941, at
    the end of the 76-3.

836. Select Committee on Convoying
Merchant Vessels (House)
  Established: January 22, 1810
    H. J. (11-2): 195.
  Authority: Res. of the House
    (11-2)
  Terminated: February 9, 1810
    Ibid. 260.

837. Select Committee on the
Regulation and Conduct of Merchant
Vessels (House)
  Established: April 14, 1808
    H. J. (10-1): 570.
  Authority: Res. of the House
    (10-1)
  Terminated: April 18, 1808
    Ibid. 584.

838. Select Committee on the
Special Message of the President
of January 8, 1861 (House)
  Established: January 9, 1861
    H. J. (36-2): 161.
  Authority: Res. of the House
    (36-2)

Terminated: February 28, 1861
  H. rpt. 91 (36-2) 1105.

839. Select Committee on the
Special Message of the President
Related to the Condition of Affairs
in Some of the States of the Union
(House)
  Established: March 23, 1871
    Cong. Globe (42-1): 249.
  Authority: Res. of the House
    (42-1)
  Terminated: April 20, 1871, at
    the end of the 42-1.

840. Select Committee on
Meteorology (House)
  Established: March 26, 1837
    H. J. (25-2): 670.
  Authority: Res. of the House
    (25-2)
  Terminated: July 21, 1840, at
    the end of the 26-1.

841. Select Committee to Investi-
gate Irregularities in Running and
Marking the U. S. Mexican Boundary
(Senate)
  Established: August 17, 1852
    S. J. (32-1): 604.
  Authority: Res. of the Senate
    (32-1)
  Terminated: March 3, 1853, at
    the end of the 32-2.

842. Select Committee on the
Appointment of a Scientific Corps
to be Attached to the Mexican
Boundary Commission (Senate)
  Established: July 8, 1850
    S. J. (31-1): 440.
  Authority: Res. of the Senate
    (31-1)
  Terminated: September 30, 1850,
    at the end of the 31-1.

843. Select Committee on a Report
of the Secretary of the Interior
to the Mexican Boundary Commission
(Senate)
  Established: July 26, 1852
    S. J. (32-1): 549.
  Authority: Res. of the Senate
    (32-1)
  Terminated: August 31, 1852, at
    the end of the 32-1.

844. Select Committee on Mexican Correspondence (House)
   Established: July 7, 1838
      H. J. (25-2): 1117.
   Authority: Res. of the House (25-2)
   Terminated: July 9, 1838, at the end of the 25-2.

845. Select Committee on Levying Duties on Mexican Ports During War with Mexico (House)
   Established: January 3, 1849
      H. J. (30-2): 190.
   Authority: Res. of the House (30-2)
   Terminated: March 3, 1849, at the end of the 30-2.

846. Select Committee to Investigate Mexican Propaganda (Senate)
   Established: December 9, 1927
      69 CR 339.
   Authority: S. Res. 7 (70-1)
   Terminated: January 9, 1929
      S. rpt. 52 (70-1) 8832.

847. Select Committee on Manner in Which the Mexican War Should be Prosecuted (House)
   Established: February 1, 1848
      H. J. (30-1): 336.
   Authority: Res. of the House (30-1)
   Terminated: August 14, 1848, at the end of the 30-1.

848. Select Committee on Families of those Who Have Died in Mexico (House)
   Established: February 1, 1848
      H. J. (30-1): 336.
   Authority: Res. of the House (30-1)
   Terminated: July 24, 1848
      H. rpt. 796 (30-1) 527.

849. Select Committee to Inquire into the Relations Between the United States and Mexico (Senate)
   Established: December 11, 1877
      S. J. (45-2): 52.
   Authority: Res. of the Senate (45-2)
   Terminated: June 20, 1878, at the end of the 45-2.

850. Select Committee on Proceedings of Board of Commissioners on Claims Against Mexico (Senate)
   Sudocs: Y4. M57:
   Established: February 25, 1852
      Cong. Globe (32-1): 630.
   Authority: Res. of the Senate (32-1)
   Terminated: March 28, 1854
      S. rpt. 182 (33-1) 708.

851. Select Committee on Protection of Friends of Peace in Mexico (House)
   Established: February 1, 1848
      H. J. (30-1): 336.
   Authority: Res. of the House (30-1)
   Terminated: August 14, 1848, at the end of the 30-1.

852. Select Committee on the Laws of the Territory of Michigan (House)
   Established: January 8, 1807
      H. J. (9-2): 124.
   Authority: Res. of the House (9-2)
   Terminated: February 24, 1807
      Ibid. 321.

853. Select Committee on the Bills to Admit Michigan and Arkansas into the Union (Senate)
   Established: January 27, 1834
      S. J. (23-1): 118.
   Authority: Res. of the Senate (28-1)
   Terminated: May 3, 1834
      Ibid. 241.

854. Select Committee on Allowing a Delegate to Congress for the Michigan Territory (House)
   Established: November 19, 1818
      H. J. (15-2): 22.
   Authority: Res. of the House (15-2)
   Terminated: November 24, 1818
      Ibid. 34.

855. Select Committee on a Letter from A. B. Woodward and Others on the Michigan Territory (House)
   Established: January 12, 1807
      H. J. (9-2): 130.

Authority: Res. of the House
  (9-2)
Terminated: January 21, 1807
  Ibid. 175.

856. Select Committee on A Letter
From William Hull, Governor of the
Michigan Territory (House)
  Established: January 12, 1807
    H. J. (9-2): 130.
  Authority: Res. of the House
    (9-2)
  Terminated: January 22, 1807
    Ibid. 177.

857. Select Committee on a Message
from the President Transmitting a
Report from the Governor and Judge
of the Michigan Territory (House)
  Established: December 23, 1805
    H. J. (9-1): 77.
  Authority: Res. of the House
    (9-1)
  Terminated: March 18, 1806
    Ibid. 333.

858. Committee on Mileage (House)
  Sudocs: Y4. M58:
  Established: September 15, 1837
    Cong. Globe (25-1): 35.
  Authority: Res. of the House
    (25-1)
  Terminated: December 5, 1927
    69 CR 13.
  Authority: H. Res. 7 (70-1)

859. Select Committee to Establish
a Uniform Rule for Computation of
Mileage of Members of Congress
(Senate)
  Established: January 6, 1830
    S. J. (21-1): 67.
  Authority: Res. of the Senate
    (21-1)
  Terminated: July 7, 1840
    S. doc. 599 (26-1) 361.

860. Special Committee on Inves-
tigation of Hazing at Military
Academy (House)
  Established: December 11, 1900
    34 CR 245.
  Authority: House Res. 307 (56-2)
  Terminated: February 9, 1901
    H. rpt. 2768 (56-2) 4215-17.

861. Committee on Military Affairs
(House)
  Sudocs: Y4. M59/1:
  Established: March 13, 1822,
    having been preceded by a
    select committee (Entry 863).
      H. J. (17-1): 357.
  Authority: Res. of the House
    (17-1)
  Terminated: January 2, 1947
    60 Stat. 812.
  Authority: PL 79-601

862. Committee on Military Affairs
(Senate)
  Sudocs: Y4. M59/2:
  Established: December 10, 1816
    Annals (14-2): 30.
  Authority: Res. of the Senate
    (14-2)
  Terminated: January 2, 1947
    60 Stat. 812.
  Authority: PL 79-601

863. Select Committee on Military
Affairs (House)
  Established: May 26, 1809,
    having been preceded by the
    Select Committee on Military
    and Naval Establishments
    (Entry 864).
      H. J. (11-1): 34.
  Authority: Res. of the House
    (11-1)
  Terminated: March 13, 1822, when
    it was made a standing commit-
    tee (Entry 861).
      H. J. (17-1): 357.
  Authority: Res. of the House
    (17-1)

864. Select Committee on the
Military and Naval Establishments
(House)
  Established: October 29, 1807
    H. J. (10-1): 24.
  Authority: Res. of the House
    (10-1)
  Terminated: May 26, 1809, when
    separate Committees on Military
    and Naval Affairs were estab-
    lished (Entries 863, 953).
      H. J. (11-1): 33.
  Authority: Res. of the House
    (11-1)

865. Select Committee on Military and Post Roads from New York to Washington (House)
  Established: January 12, 1863
    H. J. (37-3): 181.
  Authority: Res. of the House
    (37-3)
  Terminated: March 3, 1863
    H. rpt. 63 (37-3) 1173.

866. Select Committee on a Military and Postal Railroad from Washington to New York (House)
  Established: January 8, 1866
    Cong. Globe (39-1): 135.
  Authority: Res. of the House
    (39-1)
  Terminated: May 30, 1866
    S. J. (39-1): 776.

867. Select Committee on a Military Asylum Near Washington, D. C. (Senate)
  Established: April 12, 1858
    S. J. (35-1): 332.
  Authority: Res. of the Senate
    (35-1)
  Terminated: August 18, 1858, at the end of the 35-1.

868. Select Committee on the Appointment of a Commission to Examine and Decide Upon Military Claims Originating during the Present Rebellion in the State of Virginia, West of the Blue Ridge (Senate)
  Established: February 5, 1863
    S. J. (37-3): 198.
  Authority: Senate Order (37-3)
  Terminated: February 13, 1863
    Ibid. 249.

869. Select Committee on Increasing the Military Establishment, the Marine Corps, and the Number of Seamen to be Employed on Gun Boats (House)
  Established: January 19, 1808
    H. J. (10-1): 279.
  Authority: Res. of the House
    (10-1)
  Terminated: January 27, 1808
    Ibid. 309.

870. Committee on Military Pensions (House)
  Established: December 13, 1825, when Committee on Revolutionary Pensions was changed to this (Entry 1223).
    H. J. (19-1): 46.
  Authority: Res. of the House
    (19-1)
  Terminated: March 3, 1831, to be replaced by Committee on Revolutionary Pensions at the end of this session (Entry 1224).
    H. J. (21-2): 167.
  Authority: Res. of the House
    (21-2)

871. Committee on the Militia (House)
  Sudocs: Y4. M59/3:
  Established: December 10, 1835, having been preceded by a select committee (Entry 873).
    H. J. (24-1): 41.
  Authority: Res. of the House
    (24-1)
  Terminated: April 5, 1911
    47 CR 80.
  Authority: H. Res. 11 (62-1)

872. Committee on the Militia (Senate)
  Established: December 10, 1816
    Annals (14-2): 30.
  Authority: Res. of the Senate
    (14-2)
  Terminated: December 16, 1857
    Cong. Globe (35-1): 38.
  Authority: Res. of the Senate
    (35-1)

873. Select Committee on the Militia (House)
  Established: December 4, 1805
    H. J. (9-1): 23.
  Authority: Res. of the House
    (9-1)
  Terminated: December 10, 1835, when it was made a standing committee (Entry 871).
    H. J. (24-1): 41.
  Authority: Res. of the House
    (24-1)

874. Select Committee on Militia Expenses (House)

Established: December 6, 1815
H. J. (14-1): 26.
Authority: Res. of the House
(14-1)
Terminated: December 11, 1816
H. J. (14-2): 61.

875. Select Committee on the
Organization of the Militia in
the District of Columbia (House)
Established: March 26, 1806
H. J. (9-1): 370.
Authority: Res. of the House
(9-1)
Terminated: January 27, 1807
H. J. (9-2): 199.

876. Select Committee on Alter-
ations in the Militia Laws of the
U. S. (House)
Established: November 16, 1807
H. J. (10-1): 66.
Authority: Res. of the House
(10-1)
Terminated: January 2, 1808
Ibid. 216.

877. Committee on Mines and Mining
(House)
Sudocs: Y4. M66/1:
Established: December 19, 1865
Cong. Globe (39-1): 83.
Authority: Res. of the House
(39-1)
Terminated: January 2, 1947
60 Stat. 812.
Authority: PL 79-601

878. Committee on Mines and Mining
(Senate)
Sudocs: Y4. M66/2:
Established: December 5, 1865
Cong. Globe (39-1): 11.
Authority: Res. of the Senate
(39-1)
Terminated: January 2, 1947
60 Stat. 812.
Authority: PL 79-601

879. Select Committee on Alter-
ation of the Text of the Minnesota
Land Bill (House)
Established: July 21, 1854
H. J. (33-1): 1194.
Authority: Res. of the House
(33-1)

Terminated: February 23, 1855
H. rpt. 122 (33-2) 808.

880. Select Committee on the Mint
(House)
Established: January 7, 1828
H. J. (20-1): 130.
Authority: Res. of the House
(20-1)
Terminated: January 5, 1829
H. J. (20-2): 121.

881. Select Committee on Estab-
lishing Branches of the Mint
(Senate)
Established: February 5, 1835
S. J. (23-2): 137.
Authority: Res. of the Senate
(23-2)
Terminated: February 10, 1835
Ibid. 150.

882. Select Committee on a Report
of the Director of the Mint (House)
Established: January 8, 1808
H. J. (10-1): 240.
Authority: Res. of the House
(10-1)
Terminated: January 13, 1808
Ibid. 258.

883. Select Committee on Pro-
longing the Mint at Philadelphia
(House)
Established: November 12, 1812
H. J. (12-2): 34.
Authority: Res. of the House
(12-2)
Terminated: March 3, 1813, at the
end of the 12-2.

884. Select Committee on Estab-
lishing a Branch of the Mint in
North Carolina (House)
Established: December 29, 1829
H. J. (21-1): 106.
Authority: Res. of the House
(21-1)
Terminated: May 31, 1830, at the
end of the 21-1.

885. Select Committee to Study the
Problem of United States Servicemen
Missing in Action in Southeast Asia
(House)
Sudocs: Y4. M69/3:

Established: September 11, 1975
121 CR 28566.
Authority: H. Res. 335 (94-1)
Terminated: January 3, 1977
Deschler, v. 4, 314.

886. Select Committee on Affairs
in Mississippi (House)
Established: December 14, 1874
H. J. (43-2): 67.
Authority: Res. of the House
(43-2)
Terminated: February 27, 1875
H. rpt. 265 (43-2) 1659.

887. Select Committee to Inquire
into Alleged Frauds in Recent
Elections in Mississippi (Senate)
Sudocs: Y4. M69/1:
Established: March 31, 1876
S. J. (44-1): 374.
Authority: Res. of the Senate
(44-1)
Terminated: August 7, 1876
S. rpt. 527 (44-1) 1669-1670.

888. Select Committee on the
Investigation of Labor Conditions
on the Mississippi Flood Control
Project (Senate)
Established: February 22, 1933
76 CR 4692.
Authority: S. Res. 300 (72-2)
Terminated: January 5, 1937, at
the end of the 75-1.

889. Select Committee on Levees of
the Mississippi River (Senate)
Established: June 8, 1866
S. J. (39-1): 499.
Authority: Senate Order (39-1)
Terminated: July 2, 1866
S. rpt. 126 (39-1) 1240.

890. Select Committee on the Levee
System of the Mississippi River
(Senate)
Established: June 3, 1870
S. J. (41-2): 749.
Authority: Res. of the Senate
(41-2)
Terminated: March 3, 1879, at the
end of the 45-3. Replaced by
Committee on the Improvement of
the Mississippi River and its
Tributaries (Entry 893).

891. Committee on Levees and
Improvements of the Mississippi
River (House)
Sudocs: Y4. M69/2:
Established: December 10, 1875,
having been preceded by a
select committee (Entry 895).
4 CR 191.
Authority: Res. of the House
(44-1)
Terminated: April 5, 1911
47 CR 80.
Authority: H. Res. 11 (62-1)

892. Select Committee on the
Reconstruction of the Levees on
the Mississippi River (Senate)
Established: June 8, 1866
S. J. (39-1): 499.
Authority: Res. of the Senate
(39-1)
Terminated: July 2, 1866
S. rpt. 126 (39-1) 1240.

893. Committee on the Improvement
of the Mississippi River and its
Tributaries (Senate)
Established: March 19, 1879, when
it replaced Committee on the
Levee System of the Mississippi
River (Entry 890).
S. J. (46-1): 11.
Authority: Res. of the Senate
(46-1)
Terminated: April 18, 1921
61 CR 404-405.
Authority: S. Res. 43 (67 -
Special)

894. Select Committee on Leveeing
the East Bank of the Mississippi
River from Hickman to Obion River
(House)
Established: January 16, 1855
H. J. (33-2): 186.
Authority: Res. of the House
(33-2)
Terminated: February 28, 1855
Ibid. 485.

895. Select Committee on Missis-
sippi River Levees (House)
Established: March 10, 1871
H. J. (42-1): 28.
Authority: Res. of the House
(42-1)

Terminated: December 10, 1875, when it was made a standing committee (Entry 891).
4 CR 191.
Authority: Res. of the House (44-1)

896. Select Committee on the Petition of the Legislature of the Mississippi Territory (House)
Established: February 12, 1814
H. J. (13-2): 326.
Authority: Res. of the House (13-2)
Terminated: December 20, 1815
H. J. (14-1): 107.

897. Select Committee on the Right of Suffrage in the Mississippi Territory (House)
Established: November 3, 1807
H. J. (10-1): 31.
Authority: Res. of the House (10-1)
Terminated: November 12, 1807
Ibid. 60.

898. Select Committee for the Appointment of an Additional Judge for the Mississippi Territory and to Allow Jurisdiction in Certain Cases to Territorial Courts (House)
Established: November 16, 1807
H. J. (10-1): 66.
Authority: Res. of the House (10-1)
Terminated: January 25, 1810
H. J. (11-2): 206.

899. Select Committee on the Memorial of the Legislature of Mississippi Territory for Admission to the Union (Senate)
Established: January 7, 1817
S. J. (14-2): 87.
Authority: Res. of the Senate (14-2)
Terminated: January 17, 1817
Ibid. 123.

900. Select Committee on the Petition of the Mississippi Territory for an Extension of Suffrage (House)
Established: September 23, 1814
H. J. (13-3): 20.

Authority: Res. of the House (13-3)
Terminated: September 29, 1814
Ibid. 38.

901. Select Committee on the Admission of the Mississippi Territory to the Union (House)
Established: December 28, 1810
H. J. (11-3): 81.
Authority: Res. of the House (12-2)
Terminated: March 3, 1813, at the end of the 12-2.

902. Select Committee on Admission of Mississippi to the Union (Senate)
Established: December 1, 1817
S. J. (15-1): 5.
Authority: Res. of the Senate (15-1)
Terminated: December 3, 1817
Ibid. 20.

903. Select Committee on the Petition of the Mississippi Territory for Admission to the Union (House)
Established: December 9, 1816
H. J. (14-2): 42.
Authority: Res. of the House (14-2)
Terminated: December 23, 1816
Ibid. 98.

904. Select Committee on the Petition of Delegates of fifteen Mississippi Territory Counties for the Admission of that Territory into the Union without a Division (House)
Established: January 9, 1817
H. J. (14-2): 163.
Authority: Res. of the House (14-2)
Terminated: January 17, 1817
Ibid. 219.

905. Select Committee on Boundary of Missouri (House)
Established: January 3, 1828
H. J. (20-1): 116.
Authority: Res. of the House (20-1)

Terminated: January 17, 1828
  Ibid. 183.

906. Select Committee on the
Constitution of Missouri (House)
  Established: November 16, 1820
    H. J. (16-2): 17.
  Authority: Res. of the House
    (16-2)
  Terminated: November 23, 1820
    Ibid. 30.

907. Select Committee on the
Letter of the Missouri Delegation
to Senator Henderson (House)
  Established: May 18, 1868
    Cong. Globe (40-2): 2528.
  Authority: Res. of the House
    (40-2)
  Terminated: November 10, 1868,
    at the end of the 40-2.

908. Select Committee on Admission
of Missouri Into the Union (Senate)
  Established: November 14, 1820
    S. J. (16-2): 7.
  Authority: Res. of the Senate
    (16-2)
  Terminated: December 13, 1820
    Ibid. 61.

909. Select Committee on the Vari-
ous Propositions for the Admission
of Missouri into the Union (House)
  Established: February 3, 1821
    H. J. (16-2): 197.
  Authority: Res. of the House
    (16-2)
  Terminated: February 10, 1821
    Ibid. 212.

910. Select Committee on Amend-
ments in the Act for the Govern-
ment of the Missouri Territory
(House)
  Established: January 7, 1813
    H. J. (12-2): 158.
  Authority: Res. of the House
    (12-2)
  Terminated: January 29, 1813
    Ibid. 235.

911. Select Committee on the
Petition of the Inhabitants of
the Missouri Territory (House)

Established: March 30, 1816
  H. J. (14-1): 559.
Authority: Res. of the House
  (14-1)
Terminated: April 24, 1816
  Ibid. 713.

912. Select Committee on the
Petition of the Legislature of
the Missouri Territory on the
Erection of Forts (House)
  Established: February 19, 1816
    H. J. (14-1): 361.
  Authority: Res. of the House
    (14-1)
  Terminated: April 3, 1816
    Ibid. 575.

913. Select Committee on a Memorial of the American Association
for the Promotion of Science, for
an Appropriation to Enable Profes-
sor Mitchell to Construct a Machine
for Observing the Right Ascensions
and Declensions by the Aid of
Magnetism (Senate)
  Established: April 24, 1854
    S. J. (33-1): 336.
  Authority: Res. of the Senate
    (33-1)
  Terminated: August 7, 1854, at
    the end of the 33-1.

914. Select Committee on the
Contract Entered into between the
United States and Elija Mix (House)
  Established: April 22, 1822
    H. J. (17-1): 477.
  Authority: Res. of the House
    (17-1)
  Terminated: May 7, 1822
    H. rpt. 109 (17-1) 71.

915. Select Committee on the Free
Navigation of the Mobile River
(House)
  Established: February 23, 1810
    H. J. (11-2): 299.
  Authority: Res. of the House
    (11-2)
  Terminated: May 1, 1810, at the
    end of the 11-2.

916. Select Committee on the
Mohican or Stockbridge Indians
(House)

Established: January 17, 1820
H. J. (16-1): 140.
Authority: Res. of the House
(16-1)
Terminated: February 24, 1820
Ibid. 246.

917 & 918. No Entry

919. Select Committee on Investigation into the Application of
Public Moneys (House)
Established: May 24, 1809
H. J. (11-1): 20.
Authority: Res. of the House
(11-1)
Terminated: May 1, 1810, at the
end of the 11-2.

920. Select Committee on the
Faithful Application of Moneys
Drawn from the Treasury, Since the
Year 1801 (House)
Established: November 13, 1811
H. J. (12-1): 46.
Authority: Res. of the House
(12-1)
Terminated: July 6, 1812
Ibid. 869.

921. Select Committee on the
Accounts of James Monroe (House)
Established: January 6, 1825
H. J. (18-2): 110.
Authority: Res. of the House
(18-2)
Terminated: March 23, 1826
H. J. (19-1): 374.

922. Select Committee on the
Accounts of James Monroe (Senate)
Established: February 8, 1831
S. J. (21-2): 136.
Authority: Res. of the Senate
(21-2)
Terminated: February 11, 1831
Ibid. 142.

923. Select Committee to Investigate Seizure of Montgomery Ward and
Company (House)
Sudocs: Y4. W21:
Established: May 5, 1944
90 CR 4070.
Authority: H. Res. 521 (78-2)

Terminated: September 19, 1944
H. rpt. 1904 (78-2) 10848.

924. Select Committee on the
Construction and Preservation of
Monuments to Deceased Senators
(Senate)
Established: January 20, 1848
S. J. (30-1): 124.
Authority: Res. of the Senate
(30-1)
Terminated: August 14, 1848, at
the end of the 30-1.

925. Select Committee on the
Mortality of the Army at New
Orleans (House)
Established: December 19, 1810
H. J. (11-3): 57.
Authority: Res. of the House
(11-3)
Terminated: February 26, 1811
Ibid. 321.

926. Select Committee on the Memorial of W. T. G. Morton (Senate)
Established: December 28, 1846
S. J. (29-2): 71.
Authority: Res. of the Senate
(29-2)
Terminated: March 3, 1847, at
the end of the 29-2.

927. Select Committee on W. T.
Morton's Petition on Prevention
of Pain in Surgery (House)
Established: December 18, 1846
H. J. (29-2): 97.
Authority: Res. of the House
(29-2)
Terminated: February 28, 1849
H. rpt. 114 (30-2) 545.

928. Special Committee Investigating the Munitions Industry
(Senate)
Sudocs: Y4. M92:
Established: April 12, 1934
78 CR 6485.
Authority: S. Res. 206 (73-2)
Terminated: June 11, 1938, at
the end of the 75-3.

929. Committee on Muscle Shoals
(Joint)
Sudocs: Y4. M97:

Established: March 13, 1926
    67 CR 5518.
Authority: H. Con. Res. 4 (69-1)
Terminated: June 21, 1926
    S. rpt. 1120 (69-1) 8528.

930. Select Committee on Narcotics
Abuse and Control (House)
    Sudocs: Y4. N16:
    Established: July 29, 1976
        122 CR 24440.
    Authority: H. Res. 1350 (94-2)
    Terminated: Still in existence at
        the end of the 97-2.

931. Select Committee on the
National Bank (House)
    Established: April 4, 1814
        H. J. (13-2): 532.
    Authority: Res. of the House
        (13-2)
    Terminated: April 8, 1814
        Ibid. 559.

932. Select Committee on the
Establishment of a National Bank
(House)
    Established: March 22, 1810
        H. J. (11-2): 423.
    Authority: Res. of the House
        (11-2)
    Terminated: April 2, 1810
        Ibid. 480.

933. Select Committee on a
National Currency (House)
    Established: December 6, 1815
        H. J. (14-1): 25.
    Authority: Res. of the House
        (14-1)
    Terminated: January 10, 1817
        H. J. (14-2): 179.

934. Select Committee Investigating National Defense Migration
(House)
    Sudocs: Y4. N21/5:
    Established: March 31, 1941
        87 CR 2736.
    Authority: H. Res. 113 (77-1)
    Terminated: January 8, 1943
        H. rpt. 3 (78-1) 10760.

935. Special Committee Investigating National Defense Program
(Senate)

Sudocs: Y4. N21/6:
Established: March 1, 1941
    87 CR 1615.
Authority: S. Res. 71 (77-1)
Terminated: May 18, 1948
    S. rpt. 440 (80-2) 11205.

936. Select Committee to Conduct
Study and Survey of National
Defense Program in its Relation to
Small Business (House)
    Sudocs: Y4. N21/7:
    Established: January 18, 1945
        91 CR 343.
    Authority: H. Res. 64 (79-1)
    Terminated: August 2, 1946, at
        the end of the 79-2.

937. Select Committee to Investigate National Disabled Soldiers
League Inc. (House)
    Sudocs: Y4. N21/3:
    Established: January 24, 1925
        66 CR 2437.
    Authority: H. Res. 412 (68-2)
    Terminated: March 3, 1925
        H. rpt. 1638 (68-2) 8392.

938. Special Committee on the
Termination of the National
Emergency (Senate)
    Sudocs: Y4. N21/9:
    Established: January 6, 1973
        119 CR 413.
    Authority: S. Res. 9 (93-1)
    Terminated: December 20, 1974,
        at the end of the 93-2.

939. Select Committee on the
Memorial of the National Institute
(House)
    Established: February 3, 1845
        H. J. (28-2): 311.
    Authority: Res. of the House
        (28-2)
    Terminated: February 15, 1845
        H. rpt. 130 (28-2) 468.

940. Special Committee to Investigate the National Labor Relations
Board (House)
    Sudocs: Y4. N21/4:
    Established: July 20, 1939
        84 CR 9593.
    Authority: H. Res. 258 (76-1)

Terminated: December 30, 1940
   H. rpt. 3109 (76-3) 10446.

941. Committee on Conservation
of National Resources (Senate)
   Sudocs: Y4. N21/1:
   Established: March 22, 1909
      44 CR 121.
   Authority: Adoption of the rules
      (61-1)
   Terminated: April 18, 1921
      61 CR 405.
   Authority: S. Res. 43 (67 -
      Special)

942. Select Committee on National
Road from Cumberland to Wheeling
(Senate)
   Established: December 12, 1822
      S. J. (17-2): 29.
   Authority: Res. of the Senate
      (17-2)
   Terminated: May 3, 1823, at the
      end of the 17-2.

943. Special Committee to Inves-
tigate National Security League
(House)
   Sudocs: Y4. N21/2:
   Established: December 10, 1918
      57 CR 266.
   Authority: H. Res. 469 (65-3)
   Terminated: March 3, 1919
      H. rpt. 173 (65-3) 7456.

944. Select Committee on the
National Telegraph Company (Senate)
   Established: April 5, 1866
      Cong. Globe (39-1): 1224.
   Authority: Res. of the Senate
      (39-1)
   Terminated: July 28, 1866, at the
      end of the 39-1.

945. Select Committee on National
Water Resources (Senate)
   Sudocs: Y4. N21/8:
   Established: April 20, 1959
      105 CR 6307.
   Authority: S. Res. 48 (86-1)
   Terminated: January 30, 1961
      S. rpt. 29 (87-1) 12321.

946. Select Committee on Amending
the Act to Establish an Uniform
Rule of Naturalization (House)

Established: January 19, 1808
   H. J. (10-1): 277.
Authority: Res. of the House
   (10-1)
Terminated: May 26, 1808
   Ibid. 525.

947. Select Committee on Amending
and Examining Naturalization Laws
(House)
   Established: March 12, 1837
      H. J. (25-2): 576.
   Authority: Res. of the House
      (25-2)
   Terminated: July 2, 1838
      H. rpt. 1040 (25-2) 336.

948. Select Committee on Amend-
ments to the Naturalization Laws
(House)
   Established: June 27, 1812
      H. J. (12-1): 819.
   Authority: Res. of the House
      (12-1)
   Terminated: June 29, 1812
      Ibid. 824.

949. Committee on Navajo-Hopi
Indian Administration (Joint)
   Sudocs: Y4. N22/4:
   Established: April 19, 1950
      64 Stat. 47.
   Authority: PL 81-474
   Terminated: January 6, 1973
      119 CR 413.

950. Committee on Naval Affairs
(House)
   Sudocs: Y4. N22/1:
   Established: March 13, 1822,
      having been preceded by a
      select committee (Entry 953).
      H. J. (17-1): 351.
   Authority: Res. of the House
      (17-1)
   Terminated: January 2, 1947
      60 Stat. 812.
   Authority: PL 79-601

951. Committee on Naval Affairs
(Joint)
   Sudocs: Y4. N22/3:
   Established: January 12, 1894
      26 CR 754.
   Authority: S. Con. Res. (53-2)

Terminated: August 28, 1894, at
the end of the 53-2.

952. Committee on Naval Affairs
(Senate)
  Sudocs: Y4. N22/2:
  Established: December 10, 1816
    Annals (14-2): 30.
  Authority: Res. of the Senate
    (14-2)
  Terminated: January 2, 1947
    60 Stat. 812.
  Authority: PL 79-601

953. Select Committee on Naval
Affairs (House)
  Established: May 26, 1809, having
    been preceded by the Select
    Committee on Military and Naval
    Establishments (Entry 864).
      H. J. (11-1): 31.
  Authority: Res. of the House
    (11-1)
  Terminated: March 13, 1822, when
    it was made a standing commit-
    tee (Entry 950).
      H. J. (17-1): 351.
  Authority: Res. of the House
    (17-1)

954. Select Committee on Naval
Contracts and Expenditures (House)
  Established: January 18, 1859
    H. J. (35-2): 211.
  Authority: Res. of the House
    (35-2)
  Terminated: February 24, 1859
    H. rpt. 184 (35-2) 1019.

955. Select Committee on Our Naval
Peace Establishment (House)
  Established: December 4, 1805
    H. J. (9-1): 23.
  Authority: Res. of the House
    (9-1)
  Terminated: February 20, 1807
    H. J. (9-2): 305.

956. Committee on Naval Personnel
(Joint)
  Established: January 12, 1894
    S. J. (53-2): 46.
  Authority: H. Con. Res. (53-2)
  Terminated: March 3, 1895, at the
    end of the 53-3.

957. Select Committee on Naval
Reform (House)
  Established: March 15, 1814
    H. J. (13-2): 343.
  Authority: Res. of the House
    (13-2)
  Terminated: March 2, 1815
    H. J. (13-3): 766.

958. Select Committee on Naval
Supplies (Senate)
  Established: January 25, 1864
    S. J. (38-1): 109.
  Authority: Res. of the Senate
    (38-1)
  Terminated: June 29, 1864
    S. rpt. 99 (38-1) 1178.

959. Select Committee on the
Expenditure of Moneys Appropriated
Since 1803 for the Navy Department
(House)
  Established: January 18, 1811
    H. J. (11-3): 136.
  Authority: Res. of the House
    (11-3)
  Terminated: February 25, 1811
    Ibid. 308.

960. Select Committee to Inves-
tigate the Affairs of the Navy
Department (House)
  Established: March 11, 1872
    Cong. Globe (42-2): 1581.
  Authority: Res. of the House
    (42-2)
  Terminated: May 22, 1872
    H. rpt. 80-81 (42-2) 1542.

961. Select Committee on Retrench-
ments in the Expenses of the Navy
Department (House)
  Established: July 2, 1812
    H. J. (12-1): 846.
  Authority: Res. of the House
    (12-1)
  Terminated: July 6, 1812, at the
    end of the 12-1.

962. Select Committee on the
Report of the Secretary of the
Navy on Navy Hospitals (House)
  Established: May 26, 1812
    H. J. (12-1): 713.
  Authority: Res. of the House
    (12-1)

Terminated: June 11, 1812
  Ibid. 745.

963. Select Committee on the
Report of the Attorney General
on the Conflicting Claims to the
New Orleans Batture (House)
  Established: June 12, 1809
    H. J. (11-1): 109.
  Authority: Res. of the House
    (11-1)
  Terminated: June 16, 1809
    Ibid. 127.

964. Select Committee on the
New Orleans Riots (House)
  Sudocs: Y4. N42/1:
  Established: December 6, 1866
    Cong. Globe (39-2): 29.
  Authority: Res. of the House
    (39-2)
  Terminated: February 11, 1867
    H. rpt. 16 (39-2) 1304.

965. Select Committee on Finishing
and Furnishing the New York Custom
House (House)
  Established: May 13, 1842
    H. J. (27-2): 808.
  Authority: Res. of the House
    (27-2)
  Terminated: August 25, 1842
    H. rpt. 1065 (27-2) 411.

966. Select Committee on Alleged
New York Election Frauds (House)
  Sudocs: Y4. N42/2:
  Established: December 14, 1868
    Cong. Globe (40-3): 74.
  Authority: Res. of the House
    (40-3)
  Terminated: March 1, 1869
    H. rpts. 31 and 41 (40-3) 1389,
    1390.

967. Select Committee on New York
Elections (House)
  Established: July 19, 1892
    H. J. (52-1): 304.
  Authority: Res. of the House
    (52-1)
  Terminated: January 27, 1893
    H. rpt. 2365 (52-2) 3141.

968. Select Committee on Newburg,
N. Y., Monument and Centennial

Celebration of 1883 (House)
  Sudocs: Y4. N42/3:
  Established: June 20, 1882
    13 CR 5125.
  Authority: H. Res. 176 (47-1)
  Terminated: October 17, 1883
    H. misdoc. 601 (50-1) 2576.

969. Select Committee to Inves-
tigate Newsprint (House)
  Established: February 26, 1947
    93 CR 1465
  Authority: H. Res. 58 (80-1)
  Terminated: December 31, 1948,
    at the end of the 80-2.

970. Select Committee on a Ship
Canal Around the Falls of Niagara
(House)
  Established: June 24, 1862
    H. J. (37-2): 923.
  Authority: Res. of the House
    (37-2)
  Terminated: March 3, 1863
    H. J. (37-3): 602.

971. Select Committee on the
Petition of Inhabitants of the
Niagara Frontier (House)
  Established: January 13, 1816
    H. J. (14-1): 156.
  Authority: Res. of the House
    (14-1)
  Terminated: January 23, 1817
    H. J. (14-2): 269.

972. Special Committee on the
Niagara Ship-Canal (House)
  Established: March 11, 1867
    Cong. Globe (40-3): 61.
  Authority: Res. of the House
    (40-1)
  Terminated: December 2, 1867,
    at the end of the 40-1.

973. Select Committee on Grant
of Lands to the Niagara Ship Canal
(House)
  Established: March 16, 1858
    H. J. (35-1): 513.
  Authority: Res. of the House
    (35-1)
  Terminated: May 11, 1858
    H. rpt. 374 (35-1) 966.

974. Select Committee on Con-
struction of the Nicaragua Canal
(Senate)
  Established: December 30, 1895
    28 CR 421.
  Authority: Res. of the Senate
    (54-1)
  Terminated: March 3, 1901, at
    the end of the 56-2.

975. Select Committee on
Nicaraguan Claims (Senate)
  Established: February 5, 1879
    8 CR 994.
  Authority: Res. of the Senate
    (45-3)
  Terminated: March 3, 1895, at
    the end of the 53-3.

976. Select Committee on the
Credentials of the Honorable John
M. Niles (Senate)
  Established: April 30, 1844
    Cong. Globe (28-1): 594.
  Authority: Res. of the Senate
    (28-1)
  Terminated: May 16, 1844
    Ibid. 636.

977. Select Committee on a Nine
Foot Channel from Great Lakes to
the Gulf (Senate)
  Sudocs: Y4. N62:
  Established: January 25, 1923
    64 CR 2364.
  Authority: S. Res. 411 (67-4)
  Terminated: February 3, 1925
    S. rpt. 975 (68-2) 8389.

978. Select Committee on Suspen-
sion of the Non-Importation Act
(House)
  Established: December 3, 1806
    H. J. (9-2): 21.
  Authority: Res. of the House
    (9-2)
  Terminated: December 4, 1806
    Ibid. 24.

979. Select Committee on the
Petition of the General Assembly
of North Carolina (House)
  Established: January 20, 1817
    H. J. (14-2): 234.
  Authority: Res. of the House
    (14-2)

Terminated: January 28, 1817
  Ibid. 299.

980. Special Committee on Revenue
Collections in North Carolina
(Senate)
  Established: March 2, 1882
    13 CR 3128.
  Authority: Res. of the Senate
    (47-1)
  Terminated: February 12, 1883
    S. rpt. 981 (47-2) 2088.

981. Select Committee on the
Petition of the General Assembly
of North Carolina on Tennessee
Lands (House)
  Established: March 3, 1824
    H. J. (18-1): 287.
  Authority: Res. of the House
    (18-1)
  Terminated: March 6, 1824
    Ibid. 294.

982. Committee on Investigation
of Northern Pacific Railroad Land
Grants (Joint)
  Sudocs: Y4. N81:
  Established: June 5, 1924
    43 Stat. 462.
  Authority: Pub. Res. 24 (68-1)
  Terminated: April 19, 1929
    S. rpt. 5 (71-1) 9185.

983. Select Committee to Provide
for the More Effectual Defense of
the Northwestern Frontier (House)
  Established: June 22, 1813
    H. J. (13-1): 96.
  Authority: Res. of the House
    (13-1)
  Terminated: January 16, 1815
    H. J. (13-3): 518.

984. Select Committee on Nutrition
and Human Needs (Senate)
  Sudocs: Y4. N95:
  Established: July 30, 1968
    114 CR 24162.
  Authority: S. Res. 281 (90-2)
  Terminated: December 31, 1977,
    when its functions were trans-
    ferred to the Committee on
    Agriculture, Nutrition and

Forestry (Entry 15).
123 CR 3691.
Authority: S. Res. 4 (95-1)

985. Select Committee on a
National University and National
Observatory (House)
Established: December 7, 1825
H. J. (19-1): 29.
Authority: Res. of the House
(19-1)
Terminated: March 18, 1826
H. rpt. 124 (19-1) 141.

986. Select Committee making Pro-
vision for Surviving Officers and
Soldiers of the Revolution (House)
Established: December 3, 1817
H. J. (15-1): 20.
Authority: Res. of the House
(15-1)
Terminated: December 20, 1819
H. rpt. 9 (16-1) 40.

987. Select Committee on Bill
for Appointment of Officers of
the United States (House)
Established: January 14, 1839
H. J. (25-3): 222.
Authority: Res. of the House
(25-3)
Terminated: March 2, 1839
H. rpt. 325 (25-3) 352.

988. Select Committee on Memorials
of Officers of the War of 1812 for
Bounty Lands (House)
Established: March 6, 1826
H. J. (19-1): 314.
Authority: Res. of the House
(19-1)
Terminated: May 17, 1826
Ibid. 584.

989. Select Committee to Inquire
What Offices are Useless, into the
Prevention of the Combining of
Offices and of Equalizing the Pay
of Officers, Civil and Military
(House)
Established: January 24, 1817
H. J. (14-2): 276.
Authority: Res. of the House
(14-2)
Terminated: February 17, 1817
Ibid. 412.

990. Select Committee on the
Boundaries of Ohio (House)
Established: January 4, 1812
H. J. (12-1): 226.
Authority: Res. of the House
(12-1)
Terminated: July 6, 1812, at
the end of the 12-1.

991. Select Committee on Granting
Lands for the Improvement of the
Ohio (House)
Established: March 11, 1856
H. J. (34-1): 663.
Authority: Res. of the House
(34-1)
Terminated: March 24, 1856
Ibid. 716.

992. Select Committee on Offering
Relief to Purchasers of Lands Lying
Between Robert's and Ludlow's Lines
in Ohio (House)
Established: April 5, 1824
H. J. (18-1): 364.
Authority: Res. of the House
(18-1)
Terminated: May 4, 1824
Ibid. 486.

993. Select Committee to Settle
and Establish the Northern Boundary
Line of the State of Ohio (House)
Established: June 13, 1834
H. J. (23-1): 746.
Authority: Res. of the House
(23-1)
Terminated: December 28, 1835
H. J. (24-1): 90.

994. Select Committee on the Im-
provement of the Navigation of the
Ohio and Mississippi Rivers (House)
Established: March 29, 1830
H. J. (21-1): 473.
Authority: Res. of the House
(21-1)
Terminated: May 4, 1830
Ibid. 604.

995. Select Committee on Obstruc-
tions in the Navigation of the Ohio
and Mississippi Rivers (House)
Established: February 10, 1824
H. J. (18-1): 219.

Authority: Res. of the House
(18-1)
Terminated: March 31, 1824
Ibid. 353.

996. Select Committee on Fixing
Boundary Between the State of Ohio
and Territory of Michigan (House)
Established: March 2, 1826
H. J. (19-1): 305.
Authority: Res. of the House
(19-1)
Terminated: May 22, 1816, at the
end of the 19-1.

997. Select Committee on The Ohio
Michigan Boundary (Senate)
Established: December 14, 1831
S. J. (22-1): 25.
Authority: Res. of the Senate
(22-1)
Terminated: March 20, 1832
Ibid. 194.

998. Select Committee on the Ohio
Michigan Boundary (Senate)
Established: December 22, 1835
S. J. (24-1): 52.
Authority: Res. of the Senate
(24-1)
Terminated: July 4, 1836, at the
end of the 24-1.

999. Select Committee to Investi-
gate Indian Contracts in Oklahoma
(House)
Sudocs: Y4. Ok4:
Established: June 25, 1910
45 CR 9113.
Authority: H. Res. 847 (61-2)
Terminated: March 3, 1911, at the
end of the 61-3.

1000. Select Committee to Investi-
gate Old Age Pension Plans (House)
Sudocs: Y4. Ol1:
Established: March 10, 1936
80 CR 3507.
Authority: H. Res. 443 (74-2)
Terminated: August 21, 1937
H. rpt. 1 (75-1) 10086.

1001. Special Committee to Inves-
tigate Old-Age Pension System
(Senate)
Sudocs: Y4. Ol1/2:

Established: June 20, 1941
77 CR 5394.
Authority: S. Res. 129 (77-1)
Terminated: December 16, 1942,
at the end of the 77-2.

1002. Select Committee on the
Omaha Exposition (Senate)
Established: July 8, 1898
31 CR 6791.
Authority: Res. of the Senate
(55-2)
Terminated: March 3, 1899, at
the end of the 55-3.

1003. Select Committee on
Additional Arrangements for
the Preservation of Order in
the Galleries (Senate)
Established: March 8, 1861
S. J. (36-2): 413.
Authority: Res. of the Senate
(36-2)
Terminated: March 8, 1861, at
the end of the 36-2.

1004. Select Committee on Ordnance
(Joint)
Sudocs: Y4. Or2/3:
Established: March 30, 1867
S. J. (40-1): 129.
Authority: J. Res. of the House
(40-1)
Terminated: February 25, 1869
S. rpt. 266 (40-3) 1362.

1005. Select Committee on Investi-
gation of Ordnance and Ammunition
(House)
Sudocs: Y4. Or2/4:
Established: September 8, 1917
55 CR 6808.
Authority: H. Res. 134 (65-1)
Terminated: October 6, 1917, at
the end of the 65-1.

1006. Select Committee on Ordnance
and Gunnery (House)
Established: July 5, 1884
15 CR 6155.
Authority: Res. of the House
(48-1)
Terminated: March 3, 1885, when
it became a commission.
23 Stat. 470.
Authority: PL 48-359.

1007. Select Committee on Ordnance
and Gunnery (Senate)
  Established: August 2, 1882
    13 CR 6763.
  Authority: Res. of the Senate
    (47-1)
  Terminated: March 3, 1883. Name
    changed to Committee on Ord-
    nance and War-Ships in 48-1
    (Entry 1009).

1008. Select Committee on Ordnance
and Ordnance Stores (House)
  Established: December 30, 1823
    H. J. (18-1): 102.
  Authority: Res. of the House
    (18-1)
  Terminated: May 27, 1824, at
    the end of the 18-1.

1009. Select Committee on Ordnance
and War-Ships (Senate)
  Sudocs: Y4. Or2/2:
  Established: July 3, 1884, when
    name changed from Select Com-
    mittee on Ordnance and Gunnery
    (Entry 1007).
    15 CR 5937.
  Authority: Res. of the Senate
    (48-1)
  Terminated: February 8, 1886
    S. rpt. 90 (49-1) 2355.

1010. Select Committee on Heavy
Ordnance and Projectiles (Senate)
  Sudocs: Y4. Or2/1:
  Established: August 2, 1882
    13 CR 6763.
  Authority: Res. of the Senate
    (47-1)
  Terminated: February 9, 1883
    S. rpt. 969 (47-2) 2087.

1011. Select Committee to Investi-
gate all Sales of Ordnance Stores
by the Government of the U. S.
(Senate)
  Established: February 29, 1872
    Cong. Globe (42-2): 1290.
  Authority: Res. of the Senate
    (42-2)
  Terminated: March 11, 1872
    S. rpt. 183 (42-2) 1497.

1012. Select Committee on the
Oregon Railroad (Senate)

Established: June 27, 1848
  S. J. (30-1): 422.
Authority: Res. of the Senate
  (30-1)
Terminated: August 14, 1848, at
  the end of the 30-1.

1013. Select Committee on the
Oregon Territory (Senate)
  Established: December 10, 1838
    S. J. (25-3): 40.
  Authority: Res. of the Senate
    (25-3)
  Terminated: March 3, 1843, at
    the end of the 27-3.

1014. Select Committee on a Reso-
lution of the Legislature of the
Territory of Orleans Proposing
an Amendment to Their Ordinances
(House)
  Established: April 14, 1808
    H. J. (10-1): 572.
  Authority: Res. of the House
    (10-1)
  Terminated: April 25, 1808, at
    the end of the 10-1.

1015. Select Committee on the Outer
Continental Shelf (House)
  Sudocs: Y4. Ou8/2:
  Established: April 22, 1975
    121 CR 11262.
  Authority: H. Res. 412 (94-1)
  Terminated: July 31, 1980
    H. rpt. 1214 (96-2) 13374.

1016. Select Committee on Inves-
tigation of Alleged Outrages in
Southern States (Senate)
  Sudocs: Y4. Ou8:
  Established: January 19, 1871
    Cong. Globe (41-3): 598.
  Authority: Res. of the Senate
    (41-3)
  Terminated: March 12, 1873
    S. J. (42-3): 609.
  Authority: Res. of the Senate
    (42-3)

1017. Select Committee to Examine
the Condition of the Overland Mail
Service (Senate)
  Established: March 3, 1865
    S. J. (38-2): 334.

Authority: Res. of the Senate
    (38-2)
Terminated: March 3, 1865, at
    the end of the 38-2.

1018. Committee on Pacific Coast
Naval Bases (Joint)
    Sudocs: Y4. P11/4:
    Established: June 4, 1920
        41 Stat. 820.
    Authority: PL 66-243
    Terminated: December 31, 1920
        Ibid.

1019. Committee to Study Pacific
Islands (Joint)
    Established: June 18, 1948
        94 CR 8940.
    Authority: H. Con. Res. 129
        (80-2)
    Terminated: December 31, 1948, at
        the end of the 80-2.

1020. Committee on the Pacific
Islands and Puerto Rico (Senate)
    Sudocs: Y4. P11/1:
    Established: December 15, 1899
        33 CR 441.
    Authority: Res. of the Senate
        (56-1)
    Terminated: February 5, 1920,
        when name was changed to
        Committee on Pacific Islands,
        Puerto Rico, and Virgin Islands
        (Entry 1021).
            59 CR 2487.
    Authority: S. Res. 273 (66-2)

1021. Committee on the Pacific
Islands, Puerto Rico, and the
Virgin Islands (Senate)
    Sudocs: Y4. P11/1:
    Established: February 5, 1920,
        when the name of the Committee
        on the Pacific Islands and
        Puerto Rico was changed to this
        (Entry 1020).
            59 CR 2487.
    Authority: S. Res. 273 (66-2)
    Terminated: April 18, 1921
        61 CR 404-05.
    Authority: S. Res. 43 (67 -
        Special)

1022. Committee on the Pacific
Railroad (House)

Sudocs: Y4. P11/3:
Established: March 2, 1865,
    having been preceded by a
    select committee (Entry 1025).
        Cong. Globe (38-2): 1312.
Authority: Res. of the House
    (38-2)
Terminated: April 5, 1911
    47 CR 1280.
Authority: H. Res. 11 (62-1)

1023. Committee on the Pacific
Railroad (Senate)
    Sudocs: Y4. P11/2:
    Established: December 22, 1863,
        having been preceded by a
        select committee (Entry 1026).
            Cong. Globe (38-1): 76.
    Authority: Res. of the Senate
        (38-1)
    Terminated: March 12, 1873, when
        it was replaced by the Commit-
        tee on Railroads (Entry 1171).
        S. J. (42-3): 609.
    Authority: Res. of the Senate
        (42-3)

1024. Committee on Pacific Railroads (Senate)
    Established: March 15, 1893
        25 CR 16.
    Authority: Res. of the Senate
        (53-1)
    Terminated: April 18, 1921
        61 CR 404-405.
    Authority: S. Res. 43 (67 -
        Special)

1025. Select Committee on the
Pacific Railroad (House)
    Established: January 16, 1854
        H. J. (33-1): 221.
    Authority: Res. of the House
        (33-1)
    Terminated: March 2, 1865, when
        it was made a standing commit-
        tee (Entry 1022).
            Cong. Globe (38-2): 1312.
    Authority: Res. of the House
        (38-2)

1026. Select Committee on the
Pacific Railroad (Senate)
    Established: January 4, 1854
        S. J. (33-1): 81.

Authority: Res. of the Senate
(33-1)
Terminated: December 22, 1863,
when it was made a standing
committee (Entry 1023).
Cong. Globe (38-1): 76.
Authority: Res. of the Senate
(38-1)

1027. Special Committee on the
Report of the Pacific Railway
Commission (Senate)
Established: January 24, 1888
19 CR 652.
Authority: Res. of the Senate
(50-1)
Terminated: March 3, 1893, at
the end of the 52-2.

1028. Select Committee on Welfare
and Education of Congressional
Pages (House)
Sudocs: Y4. W45:
Established: September 30, 1964
110 CR 23188.
Authority: H. Res. 847 (88-2)
Terminated: January 2, 1965
H. rpt. 1945 (88-2) 12621-1.

1029. Select Committee on Canal or
Railroad across Panama (House)
Established: December 23, 1848
H. J. (30-2): 147.
Authority: Res. of the House
(30-2)
Terminated: March 3, 1849, at
the end of the 30-2.

1030. Special Committee to Inves-
tigate the Panama Canal Company
(House)
Established: January 28, 1893
24 CR 905.
Authority: Res. of the House
(52-2)
Terminated: March 3, 1893
H. rpt. 2615 (52-2) 3142-1.

1031. Committee on Disposition of
Useless Papers in the Executive
Departments (Senate)
Established: March 22, 1909,
having been preceded by a
Select Committee on Examination

and Disposition of Documents
(Entry 366).
44 CR 121.
Authority: Res. of the Senate
(61-1)
Terminated: April 18, 1921
61 CR 404-405.
Authority: S. Res. 43 (67 -
Special)

1032. Committee to Investigate
General Parcel Post (Joint)
Sudocs: Y4. P21:
Established: August 24, 1912
37 Stat. 559.
Authority: PL 62-336
Terminated: February 12, 1915
S. doc. 944 (63-3) 6787.

1033. Select Committee on the
Patent Laws (House)
Established: February 27, 1806
H. J. (9-1): 285.
Authority: Res. of the House
(9-1)
Terminated: April 21, 1806, at
the end of the 9-1.

1034. Select Committee on the
Patent Office (Senate)
Established: December 31, 1835
S. J. (24-1): 73.
Authority: Res. of the Senate
(24-1)
Terminated: April 28, 1836
S. doc. 338 (24-1) 282.

1035. Select Committee on the
Estimate of the Expense of Finish-
ing the Patent Office (House)
Established: January 20, 1812
H. J. (12-1): 281.
Authority: Res. of the House
(12-1)
Terminated: July 6, 1812, at the
end of the 12-1.

1036. Select Committee on D. P.
Holloway's Management of the Patent
Office (House)
Established: January 30, 1863
H. J. (37-3): 298.
Authority: Res. of the House
(37-3)
Terminated: March 2, 1863
H. rpt. 48 (37-3) 1173.

1037. Select Committee on the
Patent Office (House)
  Established: January 19, 1827
    H. J. (19-2): 182.
  Authority: Res. of the House
    (19-2)
  Terminated: March 1, 1827
    H. rpt. 99 (19-2) 160.

1038. Select Committee on Patenting
Medicines (House)
  Established: December 12, 1848
    H. J. (30-2): 79.
  Authority: Res. of the House
    (30-2)
  Terminated: February 6, 1849
    H. rpt. 52 (30-2) 545.

1039. Committee on Patents (House)
  Sudocs: Y4. P27/1:
  Established: September 15, 1837,
    having been preceded by a
    select committee (Entry 1042).
    Cong. Globe (25-1): 34.
  Authority: Res. of the House
    (25-1)
  Terminated: January 2, 1947
    60 Stat. 812.
  Authority: PL 79-601

1040. Committee on Patents (Senate)
  Sudocs: Y4. P27/2:
  Established: September 7, 1837
    Cong. Globe (25-1): 14.
  Authority: Res. of the House
    (25-1)
  Terminated: January 2, 1947
    60 Stat. 812.
  Authority: PL 79-601

1041. Special Committee on Charges
Against the Commissioner of Patents
(House)
  Established: February 8, 1865
    H. J. (38-2): 206.
  Authority: Res. of the House
    (38-2)
  Terminated: March 2, 1865
    H. rpt. 26 (38-2) 1235.

1042. Select Committee on Patents
and Patent Laws (House)
  Established: December 12, 1831
    H. J. (22-1): 40.
  Authority: Res. of the House
    (22-1)

Terminated: September 15, 1837,
  when the standing committee
  was established (Entry 1039).
    Cong. Globe (25-1): 34.
  Authority: Res. of the House
    (25-1)

1043. Select Committee on
Publishing a List of Patents
with the Names of The Patentees
(House)
  Established: March 22, 1830
    H. J. (21-1): 451.
  Authority: Res. of the House
    (21-1)
  Terminated: April 1, 1830
    Ibid. 491.

1044. Select Committee on Executive
Patronage (Senate)
  Established: January 7, 1835
    S. J. (23-2): 79.
  Authority: Res. of the Senate
    (23-2)
  Terminated: February 9, 1835
    S. doc. 108 (23-2) 268.

1045. Committee to Consider
Memorial on Services Rendered
by Carlisle P. Patterson (Senate)
  Established: January 11, 1882
    13 CR 342.
  Authority: H. Con. Res. (47-1)
  Terminated: August 8, 1882, at
    the end of the 47-1.

1046. Select Committee on Pay Bill
for Non-commissioned Army Officers
(House)
  Established: January 19, 1847
    H. J. (29-2): 182.
  Authority: Res. of the House
    (29-2)
  Terminated: May 3, 1847, at the
    end of the 29-2.

1047. Select Committee on the Pay
Department (House)
  Established: July 19, 1867
    Cong. Globe (40-1): 737.
  Authority: Res. of the House
    (40-1)
  Terminated: July 24, 1868
    H. rpt. 83 (40-2) 1358.

1048. Committee to Revise and
Equalize the Pay of the Employees
of Each House (Joint)
  Established: March 6, 1867
    Cong. Globe (40-1): 10.
  Authority: Con. Res. of the
    House (40-1)
  Terminated: March 3, 1869, at
    the end of the 40-3.

1049. Select Committee on Pay of
Members of Congress and Contingent
Expenses of the House (House)
  Established: February 5, 1836
    H. J. (24-1): 301.
  Authority: Res. of the House
    (24-1)
  Terminated: June 7, 1836
    Ibid. 964.

1050. Select Committee on Petition
to Reduce Pay of Members of Con-
gress and other Officers of the
Government (House)
  Established: March 30, 1840
    H. J. (26-1): 701.
  Authority: Res. of the House
    (26-1)
  Terminated: July 21, 1840, at
    the end of the 26-1.

1051. Select Committee to Equalize
Pay of Officers of the Army and
Navy (House)
  Established: December 27, 1833
    H. J. (23-1): 129.
  Authority: Res. of the House
    (23-1)
  Terminated: February 28, 1834
    Naval Affairs (23-1) Am. St.
    Papers v. 26.

1052. Select Committee on the
Assault upon U. H. Paynter (House)
  Established: July 17, 1866
    H. J. (39-1): 1031.
  Authority: Res. of the House
    (39-1)
  Terminated: July 23, 1866
    H. J. (39-1): 1088.

1053. Select Committee on an Illegal Combination Against the Peace
and Safety of the Union (House)
  Established: January 22, 1807
    H. J. (9-2): 187.

Authority: Res. of the House
  (9-2)
Terminated: April 25, 1808, at
  the end of the 10-1.

1054. Select Committee on Peale's
Portrait of Washington (Senate)
  Established: January 10, 1825
    S. J. (18-2): 73.
  Authority: Res. of the Senate
    (18-2)
  Terminated: January 17, 1825
    Ibid. 91.

1055. Select Committee to Purchase
Peale's Portrait of Washington
(House)
  Established: March 11, 1824
    H. J. (18-1): 306.
  Authority: Res. of the House
    (18-1)
  Terminated: March 20, 1824
    Ibid. 328.

1056. Committee Investigating Pearl
Harbor Attack (Joint)
  Sudocs: Y4. P31:
  Established: September 11, 1945
    91 CR 8510.
  Authority: S. Con. Res. 27 (79-1)
  Terminated: July 16, 1946
    S. doc. 244 (79-2) 11033.

1057. Select Committee on Impeach-
ment of James H. Peck (Senate)
  Established: April 26, 1830
    S. J. (21-1): 269.
  Authority: Res. of the Senate
    (21-1)
  Terminated: April 27, 1830
    Ibid. 271.

1058. Select Committee on Revising
Penitentiary System of District of
Columbia (House)
  Established: December 23, 1848
    H. J. (30-2): 147.
  Authority: Res. of the House
    (30-1)
  Terminated: March 2, 1849
    H. rpt. 140 (30-2) 545.

1059. Select Committee on Pennsylvania Militia Fines (House)
  Established: January 24, 1822
    H. J. (17-1): 181.

Authority: Res. of the House
(17-1)
Terminated: April 24, 1822
Ibid. 491.

1060. Select Committee to Inquire
Into the Circumstances of the
Surrender of the Pensacola Navy
Yard, and the Destruction of Public
Property at the Norfolk Navy Yard
and at the Harper's Ferry Armory
(Senate)
Established: July 25, 1861
S. J. (37-1): 86.
Authority: Res. of the Senate
(37-1)
Terminated: April 18, 1862
S. rpt. 37 (37-2) 1125.

1061. Select Committee on Pension
Bureau Investigation (House)
Established: February 10, 1892
23 CR 1026.
Authority: Res. of the House
(52-1)
Terminated: July 14, 1892
H. rpt. 1868 (52-1) 3049-50.

1062. Select Committee on Extending
the Provisions of the Pension Law
of 1832 to Troops Employed Against
the Indians (House)
Established: February 11, 1834
H. J. (23-1): 319.
Authority: Res. of the House
(23-1)
Terminated: July 9, 1838, at the
end of the 25-2.

1063. Committee on Pensions (House)
Sudocs: Y4. P38/1:
Established: March 2, 1880, when
it replaced the Committee on
Revolutionary Pensions (Entry
1224).
10 CR 1265.
Authority: Res. of the House
(46-2)
Terminated: January 2, 1947, when
its functions were transferred
to the Committee on Veterans
Affairs (Entry 1437).
60 Stat. 812.
Authority: PL 79-601

1064. Committee on Pensions
(Senate)
Sudocs: Y4. P38/2:
Established: December 10, 1810
Annals (14-2): 30.
Authority: Res. of the Senate
(14-2)
Terminated: January 2, 1947
60 Stat. 812.
Authority: PL 79-601

1065. Select Committee on Pensions
(House)
Established: December 15, 1864
H. J. (38-2): 48.
Authority: Res. of the House
(38-2)
Terminated: March 3, 1864, at
the end of the 38-2.

1066. Committee on Pensions and
Revolutionary Claims (House)
Established: December 22, 1813
Annals (13-1): 803.
Authority: Res. of the House
(13-1)
Terminated: December 13, 1825,
when name was changed to Com-
mittee on Revolutionary Claims
(Entry 1217).
H. J. (19-1): 46.
Authority: Res. of the House
(19-1)

1067. Select Committee on Payment
of Pensions, Bounty and Back Pay
(House)
Sudocs: Y4. P38/3:
Established: January 12, 1880
10 CR 288.
Authority: Res. of the House
(46-2)
Terminated: March 3, 1885, at the
end of the 48-2.

1068. Special Committee Investi-
gating Petroleum Resources (Senate)
Sudocs: Y4. P44:
Established: March 13, 1944
90 CR 2490.
Authority: S. Res. 253 (78-2)
Terminated: January 31, 1947
S. rpt. 9 (80-1) 11114.

1069. Select Committee on the
Extent of the Services Rendered to

the Captain and Crew of the Late
Frigate Philadelphia, by the
Danish Consul at Tripoli (House)
  Established: March 5, 1806
    H. J. (9-1): 303.
  Authority: Res. of the House
    (9-1)
  Terminated: April 11, 1806
    Ibid. 452.

1070. Committee on the Philippines
(Senate)
  Sudocs: Y4. P53:
  Established: December 15, 1899
    33 CR 441.
  Authority: Res. of the Senate
    (56-1)
  Terminated: April 18, 1921
    61 CR 404-05.
  Authority: S. Res. 43 (67 -
    Special)

1071. Special Committee on Investi-
gation of Economic Activities in
the Philippines (Senate)
  Established: June 18, 1934
    78 CR 12568.
  Authority: Senate Order (73-2)
  Terminated: May 3, 1935
    S. doc. 57 (74-1) 9909.

1072. Committee to Investigate
Phosphate Resources of the United
States (Joint)
  Sudocs: Y4. P56:
  Established: June 16, 1938
    52 Stat. 704.
  Authority: Public Res. 112 (75-3)
  Terminated: January 16, 1941
    S. doc. 5 (77-1) 10574.

1073. Select Committee on Com-
pensation for the Zebulon Pike
Expedition (House)
  Established: February 22, 1808
    H. J. (10-1): 398.
  Authority: Res. of the House
    (10-1)
  Terminated: June 12, 1809
    H. J. (11-1): 109.

1074. Select Committee on Pluero-
pneumonia Among Animals (Senate)
  Established: January 19, 1881
    11 CR 754.

Authority: Res. of the Senate
  (46-3)
Terminated: March 3, 1881, at the
  end of the 46-3.

1075. Select Committee on a Letter
from Mr. Poindexter (Senate)
  Established: February 21, 1835
    S. J. (23-2): 183.
  Authority: Res. of the Senate
    (23-2)
  Terminated: March 2, 1835
    S. doc. 148 (23-2) 269.

1076. Select Committee on Explo-
ration of Polar Regions (House)
  Established: January 15, 1827
    H. J. (19-2): 157.
  Authority: Res. of the House
    (19-2)
  Terminated: February 14, 1827
    Ibid. 298.

1077. Committee on Police and
Preservation of the Capital (Joint)
  Established: December 12, 1825
    H. J. (19-1): 80.
  Authority: Con. Res. of the House
    (19-1)
  Terminated: December 23, 1825
    Ibid. 89.

1078. Select Committee on Police
for the Capital (House)
  Established: January 6, 1825
    H. J. (18-2): 108.
  Authority: Res. of the House
    (18-2)
  Terminated: January 11, 1825
    Ibid. 122.

1079. Special Committee on Polit-
ical Activities, Lobbying, and
Campaign Contributions (Senate)
  Sudocs: Y4. P75:
  Established: February 22, 1956
    102 CR 3116.
  Authority: S. Res. 219 (84-2)
  Terminated: May 31, 1957
    S. rpt. 395 (85-1) 11977.

1080. Select Committee on Charges
Against Senator Pomeroy (Senate)
  Established: February 10, 1873
    Cong. Globe (42-3): 1215.

Authority: Res. of the Senate
(42-3)
Terminated: March 3, 1873
S. rpt. 523 (42-3) 1550.

1081. Select Committee on Popula-
tion (House)
Sudocs: Y4. P81:
Established: September 28, 1977
120 CR 31328.
Authority: H. Res. 70 (95-1)
Terminated: January 5, 1979
H. rpt. 1842 (95-2) 13203-3.

1082. Select Committee on Current
Pornographic Materials (House)
Sudocs: Y4. P82:
Established: May 12, 1952
98 CR 5069.
Authority: H. Res. 596 (82-2)
Terminated: December 31, 1952
H. rpt. 2510 (82-2) 11578.

1083. Select Committee on Pur-
chasing a Series of Portraits of
Presidents of the United States
(House)
Established: February 6, 1838
H. J. (25-2): 364.
Authority: Res. of the House
(25-2)
Terminated: July 9, 1838, at the
end of the 25-2.

1084. Select Committee on Allowing
the use of our Ports to Armed Ves-
sels of Foreign Nations Extending
the Same Privilege to American
Armed Vessels (House)
Established: December 8, 1813
H. J. (13-2): 21.
Authority: Res. of the House
(13-2)
Terminated: March 8, 1814
Ibid. 410.

1085. Select Committee on the
Petition of the Inhabitants of
Portsmouth, New Hampshire (House)
Established: March 26, 1814
H. J. (13-2): 488.
Authority: Res. of the House
(13-2)
Terminated: March 28, 1814
Ibid. 497.

1086. Select Committee to Inquire
into the Fiscal Concerns of the
General Post Office (House)
Established: January 25, 1816
H. J. (14-1): 245.
Authority: Res. of the House
(14-1)
Terminated: March 22, 1816
Ibid. 538.

1087. Select Committee on the
Petition of the Inhabitants of
Nantucket to Revise the Law
Regulating the Post Office (House)
Established: December 28, 1813
H. J. (13-2): 65.
Authority: Res. of the House
(13-2)
Terminated: March 8, 1814
Ibid. 410.

1088. Committee on Post Office and
Civil Service (House)
Sudocs: Y4. P84/10:
Established: January 2, 1947,
when the functions of several
committees were transferred to
this.
60 Stat. 812.
Authority: PL 79-601
Terminated: Still in existence at
the end of the 97-2.

1089. Committee on Post Office and
Civil Service (Senate)
Sudocs: Y4. P84/11:
Established: January 2, 1947,
when the functions of the
Committee on Civil Service and
the Committee on Post Offices
and Post Roads were transferred
to this (Entries 204, 1091).
60 Stat. 812.
Authority: PL 79-601
Terminated: February 11, 1977,
when its functions were transferred to the Committee on Governmental Affairs (Entry 587).
123 CR 3691.
Authority: S. Res. 4 (95-1)

1090. Committee on Post Offices
and Post Roads (House)
Sudocs: Y4. P84/1:
Established: November 9, 1808
Annals (10-2): 473.

Authority: Res. of the House
(10-2)
Terminated: January 2, 1947,
when its functions were
transferred to the Committee
on Post Office and Civil
Service (Entry 1088).
60 Stat. 812.
Authority: PL 79-601

1091. Committee on Post Offices
and Post Roads (Senate)
Sudocs: Y4. P84/2:
Established: December 10, 1816
Annals (14-2): 30.
Authority: Res. of the Senate
(14-2)
Terminated: January 2, 1947,
when its functions were
transferred to the Committee
on Post Office and Civil
Service (Entry 1089).
60 Stat. 812.
Authority: PL 79-601

1092. Select Committee on Post
Offices and Post Roads (House)
Established: October 29, 1807
H. J. (10-1): 25.
Authority: Res. of the House
(10-1)
Terminated: February 1, 1808
Ibid. 324.

1093. Select Committee on Post
Office Contract for Blanks, Paper,
Twine, Etc. (House)
Established: February 17, 1846
H. J. (29-1): 421.
Authority: Res. of the House
(29-1)
Terminated: August 10, 1846, at
the end of the 29-1.

1094. Select Committee on Affairs
of the Post Office Department
(House)
Established: December 19, 1820
H. J. (16-2): 80.
Authority: Res. of the House
(16-2)
Terminated: April 29, 1822
H. J. (17-1): 512.

1095. Select Committee on the
Investigation of the Post Office

Department (Senate)
Established: December 5, 1830
S. J. (21-2): 40.
Authority: Res. of the Senate
(21-2)
Terminated: March 3, 1831
Ibid. 226.

1096. Select Committee on Relations
of Members with Post Office Depart-
ments (House)
Sudocs: Y4. P84/3:
Established: March 11, 1904
38 CR 3153.
Authority: H. Res. 118 (58-2)
Terminated: April 12, 1904
H. rpt. 2372 (58-2) 4583.

1097. Select Committee on Post
Office Department Affairs (House)
Established: June 26, 1834
H. J. (23-1): 842.
Authority: Res. of the House
(23-1)
Terminated: March 3, 1835, at
the end of the 23-2.

1098. Select Committee on Purchase
of Bank of Pennsylvania for a Post
Office in Philadelphia (House)
Established: March 16, 1858
H. J. (35-1): 517.
Authority: Res. of the House
(35-1)
Terminated: June 14, 1848, at
the end of the 35-1.

1099. Select Committee on Post
Office Leases (Senate)
Sudocs: Y4. P84/6:
Established: April 18, 1930
72 CR 7276.
Authority: S. Res. 244 (71-2)
Terminated: July 1, 1932
S. rpt. 971 (72-1) 9490.

1100. Select Committee to Bring in
a Bill to Establish Certain Post
Roads (House)
Established: March 3, 1807
H. J. (9-2): 387.
Authority: Res. of the House
(9-2)
Terminated: March 3, 1807
Ibid. 388.

1101. Special Committee on Post-War Economic Policy and Planning (House)
   Sudocs: Y4. P84/9:
   Established: January 26, 1944
      90 CR 766.
   Authority: H. Res. 408 (78-2)
   Terminated: December 12, 1946
      H. rpt. 2729 (79-2) 11026.

1102. Special Committee on Post-War Economic Policy and Planning (Senate)
   Sudocs: Y4. P84/7:
   Established: March 12, 1943
      89 CR 1923.
   Authority: S. Res. 102 (78-1)
   Terminated: February 3, 1947
      S. rpt. 12 (80-1) 11114.

1103. Select Committee on Post-War Military Policy (House)
   Sudocs: Y4. P84/8:
   Established: March 28, 1944
      90 CR 3207.
   Authority: H. Res. 465 (78-2)
   Terminated: May 2, 1945
      H. rpt. 505 (79-1) 10932.

1104. Commission on Postal Salaries (Joint)
   Sudocs: Y4. P84/5:
   Established: February 28, 1919
      40 Stat. 1200.
   Authority: PL 65-299
   Terminated: March 3, 1921
      S. doc. 422 (66-3) 7789.

1105. Commission on Postal Service (Joint)
   Established: April 24, 1920
      41 Stat. 583.
   Authority: PL 66-187
   Terminated: February 8, 1924
      S. doc. 36 (68-1) 8253.

1106. Select Committee on the Postal Telegraph (House)
   Established: January 24, 1870
      Cong. Globe (41-2): 709.
   Authority: Res. of the House
      (41-2)
   Terminated: July 5, 1870
      H. rpts. 114-115 (41-2) 1438.

1107. Committee on Postage on 2d. Class Mail Matter and Compensation for Transportation of Mails (Joint)
   Sudocs: Y4. P84/4:
   Established: August 24, 1912
      37 Stat. 546.
   Authority: PL 62-336
   Terminated: March 3, 1915, at
      the end of the 63-3.

1108. Select Committee on the Potomac River Improvement (Senate)
   Established: December 13, 1881
      13 CR 79.
   Authority: Res. of the Senate
      (47-1)
   Terminated: March 3, 1911, at
      the end of the 61-3.

1109. Select Committee on Loan of Powder and Lead to Individuals and Delinquencies in the Paymaster's and Quartermaster's Departments (House)
   Established: February 24, 1820
      H. J. (16-1): 219.
   Authority: Res. of the House
      (16-1)
   Terminated: February 7, 1821
      H. rpt. 58 (16-2): 57.

1110. Select Committee on the Powers, Privileges, and Duties of the House (House)
   Established: December 14, 1876
      H. J. (44-2): 78.
   Authority: Res. of the House
      (44-2)
   Terminated: March 3, 1877
      H. rpt. 100, pt. 3 (44-2):
      1769.

1111. Select Committee on Punishing Persons Holding Offices of Profit or Trust Under the Government of the United States Who Shall Receive Money, or Accept of any Present, Emolument, Office, or Title, From Any King, Prince or Foreign State Without the Consent of Congress (House)
   Established: January 22, 1808
      H. J. (10-1): 293.
   Authority: Res. of the House
      (10-1)

Terminated: January 30, 1808
    Ibid. 316.

1112. Special Committee on Investigation of Presidential and Senatorial Campaign Expenditures (Senate)
    Sudocs: Y4. P92/2:
    Established: June 13, 1934
        78 CR 11324.
    Authority: S. Res. 173 (73-2)
    Terminated: January 10, 1935
        S. rpt. 11 (74-1) 9883.

1113. Select Committee on Presidential Campaign Activities (Senate)
    Sudocs: Y4. P92/4:
    Established: February 7, 1973
        119 CR 3849.
    Authority: S. Res. 60 (93-1)
    Terminated: June 27, 1974
        S. rpt. 981 (93-2) 13060-8.

1114. Special Committee Investigating Presidential Campaign
Expenditures (Senate)
    Sudocs: Y4. P92:
    Established: April 30, 1928
        69 CR 7431.
    Authority: S. Res. 214 (70-1)
    Terminated: January 21, 1929
        S. rpt. 1480 (70-2) 8978.

1115. Special Committee to Investigate Presidential, Vice Presidential, and Senatorial Campaign
Expenditures, 1944 (Senate)
    Sudocs: Y4. P92/3:
    Established: March 30, 1944
        90 CR 3296.
    Authority: S. Res. 263 (78-2)
    Terminated: March 15, 1945
        S. rpt. 101 (79-1) 10925.

1116. Select Committee on the
President's Message Refusing to
Furnish a Certain Paper to the
Senate (Senate)
    Established: December 19, 1833
        S. J. (23-1): 58.
    Authority: Res. of the Senate
        (23-1)
    Terminated: June 30, 1834, at
        the end of the 23-1.

1117. Select Committee to Inquire
in Reference to Prince Edward's

Island (House)
    Established: July 25, 1868
        H. J. (40-2): 1186.
    Authority: Res. of the House
        (40-2)
    Terminated: March 2, 1869
        H. rpt. 39 (40-3) 1388.

1118. Committee on Printing (House)
    Sudocs: Y4. P93/2:
    Established: January 5, 1888
        19 CR 280.
    Authority: Res. of the House
        (50-1)
    Terminated: January 2, 1947, and
        its functions were transferred
        to the Committee on House
        Administration (Entry 611).
        60 Stat. 812.
    Authority: PL 79-601

1119. Committee on Printing
(Senate)
    Sudocs: Y4. P93/3:
    Established: December 15, 1841
        Cong. Globe (27-2): 18.
    Authority: Res. of the Senate
        (27-2)
    Terminated: January 2, 1947
        60 Stat. 812.
    Authority: PL 79-601

1120. Select Committee on Printing
(House)
    Established: February 2, 1840
        H. J. (26-1): 266.
    Authority: Res. of the House
        (26-1)
    Terminated: April 14, 1840
        H. rpt. 425 (26-1) 371.

1121. Committee on Public Printing
(Joint)
    Sudocs: Y4. P93/1:
    Established: August 3, 1846
        9 Stat. 114.
    Authority: PL 29-16
    Terminated: Still in existence at
        the end of the 97-2.

1122. Select Committee to Investigate Public Printing (Senate)
    Sudocs: Y4. P93/4:
    Established: January 24, 1860
        Cong. Globe (36-1): 560.

Authority: Res. of the Senate
(36-1)
Terminated: May 31, 1860
S. rpt. 205 (36-1) 1040.

1123. Select Committee to Investigate Certain Alleged Abuses
Connected with the Public Printing
(Senate)
Established: January 24, 1860
S. J. (36-1): 97.
Authority: Res. of the Senate
(36-1)
Terminated: June 12, 1860
S. rpt. 205 (36-1) 1040.

1124. Select Committee on Public
Printing (House)
Established: March 12, 1812
H. J. (12-1): 493.
Authority: Res. of the House
(12-1)
Terminated: July 6, 1812, at the
end of the 12-1.

1125. Select Committee on Printing
Laws (House)
Established: December 9, 1857
H. J. (35-1): 50.
Authority: Res. of the House
(35-1)
Terminated: June 14, 1858, at the
end of the 35-1.

1126. Select Committee on the
Treatment of Union Prisoners
(House)
Established: July 10, 1867
H. J. (40-1): 179.
Authority: Res. of the House
(40-1)
Terminated: March 2, 1869
H. rpt. 45 (40-3) 1391.

1127. Select Committee on Establishing a Private Claims Commission
(Senate)
Established: December 18, 1854
S. J. (33-2): 53.
Authority: Res. of the Senate
(33-2)
Terminated: March 3, 1855, at the
end of the 33-2.

1128. Committee on Private Land
Claims (House)

Sudocs: Y4. P93/5:
Established: April 29, 1816
Annals (14-1): 1456.
Authority: Res. of the House
(14-1)
Terminated: April 5, 1911
47 CR 80.
Authority: H. Res. 11 (62-1)

1129. Committee on Private Land
Claims (Senate)
Sudocs: Y4. P93/7:
Established: December 26, 1826
S. J. (19-2): 63.
Authority: Res. of the Senate
(19-2)
Terminated: April 18, 1921
61 CR 404-05.
Authority: S. Res. 43 (67 -
Special)

1130. Committee on Privileges and
Elections (Senate)
Sudocs: Y4. P93/6:
Established: March 10, 1871
Cong. Globe (42-1): 33.
Authority: Res. of the Senate
(42-1)
Terminated: January 2, 1947, and
its functions were transferred
to the Committee on Rules and
Administration (Entry 1252).
60 Stat. 812.
Authority: PL 79-601

1131. Select Committee to Investigate Propaganda Affecting Taxation
and Soldiers' Bonus (Senate)
Established: January 17, 1924
65 CR 1086.
Authority: S. Res. 107 (68-1)
Terminated: March 3, 1925, at the
end of the 68-2.

1132. Special Committee to Investigate Propaganda or Money Alleged to
have been used by Foreign Governments to Influence United States
Senators (Senate)
Sudocs: Y4. P94:
Established: December 9, 1927
69 CR 339.
Authority: S. Res. 7 (70-1)
Terminated: January 9, 1929
S. rpt. 52 (70-1) 8832.

1133. Select Committee to make
Further Provision for Paying
for Property Lost in the War
With Great Britain (House)
  Established: January 18, 1819
    H. J. (15-2): 195.
  Authority: Res. of the House
    (15-2)
  Terminated: March 3, 1819, at
    the end of the 15-2.

1134. Select Committee on Payment
for Property Lost in the War of
1812 (House)
  Established: March 8, 1824
    H. J. (18-1): 299.
  Authority: Res. of the House
    (18-1)
  Terminated: April 5, 1824
    H. rpt. 1 (18-1) 122.

1135. Select Committee on the
Protest of the President of
June 22, 1860 (House)
  Established: June 25, 1860
    H. J. (36-1): 1225.
  Authority: Res. of the House
    (36-1)
  Terminated: March 3, 1861, at
    the end of the 36-2.

1136. Select Committee on the
Provost Marshall's Bureau (House)
  Established: April 30, 1866
    Cong. Globe (39-1): 2315.
  Authority: Res. of the House
    (39-1)
  Terminated: July 14, 1866
    H. rpt. 93 (39-1) 1272.

1137. Select Committee on the
System of Public Accounts (House)
  Established: December 12, 1831
    H. J. (22-1): 40.
  Authority: Res. of the House
    (22-1)
  Terminated: July 16, 1832, at
    the end of the 22-1.

1138. Select Committee on the
Mode in Which the Public Acts of
the State shall be Authenticated
(House)
  Established: January 10, 1812
    H. J. (12-1): 251.

Authority: Res. of the House
  (12-1)
Terminated: March 23, 1812
  Ibid. 527.

1139. Select Committee on Public
Buildings (House)
  Established: January 3, 1826
    H. J. (19-1): 114.
  Authority: Res. of the House
    (19-1)
  Terminated: March 17, 1826
    Ibid. 345.

1140. Select Committee on Public
Buildings (Senate)
  Established: December 16, 1819
    S. J. (16-1): 31.
  Authority: Res. of the Senate
    (16-1)
  Terminated: May 15, 1820, at the
    end of the 16-1.

1141. Select Committee on the
Report of the Surveyor of the
Public Buildings (House)
  Established: December 15, 1806
    H. J. (9-2): 47.
  Authority: Res. of the House
    (9-2)
  Terminated: April 5, 1808
    H. J. (10-1): 543.

1142. Committee on Public Buildings
and Grounds (House)
  Sudocs: Y4. P96/6:
  Established: December 15, 1837
    Cong. Globe (25-1): 34.
  Authority: Res. of the House
    (25-1)
  Terminated: January 2, 1947, when
    its functions were transferred
    to the Committee on Public
    Works (Entry 1162).
      60 Stat. 812.
  Authority: PL 79-601

1143. Committee on Public Buildings
and Grounds (Senate)
  Sudocs: Y4. P96/7:
  Established: December 16, 1819
    Annals (16-1): 26.
  Authority: Res. of the Senate
    (16-1)
  Terminated: January 2, 1947, when
    its functions were transferred

to the Committee on Public
Works (Entry 1163).
60 Stat. 812.
Authority: PL 79-601

1144. Select Committee on Rebuild-
ing the Public Buildings in the
City of Washington (House)
Established: October 20, 1814
   H. J. (13-3): 89.
Authority: Res. of the House
   (13-3)
Terminated: November 21, 1814
   Ibid. 203.

1145. Select Committee on the
Existing Public Distress (Senate)
Established: June 6, 1894
   S. J. (53-2): 227.
Authority: Res. of the Senate
   (53-2)
Terminated: August 28, 1894, at
   the end of the 53-2.

1146. Committee on Public Expendi-
tures (House)
Sudocs: Y4. P96/5:
Established: February 26, 1814
   Annals (13-2): 1695.
Authority: Res. of the House
   (13-2)
Terminated: June 16, 1880
   10 CR 1266.
Authority: Res. of the House
   (46-2)

1147. Committee on Public Expenditures (Senate)
Established: March 22, 1909
   44 CR 122.
Authority: Res. of the Senate
   (61-1)
Terminated: March 3, 1911, at the
   end of the 61-3.

1148. Select Committee on Public
Health (House)
Sudocs: Y4. P96/8:
Established: December 19, 1881
   H. J. (47-1): 178.
Authority: Res. of the House
   (47-1)
Terminated: March 3, 1885, at the
   end of the 48-2.

1149. Committee on Public Health
and National Quarantine (Senate)
Sudocs: Y4. P96/9:
Established: March 19, 1896, when
   the name of the Committee on
   Epidemic Diseases was changed
   to this (Entry 427).
   28 CR 2960.
Authority: Res. of the Senate
   (54-1)
Terminated: April 18, 1921
   61 CR 404-05.
Authority: S. Res. 43 (67 -
   Special)

1150. Committee on Public Lands
(House)
Sudocs: Y4. P96/2:
Established: December 17, 1805
   Annals (9-1): 286.
Authority: Res. of the House
   (9-1)
Terminated: February 2, 1951,
   when the name was changed to
   Committee on Interior and
   Insular Affairs (Entry 692).
   97 CR 884.
Authority: H. Res. 100 (82-1)

1151. Committee on Public Lands--
1st (Senate)
Sudocs: Y4. P96/1:
Established: December 10, 1816
   Annals (14-2): 30.
Authority: Res. of the Senate
   (14-2)
Terminated: April 18, 1921, when
   the name was changed to Commit-
   tee on Public Lands and Surveys
   (Entry 1155).
   61 CR 405.
Authority: S. Res. 43 (67 -
   Special)

1152. Committee on Public Lands--
2nd (Senate)
Sudocs: Y4. P96/1:
Established: January 2, 1947,
   when the name was changed
   from Committee on Public
   Lands and Surveys. Several
   other committees transferred
   to this committee at that
   time (Entry 1155).
   60 Stat. 812.
Authority: PL 79-601

Terminated: January 28, 1948,
when the name was changed
to Committee on Interior and
Insular Affairs (Entry 693).
94 CR 604.
Authority: S. Res. 179 (80-2)

1153. Select Committee on Adopting
New Regulations for the Sale of
Public Lands (House)
Established: December 20, 1824
H. J. (18-2): 64.
Authority: Res. of the House
(18-2)
Terminated: March 3, 1825, at
the end of the 18-2.

1154. Select Committee on the Sale
of Public Lands, and the Means of
Preventing Their Monopoly (Senate)
Established: March 31, 1836
S. J. (24-1): 255.
Authority: Res. of the Senate
(24-1)
Terminated: June 15, 1836
Ibid. 436.

1155. Committee on Public Lands
and Surveys (Senate)
Sudocs: Y4. P96/1:
Established: April 18, 1921,
when the name was changed
from the Committee on Public
Lands (Entry 1151).
61 CR 405.
Authority: S. Res. 43 (67 -
Special)
Terminated: January 2, 1947,
when the name was changed
to Committee on Public Lands
(Entry 1152).
60 Stat. 812.
Authority: PL 79-601

1156. Select Committee on Appropri-
ating Proceeds of Public Lands for
Education (House)
Established: January 19, 1830
H. J. (21-1): 187.
Authority: Res. of the House
(21-1)
Terminated: March 18, 1830
H. rpt. 312 (21-1) 201.

1157. Select Committee on Public
Lands, Past Donations and Plans

for Distributing (House)
Established: December 29, 1838
H. J. (25-3): 153.
Authority: Res. of the House
(25-3)
Terminated: February 7, 1839
H. rpt. 268 (25-3) 351.

1158. Select Committee on Separa-
tion of Patronage of Government
from Public Press (House)
Established: January 14, 1839
H. J. (25-3): 279.
Authority: Res. of the House
(25-3)
Terminated: April 14, 1840
H. rpt. 425 (26-1) 371.

1159. Select Committee on the
State of the Ancient Public Records
(House)
Established: February 21, 1810
H. J. (11-2): 292.
Authority: Res. of the House
(11-2)
Terminated: April 2, 1810
Ibid. 480.

1160. Select Committee on Appro-
priations for Prevention of Fraud
in and Depredations upon Public
Service (House)
Sudocs: Y4. P96/4:
Established: January 9, 1909
43 CR 699.
Authority: H. Res. 480 (60-2)
Terminated: March 3, 1909
H. rpt. 2320 (60-2) 5387.

1161. Select Committee on Contract
for Rent of Public Stores in New
York (House)
Established: March 26, 1860
H. J. (36-1): 590.
Authority: Res. of the House
(36-1)
Terminated: June 15, 1860
H. rpt. 647 (36-1) 1070.

1162. Committee on Public Works
(House)
Sudocs: Y4. P96/11:
Established: January 2, 1947,
when the functions of several

committees were transferred to
this.
   60 Stat. 812.
Authority: PL 79-601
Terminated: January 3, 1975,
   when the name was changed
   to the Committee on Public
   Works and Transportation
   (Entry 1164).
   120 CR 34470.
Authority: H. Res. 988 (93-2)

1163. Committee on Public Works
(Senate)
   Sudocs: Y4. P96/10:
   Established: January 2, 1947
   60 Stat. 812.
   Authority: PL 79-601
   Terminated: February 11, 1977,
      when the name was changed to
      Committee on Environment and
      Public Works (Entry 426).
      123 CR 3691.
   Authority: S. Res. 4 (95-1)

1164. Committee on Public Works
and Transportation (House)
   Sudocs: Y4. P96/11:
   Established: January 3, 1975,
      when the name of Committee
      on Public Works was changed
      to this (Entry 1162).
      120 CR 34470.
   Authority: H. Res. 988 (93-2)
   Terminated: Still in existence
      at the end of the 97-2.

1165. Select Committee on Pulp and
Paper Investigations (House)
   Sudocs: Y4. P96/3:
   Established: April 21, 1908
      42 CR 5033.
   Authority: H. Res. 344 (60-1)
   Terminated: February 19, 1909
      H. doc. 1502 (60-2) 5542-46.

1166. Select Committee on the
Quadro-Centennial (Senate)
   Established: December 12, 1889
      S. J. (51-1): 40.
   Authority: Res. of the Senate
      (51-1)
   Terminated: March 3, 1895, at
      the end of the 53-3.

1167. Select Committee on a Quarrel
Between White and Rathbun (House)
   Established: April 22, 1844
      H. J. (28-1): 847.
   Authority: Res. of the House
      (28-1)
   Terminated: May 6, 1844
      H. rpt. 470 (28-1) 446.

1168. Select Committee on the Memo-
rial of A. B. Quinby for His Steam
Engine Safety Valve (Senate)
   Established: January 26, 1837
      S. J. (24-2): 161.
   Authority: Res. of the Senate
      (24-2)
   Terminated: February 1, 1837
      S. doc. 125 (24-2) 298.

1169. Select Committee on a Rail-
road from New York to Washington
(House)
   Established: January 6, 1864
      H. J. (38-1): 106.
   Authority: Res. of the House
      (38-1)
   Terminated: July 28, 1866, at
      the end of the 39-1.

1170. Committee on Railroad Retire-
ment Legislation (Joint)
   Sudocs: Y4. R13/3:
   Established: October 18, 1951
      65 Stat. B105.
   Authority: S. Con. Res. 51 (82-1)
   Terminated: January 9, 1953
      S. rpt. 6 (83-1) 11663.

1171. Committee on Railroads
(Senate)
   Sudocs: Y4. R13/2:
   Established: March 12, 1873
      Replaced Committee on the
      Pacific Railroad (Entry 1023).
      S. J. (42-3): 609.
   Authority: Res. of the Senate
      (42-3)
   Terminated: April 18, 1821
      61 CR 404-05.
   Authority: S. Res. 43 (67 -
      Special)

1172. Committee on Railways and
Canals (House)
   Sudocs: Y4. R13:

Established: December 15, 1831
  Annals (22-1): 1442.
Authority: Res. of the House
  (22-1)
Terminated: December 5, 1927
  69 CR 12.
Authority: H. Res. 7 (70-1)

1173. Select Committee to Investigate Charges Against the Hon. Samuel J. Randall (House)
  Established: February 27, 1879
    8 CR 1897.
  Authority: Res. of the House
    (45-3)
  Terminated: March 3, 1879
    H. rpt. 139 (45-3) 1866.

1174. Select Committee on the Reading Railroad Strike (House)
  Established: February 1, 1888
    19 CR 889.
  Authority: Res. of the House
    (50-1)
  Terminated: March 3, 1889, at
    the end of the 50-2.

1175. Special Committee on Readjustment of Service Pay (House)
  Sudocs: Y4. R22/2:
  Established: March 1, 1922
    62 CR 3227.
  Authority: H. Res. 296 (67-2)
  Terminated: May 1, 1922
    H. rpt. 926 (67-2) 7956.

1176. Special Committee on Readjustment of Service Pay (Joint)
  Sudocs: Y4. R22/1:
  Established: May 18, 1820
    41 Stat. 604.
  Authority: PL 66-210
  Terminated: March 22, 1822
    H. rpt. 753 (67-2) 7955.

1177. Special Committee on Readjustment of Service Pay (Senate)
  Established: February 16, 1922
    62 CR 2646.
  Authority: S. Res. 240 (67-2)
  Terminated: March 22, 1922
    S. rpt. 572 (67-2) 7950.

1178. Select Committee on Investigation of Real Estate Bondholders' Reorganizations (House)

Sudocs: Y4. R22/3:
Established: June 15, 1934
  78 CR 11777.
Authority: H. Res. 412 (73-2)
Terminated: June 19, 1936
  H. rpt. 35 (74-2) 9995.

1179. Select Committee on the Real Estate Pool and the Jay Cooke Indebtedness (House)
  Established: January 24, 1876
    H. J. (44-1): 261.
  Authority: Res. of the House
    (44-1)
  Terminated: March 14, 1876
    H. rpt. 242 (44-1) 1708.

1180. Select Committee on Confiscation of Rebel Property (House)
  Established: April 24, 1862
    H. J. (37-2): 606.
  Authority: Res. of the House
    (37-2)
  Terminated: June 17, 1862
    H. J. (37-2): 874.

1181. Select Committee on the Rebellious States (House)
  Established: December 15, 1863
    H. J. (38-1): 57.
  Authority: Res. of the House
    (38-1)
  Terminated: March 3, 1865, at
    the end of the 38-2.

1182. Select Committee on S. 151 to Confiscate the Property and Free the Slaves of Rebels (Senate)
  Established: May 6, 1862
    S. J. (37-2): 450.
  Authority: Res. of the Senate
    (37-2)
  Terminated: May 14, 1862
    S. J. (37-2): 476.
  Authority: Senate Order (37-2)

1183. Commission on Reclassification of Salaries (Joint)
  Sudocs: Y4. R24/2:
  Established: March 1, 1919
    40 Stat. 1269.
  Authority: PL 65-314
  Terminated: March 12, 1920
    H. doc. 686 (66-2) 7672.

1184. Select Committee on Taking
Recognizances and Bail (House)
　Established: January 17, 1811
　　H. J. (11-3): 130.
　Authority: Res. of the House
　　(11-3)
　Terminated: January 19, 1811
　　Ibid. 172.

1185. Committee on Reconstruction
(Joint)
　Sudocs: Y4. R24:
　Established: December 12, 1865
　　Cong. Globe (39-1): 30.
　Authority: Con. Res. of the House
　　(39-1)
　Terminated: March 3, 1867, at the
　　end of the 39-2.

1186. Select Committee on Recon-
struction (House)
　Established: July 3, 1867
　　Cong. Globe (40-1): 479.
　Authority: Res. of the House
　　(40-1)
　Terminated: March 3, 1871, at the
　　end of the 41-3.

1187. Select Committee on Recon-
struction and Production (Senate)
　Sudocs: Y4. R24/3:
　Established: April 17, 1920
　　59 CR 5768.
　Authority: S. Res. 350 (66-2)
　Terminated: March 3, 1921
　　S. rpt. 829 (66-3) 7774.

1188. Select Committee on Inves-
tigation of Loans Made by Recon-
struction Finance Corporation
(Senate)
　Established: July 11, 1932
　　75 CR 14988.
　Authority: S. Res. 269 (72-1)
　Terminated: January 13, 1933
　　S. rpt. 1059 (72-2) 9648.

1189. Select Committee on Expunging
Remarks from the Record (House)
　Established: January 19, 1909
　　43 CR 1107.
　Authority: H. Res. 494 (60-2)
　Terminated: January 27, 1909
　　H. rpt. 1962 (60-2) 5385.

1190. Committee on Reduction of
Non-Essential Federal Expenditures
(Joint)
　Sudocs: Y4. R24/4:
　Established: September 20, 1941
　　55 Stat. 726.
　Authority: PL 77-250
　Terminated: July 12, 1974
　　88 Stat. 304.
　Authority: PL 93-344

1191. Select Committee on Refores-
tation (Senate)
　Sudocs: Y4. R25:
　Established: January 22, 1923
　　64 CR 2176.
　Authority: S. Res. 398 (67-4)
　Terminated: January 10, 1924
　　S. rpt. 28 (68-1) 8222.

1192. Select Committee on the
Report of the Commissioners Under
the Refugee Acts (House)
　Established: December 10, 1806
　　H. J. (9-2): 41.
　Authority: Res. of the House
　　(9-2)
　Terminated: December 17, 1806
　　Ibid. 57.

1193. Select Committee on Letters
and Reports for the Commissioners
Appointed Under the Act for the
Relief of Refugees from the British
Provinces of Canada and Nova Scotia
(House)
　Established: November 23, 1807
　　H. J. (10-1): 89.
　Authority: Res. of the House
　　(10-1)
　Terminated: December 22, 1807
　　Ibid. 184.

1194. Select Committee on Publish-
ing a Register of all Officers of
Government (House)
　Established: December 12, 1815
　　H. J. (14-1): 44.
　Authority: Res. of the House
　　(14-1)
　Terminated: January 5, 1816
　　Ibid. 128.

1195. Select Committee to Inquire
Whether the Privileges of the House
Have Been Violated by the Arrest

and Detention of Whitlaw Reid at
the Suit of A. R. Shepherd (House)
  Established: January 19, 1875
    H. J. (43-2): 204.
  Authority: Res. of the House
    (43-2)
  Terminated: March 2, 1875
    H. rpt. 273 (43-2) 1662.

1196. Select Committee on Boyd
Reilly's Vapor Bath (House)
  Established: April 1, 1836
    H. J. (24-1): 614.
  Authority: Res. of the House
    (24-1)
  Terminated: February 7, 1838
    H. rpt. 543 (25-2) 334.

1197. Select Committee on Purchas-
ing Boyd Reilly's Gas Apparatus
(Senate)
  Established: May 6, 1834
    S. J. (23-1): 247.
  Authority: Res. of the Senate
    (23-1)
  Terminated: March 3, 1839, at
    the end of the 25-3.

1198. Committee on Reorganization
(Joint)
  Sudocs: Y4. R29:
  Established: December 29, 1920
    41 Stat. 1083.
  Authority: Pub. Res. 54 (66-2)
  Terminated: June 3, 1924
    H. rpt. 937 (68-1) 8229.

1199. Committee on Reorganization
of the Administrative Branch of the
Government (Joint)
  Sudocs: Y4. R29:
  Established: December 29, 1920
    41 Stat. 1083.
  Authority: Public Res. 66-54
  Terminated: June 3, 1924
    H. rpt. 937 (68-1) 8229.

1200. Select Committee on Reporters
for Union Newspapers (House)
  Established: February 8, 1847
    H. J. (29-2): 313.
  Authority: Res. of the House
    (29-2)
  Terminated: March 3, 1847, at the
    end of the 29-2.

1201. Select Committee on Represen-
tative Reform (Senate)
  Established: January 13, 1869
    Cong. Globe (40-3): 320.
  Authority: Senate Order (40-3)
  Terminated: March 3, 1869
    S. rpt. 271 (40-3) 1362.

1202. Select Committee to Report
a Bill on Retaliation (House)
  Established: November 13, 1812
    H. J. (12-2): 36.
  Authority: Res. of the House
    (12-2)
  Terminated: November 17, 1812
    Ibid. 40.

1203. Select Committee on the
Retired List for the Army and
Navy (Senate)
  Established: June 12, 1848
    S. J. (30-1): 377.
  Authority: Res. of the Senate
    (30-1)
  Terminated: August 3, 1848
    Ibid. 527.

1204. Committee on Retrenchment
(Senate)
  Sudocs: Y4. R31/1:
  Established: December 9, 1844
    S. J. (28-2): 24.
  Authority: Res. of the Senate
    (28-2)
  Terminated: March 12, 1873
    S. J. (42-3): 609.
  Authority: Res. of the Senate
    (42-3)

1205. Select Committee on Retrench-
ment (House)
  Established: February 6, 1828
    H. J. (20-1): 263.
  Authority: Res. of the House
    (20-1)
  Terminated: July 16, 1832, at the
    end of the 21-2.

1206. Select Committee on Retrench-
ment (Joint)
  Established: July 19, 1866
    S. J. (39-1): 682.
  Authority: Jt. Res. of the House
    (39-1)
  Terminated: March 3, 1871, at the
    end of the 41-3.

1207. Select Committee on <u>Retrench-</u>
<u>ment</u> of the Expenses of the Govern-
ment (House)
   Established: February 19, 1822
   H. J. (17-1): 275.
   Authority: Res. of the House
   (17-1)
   Terminated: March 3, 1831, at the
   end of the 21-2.

1208. Select Committee on <u>Retrench-</u>
<u>ment</u> of Expenses of the Government
(House)
   Established: June 17, 1841
   H. J. (27-1): 150.
   Authority: Res. of the House
   (27-1)
   Terminated: March 17, 1842
   H. rpt. 451 (27-2) 408.

1209. Select Committee to Investi-
gate Frauds on the <u>Revenue</u> (House)
   Established: August 31, 1852
   S. J. (32-1): 678.
   Authority: Res. of the Senate
   (32-1)
   Terminated: August 7, 1854, at
   the end of the 33-1.

1210. Select Committee on Distrib-
uting a Part of the Public <u>Revenue</u>
Among the States (Senate)
   Established: December 14, 1826
   S. J. (19-2): 39.
   Authority: Res. of the Senate
   (19-2)
   Terminated: March 3, 1813, at the
   end of the 21-2.

1211. Select Committee to Inquire
into Placing on the Pension List
Persons Serving on <u>Revenue</u> Cutters
(House)
   Established: February 24, 1814
   H. J. (13-2): 361.
   Authority: Res. of the House
   (13-2)
   Terminated: March 14, 1814
   Ibid. 433.

1212. Select Committee on Appropri-
ation of <u>Revenue</u> Surpluses (House)
   Established: December 2, 1806
   H. J. (9-2): 15.
   Authority: Res. of the House
   (9-2)

Terminated: March 3, 1807, at the
   end of the 9-2.

1213. Select Committee on a Sup-
pression of a Duty on Salt, to a
Continuation of the Mediterranean
Fund, and to the State of Our
<u>Revenues</u> (House)
   Established: December 2, 1806
   H. J. (9-2): 15.
   Authority: Res. of the House
   (9-2)
   Terminated: February 28, 1807
   Ibid. 354.

1214. Committee on <u>Revisal</u> and
Unfinished Business (House)
   Established: December 4, 1793
   H. J. (3-1): 9.
   Authority: Res. of the House
   (3-1)
   Terminated: July 25, 1868, when
   it was replaced by the new
   Committee on Revision of Laws
   (Entry 762).
      Cong. Globe (40-2): 4495.
   Authority: Res. of the House
   (40-2)

1215. Select Committee on Provi-
sions of Act for Relief of Officers
and Soldiers of the <u>Revolution</u>
(House)
   Established: December 19, 1845
   H. J. (29-1): 131.
   Authority: Res. of the House
   (29-1)
   Terminated: August 10, 1846, at
   the end of the 29-1.

1216. Select Committee on <u>Revolu-</u>
<u>tionary</u> Bounty Lands (House)
   Established: January 10, 1828
   H. J. (20-1): 153.
   Authority: Res. of the House
   (20-1)
   Terminated: May 26, 1828, at the
   end of the 20-1.

1217. Committee on <u>Revolutionary</u>
Claims (House)
   Sudocs: Y4. R32/1:
   Established: December 13, 1825,
   when the name of Committee on
   Pensions and Revolutionary

Claims was changed to this
(Entry 1066).
  H. J. (19-1): 46.
Authority: Res. of the House
(19-1)
Terminated: December 2, 1873,
when the name changed to
Committee on War Claims
(Entry 1458).
  1 CR 23.
Authority: Res. of the House
(43-1)

1218. Committee on Revolutionary
Claims (Senate)
Sudocs: Y4. R32/2:
Established: December 28, 1832
  S. J. (22-2): 45.
Authority: Res. of the Senate
(22-2)
Terminated: March 3, 1883, at the
end of the 47-2.

1219. Committee on Revolutionary
Claims (Senate)
Sudocs: Y4. R32/2:
Established: December 16, 1889
  S. J. (51-1): 45.
Authority: Res. of the Senate
(51-1)
Terminated: April 18, 1921
  61 CR 404-05.
Authority: S. Res. 43 (67 -
Special)

1220. Select Committee on the Memo-
rial for Virginia Revolutionary
Claims (House)
Established: December 19, 1831
  H. J. (22-1): 64.
Authority: Res. of the House
(22-1)
Terminated: January 16, 1832
  Ibid. 196.

1221. Select Committee on Revolu-
tionary Officers (Senate)
Established: December 18, 1827
  S. J. (20-1): 47.
Authority: Res. of the Senate
(20-1)
Terminated: May 26, 1828, at the
end of the 20-1.

1222. Select Committee on Memorials
of Revolutionary Officers (House)

Established: December 9, 1825
  H. J. (19-1): 31.
Authority: Res. of the House
(19-1)
Terminated: January 3, 1826
  Ibid. 112.

1223. Committee on Revolutionary
Pensions (House)
Sudocs: Y4. R31/1:
Established: December 9, 1825
  H. J. (19-1): 32.
Authority: Res. of the House
(19-1)
Terminated: December 13, 1825,
when the name was changed to
the Committee on Military
Pensions (Entry 870).
  Ibid. 46.
Authority: Res. of the House
(19-1)

1224. Committee on Revolutionary
Pensions (House)
Sudocs: Y4. R31/1:
Established: December 5, 1831,
when it replaced the Committee
on Military Pensions (Entry
870).
  H. J. (21-2): 167.
Authority: Res. of the House
(21-2)
Terminated: March 2, 1880, when
it was replaced by the Committee on Pensions (Entry 1063).
  10 CR 1265.
Authority: Res. of the House
(46-2)

1225. Select Committee on the
Report Upon the Reynoldsburgh
Road (House)
Established: December 11, 1816
  H. J. (14-2): 52.
Authority: Res. of the House
(14-2)
Terminated: December 16, 1816
  Ibid. 73.

1226. Select Committee on the Rhode
Island Brigade of the Revolution
(House)
Established: December 11, 1832
  H. J. (22-2): 28.
Authority: Res. of the House
(22-2)

Terminated: February 16, 1836
H. J. (24-1): 360.

1227. Select Committee on Memorial of Democratic Members of the Rhode Island Legislature (House)
Established: February 19, 1844
H. J. (28-1): 421.
Authority: Res. of the House (28-1)
Terminated: June 17, 1844
H. rpt. 581 (28-1) 447.

1228. Committee on Rivers and Harbors (House)
Sudocs: Y4. R52:
Established: December 19, 1883
15 CR 216.
Authority: Res. of the House (48-1)
Terminated: January 2, 1947, when its functions were transferred to the Committee on Public Works (Entry 1162).
60 Stat. 812.
Authority: PL 79-601

1229. Select Committee on the Memorial of the Chicago Convention on the Rivers and Harbors of the U. S. (Senate)
Established: June 19, 1848
S. J. (30-1): 395.
Authority: Res. of the Senate (30-1)
Terminated: August 14, 1848, at the end of the 30-1.

1230. Select Committee on Opening a Road for the Greenville Treaty Line to the North Bend (House)
Established: November 14, 1811
H. J. (12-1): 50.
Authority: Res. of the House (12-1)
Terminated: November 15, 1811
Ibid. 53.

1231. Select Committee on Making a Road from Washington, Pennsylvania to the Sandusky River (House)
Established: March 30, 1816
H. J. (14-1): 549.
Authority: Res. of the House (14-1)

Terminated: April 30, 1816, at the end of the 14-1.

1232. Select Committee on Turnpiking a Road in Virginia (House)
Established: March 25, 1816
H. J. (14-1): 535.
Authority: Res. of the House (14-1)
Terminated: April 30, 1816, at the end of the 14-1.

1233. Committee on Roads (House)
Sudocs: Y4. R53/2:
Established: June 2, 1913
50 CR 1860.
Authority: H. Res. 104 (63-1)
Terminated: January 2, 1947, when its functions were transferred to the Committee on Public Works (Entry 1162).
60 Stat. 812.
Authority: PL 79-601

1234. Select Committee on Money Appropriated for Public Roads (House)
Established: December 12, 1805
H. J. (9-1): 45.
Authority: Res. of the House (9-1)
Terminated: December 30, 1805
Ibid. 104.

1235. Select Committee on a Petition of Washington Inhabitants for Roads (House)
Established: March 27, 1816
H. J. (14-1): 537.
Authority: Res. of the House (14-1)
Terminated: April 2, 1816
Ibid. 563.

1236. Committee on Roads and Canals (House)
Established: December 10, 1835
H. J. (24-1): 41.
Authority: Res. of the House (24-1)
Terminated: March 28, 1861, at the end of the 36-2.

1237. Committee on Roads and Canals (Senate)

Established: February 8, 1820
  S. J. (16-1): 148.
Authority: Res. of the Senate
  (16-1)
Terminated: December 20, 1822,
  when it was made a select
  committee (Entry 1241).
    S. J. (17-2): 45.
Authority: Res. of the Senate
  (17-2)

1238. Committee on Roads and Canals
(Senate)
  Sudocs: Y4. R53:
  Established: December 7, 1830,
    having been preceded by a
    select committee (Entry 1241).
      S. J. (21-2): 6.
  Authority: Res. of the Senate
    (21-2)
  Terminated: March 3, 1857, at the
    end of the 34-3.

1239. Select Committee on Roads and
Canals (House)
  Established: December 3, 1817
    H. J. (15-1): 19.
  Authority: Res. of the House
    (15-1)
  Terminated: May 3, 1829, at the
    end of the 20-2.

1240. Select Committee on Roads and
Canals (Senate)
  Established: December 10, 1816
    S. J. (14-2): 46.
  Authority: Res. of the Senate
    (14-2)
  Terminated: March 3, 1817, at the
    end of the 14-2.

1241. Select Committee on Roads and
Canals (Senate)
  Established: December 20, 1822,
    having been a standing commit-
    tee in the 16th Congress and
    17th Congress 1st Session
    (Entry 1237).
      S. J. (17-2): 45.
  Authority: Res. of the Senate
    (17-2)
  Terminated: December 7, 1830,
    when it was made a standing
    committee (Entry 1238).
      S. J. (21-2): 6.

Authority: Res. of the Senate
  (21-2)

1242. Select Committee on Roads
and Canals Leading to Illinois,
Indiana, and Missouri (House)
  Established: December 10, 1822
    H. J. (17-2): 32.
  Authority: Res. of the House
    (17-2)
  Terminated: February 12, 1824
    H. J. (18-1): 229.

1243. Select Committee on Repairing
Certain Roads in Tennessee and
Mississippi Territory (House)
  Established: January 18, 1815
    H. J. (13-3): 530.
  Authority: Res. of the House
    (13-3)
  Terminated: February 9, 1815
    Ibid. 630.

1244. Select Committee on Petition
for Opening Roanoke Inlet (House)
  Established: March 2, 1830
    H. J. (21-1): 359.
  Authority: Res. of the House
    (21-1)
  Terminated: March 19, 1830
    Ibid. 441.

1245. Select Committee on the Case
of Brigham H. Roberts (House)
  Established: December 5, 1899
    33 CR 53.
  Authority: Res. of the House
    (56-1)
  Terminated: January 20, 1900
    H. rpt. 85 (56-1) 4021.

1246. Select Committee on the
Letter from Commodore Rodgers
(House)
  Established: February 3, 1816
    H. J. (14-1): 267.
  Authority: Res. of the House
    (14-1)
  Terminated: February 7, 1816
    Ibid. 294.

1247. Select Committee on the
Assault of Mr. Rousseau upon
Mr. Grinnell (House)
  Established: June 15, 1866
    H. J. (39-1): 842.

Authority: Res. of the House
(39-1)
Terminated: July 2, 1866
H. rpt. 90 (39-1) 1272.

1248. Select Committee on the
Letter of the Honorable Mr. Ruggles
(Senate)
Established: February 22, 1838
S. J. (25-2): 245.
Authority: Res. of the Senate
(25-2)
Terminated: April 12, 1838
S. doc. 377 (25-2) 317.

1249. Committee on Rules (House)
Sudocs: Y4. R86/1:
Established: March 2, 1880,
having been preceded by a
select committee (Entry 1251).
10 CR 1266.
Authority: Res. of the House
(46-2)
Terminated: Still in existence
at the end of the 97-2.

1250. Committee on Rules (Senate)
Sudocs: Y4. R86/2:
Established: December 9, 1874,
having been preceded by the
Select Committee to Revise
the Rules of the Senate
(Entry 1279).
3 CR 28.
Authority: Res. of the Senate
(43-2)
Terminated: January 2, 1947,
when the name was changed to
Committee on Rules and Admin-
istration (Entry 1252).
60 Stat. 812.
Authority: PL 79-601

1251. Select Committee on Rules
(House)
Sudocs: Y4. R86/1:
Established: April 2, 1789
H. J. (1-1): 6.
Authority: Res. of the House
(1-1)
Terminated: March 2, 1880, when
it became a standing committee
(Entry 1249).
10 CR 1266.
Authority: Res. of the House
(46-2)

1252. Committee on Rules and
Administration (Senate)
Sudocs: Y4. R86/2:
Established: January 2, 1947,
when the name was changed
from Committee on Rules
(Entry 1250).
60 Stat. 812.
Authority: PL 79-601
Terminated: Still in existence
at the end of the 97-2.

1253. Committee on Rural Credits
(Joint)
Sudocs: Y4. R88:
Established: March 4, 1915
38 Stat. 1116.
Authority: PL 63-293
Terminated: January 4, 1916
H. doc. 494 (64-1) 7098.

1254. Committee to Investigate the
System of Shortime Rural Credits
(Joint)
Sudocs: Y4. Sh8:
Established: May 31, 1920
41 Stat. 730.
Authority: PL 66-234
Terminated: June 30, 1922
H. rpt. 1174 (67-2) 7957.

1255. Special Committee to Inves-
tigate Safety of Roofs over Senate
and House Wings of the Capital
(Joint)
Established: June 16, 1939
53 Stat. 832.
Authority: PL 76-130
Terminated: May 27, 1940
H. rpt. 2310 (76-3) 10442.

1256. Select Committee on Reduction
of Salaries (House)
Established: January 13, 1821
H. J. (16-2): 135.
Authority: Res. of the House
(16-2)
Terminated: February 6, 1821
Ibid. 201.

1257. Special Committee on the
Reduction of Salaries (House)
Established: December 4, 1873
H. J. (43-1): 43.
Authority: Res. of the House
(43-1)

Terminated: March 3, 1875, at
the end of the 43-2.

1258. Committee to Investigate the
Salaries of Officers and Employees
of the Senate and the House (Joint)
  Established: February 28, 1929
    45 Stat. 1402.
  Authority: PL 70-844
  Terminated: June 14, 1929
    S. rpt. 35 (71-1) 9185.

1259. Select Committee on Reducing
Salaries of Officers of the Govern-
ment (House)
  Established: April 19, 1834
    H. J. (23-1): 542.
  Authority: Res. of the House
    (23-1)
  Terminated: June 25, 1834
    Ibid. 831.

1260. Select Committee on Salaries
of Secretaries and Judges of the
Indiana, Louisiana, and Michigan
Territories (House)
  Established: February 9, 1807
    H. J. (9-2): 249.
  Authority: Res. of the House
    (9-2)
  Terminated: November 17, 1807
    H. J. (10-1): 68.

1261. Select Committee to Inquire
to What Extent Salt Can be Supplied
from Within the United States
(House)
  Established: December 23, 1808
    H. J. (10-2): 174.
  Authority: Res. of the House
    (10-2)
  Terminated: January 13, 1809
    Ibid. 275.

1262. Special Committee on San
Francisco Disaster (Joint)
  Established: January 16, 1854
    S. J. (33-1): 102.
  Authority: House Jt. Res. 160
    (33-1)
  Terminated: February 16, 1854
    H. rpt. 113 (33-1) 742.

1263. Committee on Science and
Astronautics (House)
  Sudocs: Y4. Sci2:

Established: July 21, 1958, when
it replaced the Select Commit-
tee on Astronautics and Space
Exploration (Entry 83).
    104 CR 14514.
  Authority: H. Res. 580 (85-2)
  Terminated: January 3, 1975, when
the name was changed to the
Committee on Science and Tech-
nology (Entry 1264).
    120 CR 34470.
  Authority: H. Res. 988 (93-2)

1264. Committee on Science and
Technology (House)
  Sudocs: Y4. Sci2:
  Established: January 3, 1975,
when the name was changed
from Committee on Science and
Astronautics (Entry 1263).
    120 CR 34470.
  Authority: H. Res. 580 (85-2)
  Terminated: Still in existence
at the end of the 97-2.

1265. Commission on Scientific
Bureaus (Joint)
  Established: July 7, 1884
    23 Stat. 219.
  Authority: PL 48-332
  Terminated: June 8, 1886
    S. rpt. 1285 (49-1) 2361.

1266. Select Committee on American
Seamen (House)
  Established: May 31, 1809
    H. J. (11-1): 62.
  Authority: Res. of the House
    (11-1)
  Terminated: June 7, 1809
    Ibid. 87.

1267. Select Committee to Make
Farther Provision for the Benefit
of Seamen (House)
  Established: January 10, 1809
    H. J. (10-2): 256.
  Authority: Res. of the House
    (10-2)
  Terminated: February 18, 1809
    Ibid. 410.

1268. Select Committee on the
Removal of the Seat of Government
(House)

Established: September 26, 1814
  H. J. (13-3): 23.
Authority: Res. of the House
  (13-3)
Terminated: October 5, 1814
  Ibid. 49.

1269. Select Committee to Inquire
into a Violation of an Injunction
of Secrecy (Senate)
  Established: April 29, 1844
    Ex. J. of the Senate (28-1):
    264.
  Authority: Res. of the Senate in
    Ex. Session (28-1)
  Terminated: May 8, 1844
    Ibid. 268.

1270. Special Committee to Study
Secret and Confidential Government
Documents (Senate)
  Established: August 15, 1972
    118 CR 28250.
  Authority: S. Res. 299 (92-2)
  Terminated: October 12, 1973
    S. rpt. 466 (93-1) 13017-7.

1271. Committee on President's
Message Relating to the Secret
Service (House)
  Established: December 11, 1908
    43 CR 140.
  Authority: H. Res. 451 (60-2)
  Terminated: January 8, 1909
    H. rpt. 1826 (60-2) 5385.

1272. Select Committee on Requiring
Security on Appeals from District
to Circuit Courts (House)
  Established: January 6, 1812
    H. J. (12-1): 230.
  Authority: Res. of the House
    (12-1)
  Terminated: May 13, 1812
    Ibid. 586.

1273. Committee on Selective
Service Deferments (Joint)
  Established: April 8, 1943
    57 Stat. 58.
  Authority: PL 78-23
  Terminated: March 31, 1947
    50 U.S.C. 391.

1274. Select Committee on the
Seminole War (Senate)

Established: December 18, 1818
  S. J. (15-2): 87.
Authority: Res. of the Senate
  (15-2)
Terminated: May 15, 1820, at the
  end of the 16-1.

1275. Committee to Audit and
Control the Contingent Expenses
of the Senate (Senate)
  Sudocs: Y4. Se5/3:
  Established: November 20, 1820
    S. J. (16-2): 22.
  Authority: Res. of the Senate
    (10-1)
  Terminated: January 2, 1947, and
    its functions were transferred
    to the Committee on Rules and
    Administration (Entry 1252).
    60 Stat. 812.
  Authority: PL 79-601

1276. Select Committee on Compen-
sation of Employees of the Senate
(Senate)
  Established: March 30, 1885
    S. J. (48-2): 527.
  Authority: Res. of the Senate
    (48-2)
  Terminated: December 7, 1885, at
    the beginning of the 49-1.

1277. Select Committee on Evidence
Affecting Certain Members of the
Senate (Senate)
  Established: February 4, 1873
    Cong. Globe (42-3): 1076.
  Authority: Res. of the Senate
    (42-3)
  Terminated: February 27, 1873
    S. rpt. 519 (42-3) 1550.

1278. Select Committee on the State
of the Administrative Service of
the Senate (Senate)
  Established: June 20, 1890
    S. J. (51-1): 386.
  Authority: Res. of the Senate
    (51-1)
  Terminated: March 3, 1891, at the
    end of the 51-2.

1279. Select Committee to Revise
the Rules of the Senate (Senate)
  Established: December 3, 1867
    S. J. (40-2): 9.

Authority: Res. of the Senate
(40-3)
Terminated: June 23, 1874, at the
end of the 43-1. Standing committee created at the beginning
of 43-2 (Entry 1250).

1280. Committee on the Senate
Chamber and Hall of the House of
Representatives (Joint)
Established: May 10, 1864
H. J. (38-1): 639.
Authority: S. Con. Res. (38-1)
Terminated: February 20, 1865
S. rpt. 128 (38-2) 1211.

1281. Select Committee on the Bill
to Alter and Improve the Senate
Chamber (Senate)
Established: May 19, 1860
S. J. (36-1): 475.
Authority: Senate Order (36-1)
Terminated: August 6, 1861, at
the end of the 37-1.

1282. Temporary Select Committee to
Study the Senate Committee System
(Senate)
Sudocs: Y4. Se5/4:
Established: March 31, 1976
122 CR 8846.
Authority: S. Res. 109 (94-2)
Terminated: February 11, 1977
123 CR 3691.
Authority: S. Res. 4 (95-1)

1283. Committee on Senate Contin-
gent Expenses (Senate)
Sudocs: Y4. Se5:
Established: January 5, 1820
S. J. (16-1): 65.
Authority: Res. of the Senate
(16-1)
Terminated: April 18, 1921
61 CR 404-05.
Authority: S. Res. 43 (67 -
Special)

1284. Special Committee to Investigate Senatorial Campaign Expenditures (Senate)
Sudocs: Y4. Se5/2:
Established: May 27, 1938
83 CR 7632.
Authority: S. Res. 283 (75-3)

Terminated: July 7, 1943
S. rpt. 405 (78-1) 10756.

1285. Select Committee to Investi-
gate Senatorial Elections (Senate)
Established: May 19, 1926
67 CR 9678.
Authority: S. Res. 195 (69-1)
Terminated: March 22, 1928
S. rpt. 603 (70-1) 8832.

1286. Select Committee on Clerical
Assistance to Senators (Senate)
Established: January 26, 1917
54 CR 2027.
Authority: S. Res. 330 (64-2)
Terminated: March 3, 1917, at
the end of the 64-2.

1287. Select Committee on Sergeant-
at-arms Communication on Error in
Paying Members at Metropolis Bank
(House)
Established: January 11, 1837
H. J. (25-2): 253.
Authority: Res. of the House
(25-2)
Terminated: January 31, 1838
H. rpt. 513 (25-2) 334.

1288. Select Committee on the Elec-
tion of Sheriffs in the Indiana
Territory (House)
Established: November 28, 1811
H. J. (12-1): 89.
Authority: Res. of the House
(12-1)
Terminated: December 7, 1811
Ibid. 123.

1289. Special Committee on the
Eligibility of the Honorable
James Shields to a Seat in the
Senate (Senate)
Established: March 6, 1849
S. J. (30-2): 357.
Authority: Res. of the Senate
(30-2)
Terminated: March 15, 1849
Cong. Globe (30-2): 342
Appendix.

1290. Select Committee on Investigation of the Superintendent of
the Shiloh National Park (Senate)

Established: June 13, 1934
78 CR 11328.
Authority: S. Res. 198 (73-2)
Terminated: June 18, 1934, at
the end of the 73-2.

1291. Special Committee to Inves-
tigate Alleged Ship Purchase Lobby
(Senate)
Sudocs: Y4. Sh6/2:
Established: February 15, 1915
52 CR 3777.
Authority: S. Res. 543 (63-3)
Terminated: January 5, 1916
S. rpt. 25 (64-1) 6900.

1292. Select Committee to Inves-
tigate Alleged Ship Subsidy Lobby
(House)
Sudocs: Y4. Sh6:
Established: March 29, 1910
45 CR 3896.
Authority: H. Res. 543 (61-2)
Terminated: March 2, 1911
H. rpt. 2297 (61-3) 5857
& 5858.

1293. Select Committee on American
Shipbuilding (Joint)
Established: August 7, 1882
13 CR 7018.
Authority: H. R. Res. 266 (47-1)
Terminated: December 15, 1882
H. rpt. 1827 (47-2) 2159.

1294. Select Committee on the
Shipping Board Emergency Fleet
Corporation (House)
Sudocs: Y4. Sh6/4:
Established: March 4, 1924
65 CR 3555.
Authority: H. Res. 186 (68-1)
Terminated: 1925
H. rpt. 2 (69-1) 8535.

1295. Select Committee on Shipping
Board Operations (House)
Sudocs: Y4. Sh6/3:
Established: July 24, 1919
58 CR 3111.
Authority: H. Res. 171 (66-1)
Terminated: March 2, 1921
H. rpt. 1399 (66-3) 7777.

1296. Select Committee on Protection of Life and Health in

Passenger Ships (Senate)
Established: December 20, 1854
S. J. (33-2): 60.
Authority: Res. of the Senate
(33-2)
Terminated: March 3, 1855, at
the end of the 33-2.

1297. Select Committee to Consider
the Causes and Extent of Sickness
on Emigrant Ships (Senate)
Sudocs: Y4. Si1:
Established: December 7, 1853
S. J. (33-1): 27.
Authority: Res. of the Senate
(33-1)
Terminated: August 2, 1854
S. rpt. 386 (33-1) 707.

1298. Special Committee on the
Investigation of Silver (Senate)
Sudocs: Y4. Si3:
Established: August 16, 1935
79 CR 13391.
Authority: S. Res. 187 (74-1)
Terminated: August 2, 1946, at
the end of the 79-2.

1299. Special Committee on the
Silver Pool Investigation (House)
Established: January 12, 1891
22 CR 1208.
Authority: Res. of the House
(51-2)
Terminated: February 25, 1891
H. rpt. 4006 (51-2) 2889.

1300. Select Committee to Investi-
gate Assault on Representative Sims
of Tennessee (House)
Established: April 21, 1913
50 CR 283.
Authority: H. Res. 59 (63-1)
Terminated: April 26, 1913
H. rpt. 6 (63-1) 6515.

1301. Select Committee to Examine
into the Condition of the Sioux
and Crow Indians (Senate)
Established: March 2, 1883
14 CR 3556.
Authority: Res. of the Senate
(47-2)
Terminated: March 7, 1884
S. rpt. 283 (48-1) 2174.

1302. Select Committee on the
Slave Trade (Senate)
   Established: December 10, 1816
      S. J. (14-2): 46.
   Authority: Res. of the Senate
      (14-2)
   Terminated: March 3, 1819, at
      the end of the 15-2.

1303. Select Committee on the
Prohibition of the Slave Trade
(House)
   Established: February 7, 1806
      H. J. (9-1): 201.
   Authority: Res. of the House
      (9-1)
   Terminated: April 21, 1806, at
      the end of the 9-1.

1304. Select Committee on the
Prohibition of the African Slave
Trade (House)
   Established: December 4, 1816
      H. J. (14-2): 25.
   Authority: Res. of the House
      (14-2)
   Terminated: March 3, 1827, at
      the end of the 19-2.

1305. Select Committee on Slavery
(House)
   Established: February 8, 1836
      H. J. (24-1): 846.
   Authority: Res. of the House
      (24-1)
   Terminated: March 26, 1836
      Ibid. 879.

1306. Select Committee on the
Petition of the Convention for
Promoting the Abolition of Slavery
(House)
   Established: February 27, 1816
      H. J. (14-1): 405.
   Authority: Res. of the House
      (14-1)
   Terminated: August 30, 1816, at
      the end of the 14-1.

1307. Select Committee on Slavery
and the Treatment of Freedmen
(Senate)
   Established: January 13, 1864
      S. J. (38-1): 74.
   Authority: Res. of the Senate
      (38-1)

   Terminated: February 29, 1864
      S. rpt. 24-25 (38-1) 1178.

1308. Select Committee on
Prohibiting Slavery in the
Territories (House)
   Established: December 15, 1819
      H. J. (16-1): 44.
   Authority: Res. of the House
      (16-1)
   Terminated: December 28, 1819
      Ibid. 82.

1309. Select Committee to Bring
in a Bill to Explain the Act to
Prohibit the Importation of Slaves
(House)
   Established: February 27, 1807
      H. J. (9-2): 338.
   Authority: Res. of the House
      (9-2)
   Terminated: February 27, 1807
      Ibid. 339.

1310. Select Committee on Illicit
Introduction of Slaves From Amelia
Island (House)
   Established: December 3, 1817
      H. J. (15-1): 19.
   Authority: Res. of the House
      (15-1)
   Terminated: January 10, 1818
      Ibid. 131.

1311. Committee on Small Business
(House)
   Sudocs: Y4. Sml:
   Established: January 3, 1975,
      having been preceded by a
      select committee (Entry 1312).
         120 CR 34470.
   Authority: H. Res. 988 (93-2)
   Terminated: Still in existence
      at the end of the 97-2.

1312. Select Committee on Small
Business (House)
   Sudocs: Y4. Sml:
   Established: December 4, 1941
      87 CR 9428.
   Authority: H. Res. 294 (77-1)
   Terminated: January 3, 1975,
      when a standing committee was
      established (Entry 1311).
         120 CR 34470
   Authority: H. Res. 988 (93-2)

1313. Select Committee on Small
Business (Senate)
  Sudocs: Y4. Sm1/2:
  Established: February 20, 1950,
    having been preceded by the
    Special Committee to Study
    Problems of American Small
    Business (Entry 43).
    96 CR 1944.
  Authority: S. Res. 58 (81-2)
  Terminated: Still in existence
    at the end of the 97-2.

1314. Select Committee on the
Resolution for the Expulsion of
W. Scott Smith from the Reporters'
Gallery (House)
  Established: June 10, 1870
    Cong. Globe (41-2): 4322.
  Authority: Res. of the House
    (41-2)
  Terminated: June 22, 1870
    H. rpt. 104 (41-2) 1438.

1315. Select Committee on Smith-
sonian Bequest (House)
  Established: December 10, 1838
    H. J. (25-3): 45.
  Authority: Res. of the House
    (25-3)
  Terminated: August 31, 1842,
    at the end of the 27-2.

1316. Committee on the Smithsonian
Bequest (Joint)
  Established: January 12, 1839
    H. J. (25-3): 264.
  Authority: S. Con. Res. 7 (25-3)
  Terminated: February 18, 1839
    S. doc. 234 (25-3) 340.

1317. Select Committee on Smith-
sonian Fund (House)
  Established: February 19, 1844
    H. J. (28-1): 437.
  Authority: Res. of the House
    (28-1)
  Terminated: August 10, 1846, at
    the end of the 29-1.

1318. Select Committee on the
Smithsonian Institution (Senate)
  Established: April 30, 1846
    S. J. (29-1): 269.
  Authority: Res. of the Senate
    (29-1)

Terminated: August 10, 1846, at
  the end of the 29-1.

1319. Select Committee on Letter of
Rufus Choate on the Management of
the Smithsonian Institution (House)
  Established: January 18, 1855
    H. J. (33-2): 189.
  Authority: Res. of the House
    (33-2)
  Terminated: March 3, 1855
    H. rpt. 141 (33-2) 808.

1320. Select Committee on
Reinvesting the Funds of the
Smithsonian Institution (House)
  Established: January 3, 1854
    H. J. (33-1): 156.
  Authority: Res. of the House
    (33-1)
  Terminated: March 3, 1855
    H. rpt. 144 (33-2) 808.

1321. Committee on Construction of
Building for Museum of History and
Technology for Smithsonian (Joint)
  Sudocs: Y4. C76/5:
  Established: June 28, 1955
    69 Stat. 189.
  Authority: PL 84-106
  Terminated: September 15, 1965
    S. doc. 58 (89-1) 12668-2.

1322. Select Committee on Smith-
sonian Legacy and Institution
(House)
  Established: December 21, 1835
    H. J. (24-1): 79.
  Authority: Res. of the House
    (24-1)
  Terminated: January 19, 1836
    H. rpt. 181 (24-1) 293.

1323. Select Committee on the
Petition of the Society for
Propagating the Gospel (House)
  Established: February 5, 1817
    H. J. (14-2): 342.
  Authority: Res. of the House
    (14-2)
  Terminated: February 27, 1817
    Ibid. 479.

1324. Select Committee on Soldiers'
and Sailors' Bounty (House)

Established: July 18, 1867
  Cong. Globe (40-1): 718.
Authority: Res. of the House
  (40-1)
Terminated: December 19, 1867
  H. rpt. 5 (40-2) 1357.

1325. Select Committee on Provision
for Soldiers Who Served Under Gen-
erals St. Clair and Wayne (House)
  Established: January 20, 1842
    H. J. (27-2): 511.
  Authority: Res. of the House
    (27-2)
  Terminated: March 8, 1842
    Ibid. 511.

1326. Select Committee on the
Murder of United States Soldiers
in South Carolina (House)
  Established: December 10, 1866
    Cong. Globe (39-2): 49.
  Authority: Res. of the House
    (39-2)
  Terminated: March 2, 1867
    H. rpt. 32 (39-2) 1305.

1327. Select Committee to Investi-
gate all Aspects of United States
Military Involvement in Southeast
Asia (House)
  Established: June 8, 1970
    116 CR 18670.
  Authority: H. Res. 976 (91-2)
  Terminated: July 6, 1970
    H. rpt. 91-1276 (91-2) 12886-1.

1328. Select Committee on Southern
Railroads (House)
  Established: December 10, 1866
    Cong. Globe (39-2): 49.
  Authority: Res. of the House
    (39-2)
  Terminated: November 10, 1868,
    at the end of the 40-2.

1329. Select Committee on the
Southern States (House)
  Established: January 22, 1877
    H. J. (44-2): 285.
  Authority: Res. of the House
    (44-2)
  Terminated: March 3, 1877, at
    the end of the 44-2.

1330. Special Committee on Space
and Astronautics (Senate)
  Sudocs: Y4. Sp1:
  Established: February 6, 1958
    104 CR 1806.
  Authority: S. Res. 256 (85-2)
  Terminated: March 11, 1959
    S. rpt. 100 (86-1) 12148.

1331. Select Committee on the
Spanish American Colonies (House)
  Established: November 12, 1811
    H. J. (12-1): 36.
  Authority: Res. of the House
    (12-1)
  Terminated: July 6, 1812, at
    the end of the 12-1.

1332. Select Committee on Charges
Against Speaker on Mutilating
Journal (House)
  Established: March 26, 1850
    H. J. (31-1): 713.
  Authority: Res. of the House
    (31-1)
  Terminated: March 29, 1850
    H. rpt. 218 (31-1) 584.

1333. Select Committee on Profes-
sional Sports (House)
  Sudocs: Y4. Sp6:
  Established: May 18, 1976
    122 CR 14312.
  Authority: H. Res. 1186 (94-2)
  Terminated: January 3, 1977
    H. rpt. 1786 (94-2) 13186-1.

1334. Select Committee to Investi-
gate Loss of Stamps in the Sub-
treasury New York (House)
  Established: December 19, 1872
    Cong. Globe (42-3): 306.
  Authority: Res. of the House
    (42-3)
  Terminated: February 11, 1873
    H. rpt. 70 (42-3) 1576.

1335. Select Committee on Standards
and Conduct (House)
  Established: October 19, 1966
    112 CR 27729.
  Authority: H. Res. 1013 (89-2)
  Terminated: December 27, 1966
    Deschler, v. 4, p. 305.

1336. Select Committee on Standards and Conduct (Senate)
   Sudocs: Y4. St2/2:
   Established: July 24, 1964
      110 CR 16939.
   Authority: S. Res. 338 (88-2)
   Terminated: February 11, 1977,
      when it was transferred to
      the Committee on Ethics (Entry
      435).
         123 CR 3691.
   Authority: S. Res. 4 (95-1)

1337. Committee on Standards of Official Conduct (House)
   Sudocs: Y4. St2/3:
   Established: April 13, 1967
      113 CR 9448.
   Authority: H. Res. 418 (90-1)
   Terminated: Still in existence
      at the end of the 97-2.

1338. Committee on Standards, Weights and Measures (Senate)
   Sudocs: Y4. St2:
   Established: March 22, 1909,
      having been preceded by a
      select committee (Entry 1339).
         42 CR 122.
   Authority: Res. of the Senate
      (61-1)
   Terminated: April 18, 1921
      61 CR 404-405.
   Authority: S. Res. 43 (67 -
      Special)

1339. Select Committee on Standards, Weights, and Measures (Senate)
   Sudocs: Y4. St2:
   Established: December 18, 1901
      35 CR 388.
   Authority: Res. of the Senate
      (57-1)
   Terminated: March 22, 1909,
      when it was made a standing
      committee (Entry 1338).
         44 CR 122.
   Authority: Res. of the Senate
      (61-1)

1340. Select Committee to Investigate the Charges Preferred Against Benjamin Stark (Senate)
   Established: March 18, 1862
      S. J. (37-2): 317.

Authority: Res. of the Senate
   (37-2)
Terminated: April 22, 1862
   S. rpt. 38 (37-2) 1125.

1341. Select Committee on Petition of the Citizens of Pennsylvania on Constitutionality of State Banks (House)
   Established: December 29, 1836
      H. J. (24-2): 143.
   Authority: Res. of the House
      (24-2)
   Terminated: February 22, 1837
      Ibid. 506.

1342. Select Committee on Further Provisions Needed in State Public Records, Acts, and Judicial Proceedings and their Proof (House)
   Established: January 22, 1806
      H. J. (9-1): 153.
   Authority: Res. of the House
      (9-1)
   Terminated: December 20, 1808
      H. J. (10-2): 160.

1343. Select Committee on State, War and Navy Department Building (Joint)
   Established: August 5, 1882
      22 Stat. 256.
   Authority: PL 47-389
   Terminated: March 3, 1883, at
      the end of the 47-2.

1344. Select Committee on Giving to the States Jurisdiction in Selecting Sites for Forts and Arsenals (House)
   Established: February 2, 1820
      H. J. (16-1): 189.
   Authority: Res. of the House
      (16-1)
   Terminated: May 15, 1820, at
      the end of the 16-1.

1345. Select Committee on Stationery (House)
   Established: April 17, 1840
      H. J. (26-1): 804.
   Authority: Res. of the House
      (26-1)
   Terminated: July 21, 1840, at
      the end of the 26-1.

1346. Select Committee on Stationery Furnished to Persons Not
Entitled (House)
    Established: March 23, 1840
        H. J. (26-1): 671.
    Authority: Res. of the House
        (26-1)
    Terminated: July 21, 1840, at
        the end of the 26-1.

1347. Select Committee on Sta-
tistics (House)
    Established: January 29, 1844
        H. J. (28-1): 316.
    Authority: Res. of the House
        (28-2)
    Terminated: February 25, 1845
        H. rpt. 186 (28-2) 468.

1348. Select Committee on What
Description of Claims Against
the United States are Barred by
the Statute of Limitations (House)
    Established: December 5, 1805
        H. J. (9-1): 29.
    Authority: Res. of the House
        (9-1)
    Terminated: December 22, 1807
        H. J. (10-1): 181.

1349. Select Committee on Steam
Boilers (House)
    Established: December 29, 1837
        H. J. (25-2): 160.
    Authority: Res. of the House
        (25-2)
    Terminated: August 22, 1842
        H. rpt. 1033 (27-2) 411.

1350. Select Committee on Explosion
of Steam Boilers (House)
    Established: March 2, 1832
        H. J. (22-1): 431.
    Authority: Res. of the House
        (22-1)
    Terminated: April 26, 1834
        H. rpt. 426 (23-1) 262.

1351. Select Committee on Steam
Engines (House)
    Established: December 13, 1838
        H. J. (25-3): 73.
    Authority: Res. of the House
        (25-3)
    Terminated: March 3, 1839, at
        the end of the 25-3.

1352. Select Committee on the
Condition of Steam Navigation,
and Causes of Disasters (House)
    Established: December 19, 1836
        H. J. (24-2): 63.
    Authority: Res. of the House
        (24-2)
    Terminated: March 3, 1837, at
        the end of the 24-2.

1353. Select Committee on the
Danger of Steam Vessels (Senate)
    Established: December 6, 1837
        S. J. (25-2): 25.
    Authority: Res. of the Senate
        (25-2)
    Terminated: July 9, 1838, at
        the end of the 25-2.

1354. Select Committee to Investigate the Steel Producing Capacity
of the United States (Senate)
    Established: July 3, 1884
        S. J. (48-1): 902.
    Authority: Res. of the Senate
        (48-1)
    Terminated: March 3, 1885, at
        the end of the 48-2.

1355. Select Committee on Disburse-
ments by Lawrence Stone and Company
(House)
    Established: January 15, 1858
        H. J. (35-1): 177.
    Authority: Res. of the House
        (35-1)
    Terminated: June 14, 1858, at
        the end of the 35-1.

1356. Select Committee on R. M. T.
Hunter's Sub-Treasury Plan (House)
    Established: January 14, 1839
        H. J. (25-3): 282.
    Authority: Res. of the House
        (25-3)
    Terminated: March 3, 1839, at
        the end of the 25-3.

1357. Select Committee on Alleged
Assault on Senator Sumner (House)
    Established: May 23, 1856
        H. J. (34-1): 1029.
    Authority: Res. of the House
        (34-1)
    Terminated: June 2, 1856
        H. rpt. 182 (34-1) 868.

1358. Select Committee to Inquire into the Circumstances Attending the Assault Upon the Honorable Charles Sumner (Senate)
　　Established: May 23, 1856
　　　S. J. (34-1): 351.
　　Authority: Res. of the Senate
　　　(34-1)
　　Terminated: May 28, 1856
　　　S. rpt. 191 (34-1) 836.

1359. Select Committee on Additional Compensation to the Superintendent of the Indian Trade (House)
　　Established: April 7, 1812
　　　H. J. (12-1): 567.
　　Authority: Res. of the House
　　　(12-1)
　　Terminated: April 28, 1812
　　　Ibid. 644.

1360. Select Committee on the Accounts of the Late Superintendent of Public Printing (House)
　　Established: December 23, 1858
　　　H. J. (35-2): 110.
　　Authority: Res. of the House
　　　(35-2)
　　Terminated: February 28, 1859
　　　H. rpt. 189 (35-2) 1020.

1361. Select Committee on Suppression of Part of the Document from the Secretary of the Treasury to the House (House)
　　Established: February 6, 1823
　　　H. J. (17-2): 202.
　　Authority: Res. of the House
　　　(17-2)
　　Terminated: March 3, 1823, at the end of the 17-2.

1362. Select Committee on Proceedings of the Supreme Court (House)
　　Established: January 22, 1827
　　　H. J. (19-2): 191.
　　Authority: Res. of the House
　　　(19-2)
　　Terminated: March 3, 1827, at the end of the 19-2.

1363. Select Committee on Altering the Terms of the Supreme Court of the United States (House)

Established: February 27, 1807
　　H. J. (9-2): 267.
　Authority: Res. of the House
　　(9-2)
　Terminated: March 3, 1807, at the end of the 9-2.

1364. Select Committee to Investigate Disposition of Surplus Property (House)
　　Sudocs: Y4. Su7:
　　Established: May 9, 1946
　　　92 CR 4750.
　　Authority: H. Res. 385 (79-2)
　　Terminated: December 31, 1946
　　　H. rpt. 2738 (79-2) 11026.

1365. Select Committee on Distribution of Surplus Revenue (House)
　　Established: December 9, 1830
　　　H. J. (21-2): 36.
　　Authority: Res. of the House
　　　(21-2)
　　Terminated: January 28, 1831
　　　H. rpt. 51 (21-2) 210.

1366. Select Committee on Survivors Benefits (House)
　　Sudocs: Y4. Su7/2:
　　Established: August 4, 1954
　　　100 CR 13354.
　　Authority: H. Res. 549 (83-2)
　　Terminated: June 28, 1955
　　　H. rpt. 993 (84-1) 11823.

1367. Select Committee on Draining or Reclaiming Swamp or Submerged Lands (House)
　　Established: December 23, 1848
　　　H. J. (30-2): 147.
　　Authority: Res. of the House
　　　(30-2)
　　Terminated: February 28, 1849
　　　H. rpt. 130 (30-2) 545.

1368. Select Committee on Defalcation of Samuel Swartwout, Collector of New York (House)
　　Established: January 17, 1839
　　　H. J. (25-3): 312.
　　Authority: Res. of the House
　　　(25-3)
　　Terminated: February 27, 1839
　　　H. rpt. 313 (25-3) 352.

1369. Select Committee on Impeachment of Charles Swayne (House)
  Established: December 13, 1904
    39 CR 249.
  Authority: Res. of the House
    (58-3)
  Terminated: January 10, 1905
    H. rpt. 3477 (58-3) 4761.

1370. Select Committee on Impeachment of Charles Swayne (Senate)
  Established: December 14, 1904
    39 CR 265.
  Authority: Res. of the Senate
    (58-3)
  Terminated: March 3, 1905, at
    the end of the 58-3.

1371. Select Committee on Removing Henry H. Sylvester from Office (House)
  Established: May 16, 1842
    H. J. (27-2): 821.
  Authority: Res. of the House
    (27-2)
  Terminated: July 27, 1842
    H. rpt. 945 (27-2) 410.

1372. Select Committee to Inquire Into the Official Conduct of Judge Tallmadge (House)
  Established: March 27, 1816
    H. J. (14-1): 545.
  Authority: Res. of the House
    (14-1)
  Terminated: February 17, 1819
    H. J. (15-2): 279.

1373. Select Committee on the Bill to Modify the Tariff (Senate)
  Established: February 13, 1833
    S. J. (22-2): 175.
  Authority: Res. of the Senate
    (22-2)
  Terminated: March 2, 1833, at
    the end of the 22-2.

1374. Special Committee on Repealing the First Section of the Tariff Bill of 1828 (Senate)
  Established: January 2, 1849
    S. J. (30-2): 93.
  Authority: Res. of the Senate
    (30-2)
  Terminated: March 3, 1849, at
    the end of the 30-2.

1375. Select Committee on Investigation of the Tariff Commission (Senate)
  Sudocs: Y4. T17:
  Established: March 11, 1926
    67 CR 5390.
  Authority: S. Res. 162 (69-1)
  Terminated: May 28, 1928
    S. rpt. 1325 (70-1) 8832.

1376. Select Committee on Tariff Regulation (Senate)
  Established: February 25, 1823
    S. J. (17-2): 189.
  Authority: Res. of the Senate
    (17-2)
  Terminated: March 3, 1823, at
    the end of the 17-2.

1377. Committee on Tax Evasion and Avoidance (Joint)
  Sudocs: Y4. T19:
  Established: June 11, 1937
    50 Stat. 253.
  Authority: Public Res. 40 (75-1)
  Terminated: August 5, 1937
    H. doc. 337 (75-1) 10126.

1378. Select Committee to Investigate Tax-Exempt Foundations and Comparable Organizations (House)
  Sudocs: Y4. T19/4:
  Established: April 4, 1952
    98 CR 3504.
  Authority: H. Res. 561 (82-2)
  Terminated: December 16, 1954
    H. rpt. 2681 (83-2) 11748.

1379. Committee on Taxation (Joint)
  Sudocs: Y4. T19/4:
  Established: October 4, 1976,
    when it replaced the Joint
    Committee on Internal Revenue
    Taxation (Entry 699).
    90 Stat. 1835.
  Authority: PL 94-455
  Terminated: Still in existence
    at the end of the 97-2.

1380. Special Committee on Taxation of Governmental Securities and Salaries (Senate)
  Sudocs: Y4. T19/2:
  Established: June 16, 1938
    83 CR 9549.
  Authority: S. Res. 303 (75-3)

Terminated: September 18, 1940
    S. rpt. 2140 (76-3) 10432.

1381. Special Committee to Investigate Taylor and other Systems of
Shop Management (House)
    Sudocs: Y4. T21:
    Established: August 21, 1911
        48 CR 4364.
    Authority: H. Res. 90 (62-2)
    Terminated: March 9, 1912
        H. rpt. 403 (62-2) 6135.

1382. Select Committee on Construction of an Atmospheric Telegraph
Between Washington and Baltimore
for the Conveyance of Letters and
Packages (Senate)
    Established: February 23, 1854
        S. J. (33-1): 204.
    Authority: Res. of the Senate
        (33-1)
    Terminated: August 7, 1854, at
        the end of the 33-1.

1383. Select Committee on Telephone
Investigation (House)
    Established: February 26, 1886
        17 CR 1831.
    Authority: Res. of the House
        (49-1)
    Terminated: June 30, 1886
        H. rpt. 3142 (49-1) 2444.

1384. Select Committee to Investigate the Telepost (Senate)
    Established: July 17, 1914
        51 CR 12259.
    Authority: S. Res. 405 (63-2)
    Terminated: March 4, 1915
        S. doc. 983 (63-3) 6784.

1385. Select Committee on a Grant
of Certain Vacant Lands to Tennessee (House)
    Established: January 23, 1826
        H. J. (19-1): 178.
    Authority: Res. of the House
        (19-1)
    Terminated: February 9, 1826
        H. rpt. 68 (19-1) 141.

1386. Select Committee on Petition
of Inhabitants of Tennessee Between
the Tennessee and Big Pigeon Rivers
(House)

Established: February 9, 1824
    H. J. (18-1): 215.
Authority: Res. of the House
    (18-1)
Terminated: May 27, 1824, at
    the end of the 18-1.

1387. Select Committee on the
Tennessee Centennial Exposition
(Senate)
    Established: May 12, 1896
        28 CR 5093.
    Authority: Res. of the Senate
        (54-1)
    Terminated: March 3, 1897, at
        the end of the 54-2.

1388. Select Committee on Tennessee
Lands (House)
    Established: December 17, 1833
        H. J. (23-1): 85.
    Authority: Res. of the House
        (23-1)
    Terminated: January 2, 1834
        Ibid. 149.

1389. Committee on the Tennessee
Valley Authority (Joint)
    Sudocs: Y4. T25:
    Established: April 5, 1938
        83 CR 4703.
    Authority: Public Res. 83 (75-3)
    Terminated: April 1, 1939
        S. doc. 56 (76-1) 10308.

1390. Committee on Territories
(House)
    Sudocs: Y4. T27/1:
    Established: December 13, 1825
        H. J. (19-1): 46.
    Authority: Res. of the House
        (19-1)
    Terminated: January 2, 1947,
        when its functions were trans-
        ferred to the Committee on
        Public Lands (Entry 1150).
        60 Stat. 812.
    Authority: PL 79-601

1391. Committee on Territories
(Senate)
    Sudocs: Y4. T27/2:
    Established: March 25, 1844
        Cong. Globe (28-1): 438.
    Authority: Res. of the Senate
        (28-1)

Terminated: April 18, 1921, when the name was changed to Committee on Territories and Insular Affairs (Entry 1392).
61 CR 405.
Authority: S. Res. 43 (67 - Special)

1392. Committee on Territories and Insular Affairs (Senate)
Sudocs: Y4. T27/2:
Established: April 18, 1921, when the name was changed from Committee on Territories (Entry 1391).
61 CR 405.
Authority: S. Res. 43 (67 - Special)
Terminated: January 2, 1947, when functions were transferred to the newly created Committee on Public Lands (Entry 1152).
60 Stat. 812.
Authority: PL 79-601

1393. Select Committee on Repealing a Part of the Ordinance of the Government of the Several Territories of the U. S. (House)
Established: February 17, 1808
H. J. (10-1): 383.
Authority: Res. of the House (10-1)
Terminated: November 16, 1809
H. J. (10-2): 41.

1394. Select Committee to Investigate Alleged Traffic with Rebels in Texas (Senate)
Established: January 4, 1871
S. J. (41-3): 91.
Authority: Res. of the Senate (41-3)
Terminated: March 3, 1871
S. rpt. 377 (41-3) 1443.

1395. Select Committee on the Texas Frontier Troubles (House)
Established: January 6, 1876
H. J. (44-1): 128.
Authority: Res. of the House (44-1)
Terminated: February 29, 1876
H. rpt. 343 (44-1) 1709.

1396. Committee to Investigate the Third Degree Ordeal (Senate)
Established: April 30, 1910
45 CR 5600.
Authority: S. Res. 186 (61-2)
Terminated: August 4, 1911
S. rpt. 128 (62-1) 6077.

1397. Special Committee of Thirteen on the Disturbed Condition of the Country (Senate)
Established: December 18, 1860
S. J. (36-2): 49.
Authority: Res. of the Senate (36-2)
Terminated: December 31, 1860
S. rpt. 288 (36-2) 1090.

1398. Select Committee of Thirty Three on the Disturbed Condition of the Country (House)
Established: December 4, 1860
H. J. (36-2): 37.
Authority: Res. of the House (36-2)
Terminated: January 14, 1861
H. rpt. 31 (36-2) 1104.

1399. Select Committee to Inquire Into the Settlement of the Accounts of Quarter-Master James Thomas (House)
Established: March 6, 1816
H. J. (14-1): 465.
Authority: Res. of the House (14-1)
Terminated: April 24, 1816
Ibid. 701.

1400. Select Committee on the Memorial of Edward D. Tippett (Senate)
Established: February 24, 1838
S. J. (25-2): 311.
Authority: Res. of the Senate (25-2)
Terminated: July 9, 1838, at the end of the 25-2.

1401. Select Committee on High Duties on Tobacco (House)
Established: January 30, 1837
H. J. (24-2): 310.
Authority: Res. of the House (24-2)
Terminated: February 18, 1837
H. rpt. 239 (24-2) 306.

1402. Select Committee on Tobacco
Trade (House)
  Established: December 20, 1838
    H. J. (25-3): 117.
  Authority: Res. of the House
    (25-3)
  Terminated: July 21, 1840, at
    the end of the 26-1.

1403. Select Committee on Tobacco
Trade (House)
  Established: March 13, 1848
    H. J. (30-1): 539.
  ·Authority: Res. of the House
    (30-1)
  Terminated: July 25, 1848
    H. rpt. 810 (30-1) 527.

1404. Select Committee on the
Present Condition of the Tobacco
Trade (House)
  Established: March 23, 1860
    H. J. (36-1): 592.
  Authority: Res. of the House
    (36-1)
  Terminated: June 25, 1860
    H. rpt. 667 (36-1) 1070.

1405. Select Committee on the
Settlement of the Accounts of
Daniel D. Tompkins (House)
  Established: January 9, 1823
    H. J. (17-2): 113.
  Authority: Res. of the House
    (17-2)
  Terminated: February 8, 1823
    H. rpt. 88 (17-2) 87.

1406. Select Committee on the Cause
of Reduction of American Tonnage
(House)
  Sudocs: Y4. T61:
  Established: March 22, 1869
    Cong. Globe (41-1): 281.
  Authority: Res. of the House
    (41-1)
  Terminated: February 27, 1870
    H. rpt. 28 (41-2) 1436.

1407. Committee on Transportation
Routes to the Seaboard (Senate)
  Sudocs: Y4. T68:
  Established: March 19, 1879,
    having been preceded by a
    select committee (Entry 1408).
    Cong. Globe (42-3): 206.

Authority: Res. of the Senate
  (46-1)
Terminated: April 18, 1921
  61 CR 404-05.
Authority: S. Res. 43 (67 -
  Special)

1408. Select Committee on Trans-
portation Routes to the Seaboard
(Senate)
  Sudocs: Y4. T68:
  Established: December 16, 1872
    Cong. Globe (42-3): 206.
  Authority: Res. of the Senate
    (42-3)
  Terminated: March 19, 1879,
    when it was made a standing
    committee (Entry 1407).
    S. J. (46-1): 9.
  Authority: Res. of the Senate
    (46-1)

1409. Select Committee on Petition
of Trustees of Transylvania Univer-
sity (House)
  Established: March 2, 1830
    H. J. (21-1): 359.
  Authority: Res. of the House
    (21-1)
  Terminated: January 4, 1832
    H. rpt. 138 (22-1) 224.

1410. Select Committee to Endow
Transylvania University, Kentucky,
and Brown University, Rhode Island
(House)
  Established: December 22, 1832
    H. J. (22-2): 91.
  Authority: Res. of the House
    (22-2)
  Terminated: March 2, 1833, at
    the end of the 22-2.

1411. Select Committee on Alleged
Frauds in the Treasury Department
(House)
  Established: April 30, 1864
    H. J. (38-1): 597.
  Authority: Res. of the House
    (38-1)
  Terminated: June 30, 1864
    H. rpt. 140 (38-1) 1207.

1412. Select Committee to Reorganize the Treasury Department
(House)

Established: December 8, 1834
  H. J. (23-2): 46.
Authority: Res. of the House
  (23-2)
Terminated: March 3, 1835, at
  the end of the 23-2.

1413. Select Committee to Examine
the Management of the Treasury
Printing Bureau (Senate)
  Established: March 13, 1867
    Cong. Globe (40-1): 81.
  Authority: Res. of the Senate
    (40-1)
  Terminated: December 2, 1867,
    at the end of the 40-1.

1414. Select Committee to Investi-
gate the Books and Accounts of the
Treasury Department in Relation to
the Discrepancies and Alterations
of the Official Report (Senate)
  Established: November 19, 1877
    S. J. (45-1): 73.
  Authority: Res. of the Senate
    (45-1)
  Terminated: April 28, 1880
    S. rpt. 539 (46-2) 1897.

1415. Select Committee to Investi-
gate How and by Whom the Treaty of
Washington was Made Public (Senate)
  Established: May 12, 1871
    S. rpt. 5 (42-Sp) 1468.
  Authority: Res. of the Senate
    (42-Special)
  Terminated: May 25, 1871
    S. rpt. 5 (42-Sp) 1468.

1416. Select Committee on a Letter
and Representation from William
Eaton, Inclosing a Communication
from Hamet Bashow Carameli, ex-
Bashaw of Tripoli (House)
  Established: November 3, 1807
    H. J. (10-1): 31.
  Authority: Res. of the House
    (10-1)
  Terminated: December 18, 1807
    Ibid. 180.

1417. Select Committee on Purchas-
ing the Right to Use an Improved
Truss in the Army and Navy (House)
  Established: June 3, 1836
    H. J. (24-1): 926.

Authority: Res. of the House
  (24-1)
Terminated: July 4, 1836, at the
  end of the 24-1.

1418. Select Committee on Estab-
lishment of a Pension Office at
Tuscaloosa, Alabama (House)
  Established: January 17, 1838
    H. J. (25-2): 293.
  Authority: Res. of the House
    (25-2)
  Terminated: July 9, 1838, at the
    end of the 25-2.

1419. Committee on Un-American
Activities (House)
  Sudocs: Y4. Un1/2:
  Established: January 3, 1945,
    having been preceded by a
    select committee (Entry 1421).
    91 CR 91.
  Authority: H. Res. 5 (79-1)
  Terminated: February 18, 1969,
    when the name was changed to
    Committee on Internal Security
    (Entry 700).
    115 CR 3746.
  Authority: H. Res. 89 (91-1)

1420. Special Committee on Un-
American Activities (House)
  Sudocs: Y4. Un1:
  Established: March 20, 1934
    78 CR 4949.
  Authority: H. Res. 198 (73-2)
  Terminated: February 15, 1935
    H. rpt. 153 (74-1) 9890.

1421. Special Committee on Un-
American Activities (House)
  Sudocs: Y4. Un1/2:
  Established: May 26, 1938
    83 CR 7586.
  Authority: H. Res. 282 (75-3)
  Terminated: January 3, 1945,
    when it was made a standing
    committee (Entry 1419).
    91 CR 91.
  Authority: H. Res. 5 (79-1)

1422. Special Committee to Inves-
tigate Unemployment and Relief
(Senate)
  Sudocs: Y4. Un2/2:

Established: June 30, 1937
  81 CR 5515.
Authority: S. Res. 36 (75-1)
Terminated: January 16, 1939
  S. rpt. 2 (76-1) 10292.

1423. Committee on Unemployment
Insurance (Senate)
  Sudocs: Y4. Un2:
  Established: February 28, 1931
  74 CR 6451.
  Authority: S. Res. 483 (71-3)
  Terminated: 1932
  S. rpt. 964 (72-1) 9490.

1424. Special Committee on
Unemployment Problems (Senate)
  Sudocs: Y4. Un2/3:
  Established: September 12, 1959
  105 CR 19259.
  Authority: S. Res. 196 (86-1)
  Terminated: March 30, 1960
  S. rpt. 1206 (86-2) 12234.

1425. Select Committee on a
Transfer of Lands From the
United Brethren for Propagating
the Gospel Among the Heathen of
the U. S. (House)
  Established: March 26, 1824
  H. J. (18-1): 340.
  Authority: Res. of the House
  (18-1)
  Terminated: April 2, 1824
  H. rpt. 99 (18-1) 106.

1426. Committee on the Investi-
gation of the United States Steel
Corporation (House)
  Sudocs: Y4. Un3/2:
  Established: May 16, 1911
  47 CR 1234.
  Authority: H. Res. 148 (62-1)
  Terminated: August 2, 1912
  H. rpt. 1127 (62-2) 6138.

1427. Select Committee on a
National University (House)
  Established: December 10, 1810
  H. J. (11-3): 23.
  Authority: Res. of the House
  (11-3)
  Terminated: February 18, 1811
  Ibid. 274.

1428. Select Committee on a
National University (Senate)
  Established: December 10, 1810
  S. J. (14-2): 46.
  Authority: Res. of the Senate
  (14-2)
  Terminated: March 3, 1817, at
  the end of the 14-2.

1429. Select Committee on Estab-
lishing a National University
(House)
  Established: December 6, 1815
  H. J. (14-1): 25.
  Authority: Res. of the House
  (14-1)
  Terminated: March 30, 1818
  H. J. (15-1): 396.

1430. Committee to Establish a
University of the United States
(Senate)
  Sudocs: Y4. Un3/1:
  Established: March 19, 1896,
  having been preceded by a
  select committee (Entry 1431).
  28 CR 2960.
  Authority: Res. of the Senate
  (54-1)
  Terminated: April 18, 1921
  61 CR 404-05.
  Authority: S. Res. 43 (65 -
  Special)

1431. Select Committee to Estab-
lish the University of the United
States (Senate)
  Sudocs: Y4. Un3/1:
  Established: June 2, 1890
  S. J. (51-1): 339.
  Authority: Order of the Senate
  (51-1)
  Terminated: March 19, 1896, when
  it was made a standing commit-
  tee (Entry 1430).
  28 CR 2960.
  Authority: Res. of the Senate
  (54-1)

1432. Select Committee on the Sub-
ject of Unsettled Balances (House)
  Established: February 27, 1816
  H. J. (14-1): 408.
  Authority: Res. of the House
  (14-1)

Terminated: April 24, 1816
  Ibid. 701.

1433. Select Committee on
Vaccination (House)
  Established: December 13, 1825
  H. J. (19-1): 322.
  Authority: Res. of the House
    (19-1)
  Terminated: March 1, 1827
  H. rpt. 95 (19-2) 160.

1434. Select Committee on
Vaccination (Senate)
  Established: January 22, 1828
  S. J. (20-1): 110.
  Authority: Res. of the Senate
    (20-1)
  Terminated: February 21, 1828
  Ibid. 178.

1435. Select Committee on Modifying
the Act to Encourage Vaccination
(House)
  Established: February 6, 1822
  H. J. (17-1): 240.
  Authority: Res. of the House
    (17-1)
  Terminated: April 13, 1822
  H. rpt. 93 (17-1) 71.

1436. Select Committee on the
Petition of the National Vaccine
Institute (House)
  Established: January 5, 1820
  H. J. (16-1): 106.
  Authority: Res. of the House
    (16-1)
  Terminated: January 10, 1820
  Ibid. 119.

1437. Committee on Veterans Affairs
(House)
  Sudocs: Y4. V64/3:
  Established: January 2, 1947,
    when the functions of several
    committees were transferred to
    this.
      60 Stat. 812.
  Authority: PL 79-601
  Terminated: Still in existence at
    the end of the 97-2.

1438. Committee on Veterans Affairs
(Senate)
  Sudocs: Y4. V64/4:

Established: October 26, 1970
  84 Stat. 1164.
Authority: PL 91-510
Terminated: Still in existence at
  the end of the 97-2.

1439. Committee on Veterans'
Affairs (Joint)
  Sudocs: Y4. V64/2:
  Established: June 30, 1932
    47 Stat. 419.
  Authority: PL 72-212
  Terminated: May 26, 1933
  S. doc. 63 (73-1) 9748.

1440. Select Committee on Veterans
Bureau Investigation (Senate)
  Sudocs: Y4. V64:
  Established: March 2, 1923
    64 CR 5102.
  Authority: S. Res. 466 (67-4)
  Terminated: March 3, 1925, at
    the end of the 68-2.

1441. Select Committee to Inves-
tigate Veteran's Education and
Training Program (House)
  Established: August 28, 1950
    96 CR 13632.
  Authority: H. Res. 474 (81-2)
  Terminated: January 2, 1951
  H. rpt. 3253 (81-2) 11385.

1442. Select Committee on Opening
a Road from Vincennes to Dayton
(House)
  Established: January 4, 1811
  H. J. (11-3): 98.
  Authority: Res. of the House
    (11-3)
  Terminated: January 17, 1811
  Ibid. 129.

1443. Select Committee on the
Extension of a Road from Vincennes
to Dearborn County, Indiana Terri-
tory (House)
  Established: December 19, 1810
  H. J. (11-3): 55.
  Authority: Res. of the House
    (11-3)
  Terminated: December 31, 1810
  Ibid. 87.

1444. Special Committee on Investigation of Administration of

Government of the Virgin Islands
(Senate)
  Established: April 1, 1935
    79 CR 4728.
  Authority: S. Res. 98 (74-1)
  Terminated: January 20, 1936,
    at the end of the 74-2.

1445. Select Committee on the
Defense of the Eastern Frontier
of Virginia (House)
  Established: February 29, 1808
    H. J. (10-1): 424.
  Authority: Res. of the House
    (10-1)
  Terminated: April 25, 1808, at
    the end of the 10-1.

1446. Select Committee on Paying
Virginia Claims (House)
  Established: January 24, 1839
    H. J. (25-3): 370.
  Authority: Res. of the House
    (25-3)
  Terminated: March 3, 1839, at
    the end of the 25-3.

1447. Select Committee on Giving
Further Time for Locating Virginia
Land Warrants (House)
  Established: December 30, 1816
    H. J. (14-2): 120.
  Authority: Res. of the House
    (14-2)
  Terminated: January 4, 1817
    Ibid. 137.

1448. Select Committee on Repealing
the Law Locating Virginia Land
Warrants and Returning Surveys
(House)
  Established: January 14, 1839
    H. J. (25-3): 283.
  Authority: Res. of the House
    (25-3)
  Terminated: March 3, 1839, at
    the end of the 25-3.

1449. Select Committee on Entries
in Virginia Military District in
Ohio (House)
  Established: January 18, 1859
    H. J. (35-2): 209.
  Authority: Res. of the House
    (35-2)

Terminated: March 3, 1859, at
  the end of the 35-2.

1450. Select Committee on Selling
Virginia Military District Land in
Ohio (House)
  Established: March 5, 1837
    H. J. (25-2): 532.
  Authority: Res. of the House
    (25-2)
  Terminated: July 9, 1838, at
    the end of the 25-2.

1451. Select Committee on Fines
Imposed on Virginia Militia (House)
  Established: January 27, 1823
    H. J. (17-2): 162.
  Authority: Res. of the House
    (17-2)
  Terminated: March 3, 1823, at
    the end of the 17-2.

1452. Select Committee on Virginia
Resolutions (House)
  Established: March 6, 1844
    H. J. (28-1): 531.
  Authority: Res. of the House
    (28-1)
  Terminated: June 17, 1844, at
    the end of the 28-1.

1453. Select Committee on Raising
and Organizing Volunteer Troops
for the U. S. (House)
  Established: February 18, 1808
    H. J. (10-1): 387.
  Authority: Res. of the House
    (10-1)
  Terminated: April 25, 1808, at
    the end of the 10-1.

1454. Select Committee on Alleged
Fraudulent Registration and Fraud-
ulent Voting in the Cities of New
York, Philadelphia, Brooklyn, and
Jersey City (House)
  Established: December 11, 1876
    H. J. (44-2): 62.
  Authority: Res. of the House
    (44-2)
  Terminated: March 3, 1877
    H. rpt. 218 (44-2) 1770.

1455. Select Committee on Grant
of Land for Wabash and Erie Canal
(House)

Established: April 10, 1844
    H. J. (28-1): 757.
Authority: Res. of the House
    (28-1)
Terminated: June 7, 1844
    H. rpt. 544 (28-1) 447.

1456. Select Committee to Investigate Wages and Prices of Commodi-
ties (Senate)
    Sudocs: Y4. W12:
    Established: February 9, 1910
        45 CR 1638.
    Authority: S. Res. 165 (61-2)
    Terminated: June 23, 1910
        S. rpt. 912 (61-2) 5584.

1457. Committee on Conduct of the
War (Joint)
    Sudocs: Y4. C75:
    Established: December 10, 1861
        Cong. Globe (37-2): 40.
    Authority: Con. Res. of the
        Senate (37-2)
    Terminated: June 20, 1866
        S. rpt. (39-1) 1242. (no report
        number given)

1458. Committee on War Claims
(House)
    Sudocs: Y4. W19:
    Established: December 2, 1873,
        when the name of the Committee
        on Revolutionary Claims was
        changed to this (Entry 1217).
        1 CR 23.
    Authority: Res. of the House
        (43-1)
    Terminated: January 2, 1947,
        when its functions were trans-
        ferred to the Judiciary Commit-
        tee (Entry 731).
        60 Stat. 812.
    Authority: PL 79-601

1459. Select Committee to Investigate Certain Loans Made by the War
Finance Corporation (Senate)
    Established: June 7, 1924
        65 CR 11127.
    Authority: S. Res. 208 (68-1)
    Terminated: March 9, 1925
        S. rpt. 1 (69-Special) 8527.

1460. Select Committee on the
Spirit and Manner in Which the War

has Been Waged by the Enemy (House)
    Established: May 26, 1813
        H. J. (13-1): 19.
    Authority: Res. of the House
        (13-1)
    Terminated: July 31, 1813
        Ibid. 309.

1461. Select Committee on Construction of a War Steamer on Lake Erie
(House)
    Established: February 24, 1842
        H. J. (27-2): 1006.
    Authority: Res. of the House
        (27-2)
    Terminated: August 2, 1842
        Ibid. 1202.

1462. Select Committee on Bill to
Remove the Building over Statue of
Washington (House)
    Established: May 25, 1844
        H. J. (28-1): 969.
    Authority: Res. of the House
        (28-1)
    Terminated: June 17, 1844, at
        the end of the 28-1.

1463. Select Committee on the
Capture of the City of Washington
(House)
    Established: September 22, 1814
        H. J. (13-3): 19.
    Authority: Res. of the House
        (13-3)
    Terminated: March 3, 1815, at
        the end of the 13-3.

1464. Select Committee on Modifying
the Charter of the City of Washington June 5, 1840 (Senate)
    Established: June 5, 1840
        S. J. (26-1): 409.
    Authority: Res. of the Senate
        (26-1)
    Terminated: July 21, 1840, at
        the end of the 26-1.

1465. Select Committee on Entomb-
ment of General Washington (House)
    Established: February 22, 1830
        H. J. (21-1): 327.
    Authority: Res. of the House
        (21-1)
    Terminated: March 15, 1830
        H. rpt. 318 (21-1) 201.

1466. Select Committee on Publi-
cation of the Works of General
Washington (House)
   Established: February 9, 1835
     H. J. (23-2): 347.
   Authority: Res. of the House
     (23-2)
   Terminated: February 16, 1835
     Ibid. 398.

1467. Select Committee to Inves-
tigate the Work on the Washington
Aqueduct Tunnel (Joint)
   Established: October 9, 1888
     S. J. (50-1): 1526.
   Authority: Con. Res. of the
     House (50-1)
   Terminated: February 26, 1889
     S. rpt. 2686 (50-2) 2620.

1468. Select Committee on Washing-
ton City Centennial (House)
   Established: December 12, 1899
     33 CR 279.
   Authority: H. Res. 28 (56-1)
   Terminated: December 12, 1900
     H. doc. 552 (56-2) 4207.

1469. Select Committee on the
Washington City Centennial (Senate)
   Established: December 7, 1898
     32 CR 29.
   Authority: Res. of the Senate
     (55-3)
   Terminated: December 12, 1900
     H. doc. 552 (56-2) 4207.

1470. Select Committee on Sales of
Public Lots in Washington, D. C.
(House)
   Established: December 18, 1822
     H. J. (17-2): 58.
   Authority: Res. of the House
     (17-2)
   Terminated: February 28, 1825
     H. rpt. 90 (18-2) 123.

1471. Committee on Washington
Metropolitan Problems (Joint)
   Sudocs: Y4. W27/2:
   Established: August 29, 1957
     71 Stat. B50.
   Authority: H. Con. Res. 172
     (85-1)
   Terminated: August 23, 1960
     S. rpt. 1903 (86-2) 12238.

1472. Select Committee on the
Washington Monument (House)
   Established: December 7, 1825
     H. J. (19-1): 30.
   Authority: Res. of the House
     (19-1)
   Terminated: January 16, 1826
     Ibid. 196.

1473. Select Committee on the
Washington Monument (House)
   Established: January 27, 1873
     Cong. Globe (42-3): 891.
   Authority: Res. of the House
     (42-3)
   Terminated: February 22, 1873
     H. rpt. 79 (42-3) 1576.

1474. Select Committee on the
Completion of the Washington
Monument (House)
   Established: January 12, 1874
     H. J. (43-1): 224.
   Authority: Res. of the House
     (43-1)
   Terminated: May 1, 1874
     H. rpt. 485 (43-1) 1625.

1475. Select Committee on the
Washington National Monument
(House)
   Established: July 13, 1854
     Cong. Globe (33-1): 1711.
   Authority: Res. of the House
     (33-1)
   Terminated: February 22, 1855
     H. rpt. 94 (33-2) 808.

1476. Special Committee to Inves-
tigate Washington Railway and
Electrical Company (Senate)
   Sudocs: Y4. W27:
   Established: April 16, 1917
     55 CR 714.
   Authority: S. Res. 23 (65-1)
   Terminated: October 6, 1917
     S. rpt. 176 (65-1) 7251.

1477. Committee for Making Arrange-
ments for Inaugurating Washington's
Statue (Joint)
   Established: February 16, 1860
     H. J. (36-1): 320.
   Authority: H. J. Res. 8 (36-1)
   Terminated: June 25, 1860, at
     the end of the 36-1.

1478. Select Committee to Open an Inland Water Communication from the Chesapeake to St. Mary's, in Georgia (House)
Established: March 1, 1814
H. J. (13-2): 373.
Authority: Res. of the House (13-2)
Terminated: March 14, 1814
Ibid. 428.

1479. Committee on Water Power (House)
Sudocs: Y4. W29:
Established: January 11, 1918
56 CR 851.
Authority: H. Res. 220 (65-2)
Terminated: March 3, 1921, at the end of the 66th Congress.

1480. Select Committee on Watson's Charges (House)
Established: July 29, 1892
23 CR 6944.
Authority: Res. of the House (52-1)
Terminated: August 5, 1892
H. rpt. 2132 (52-1) 3051.

1481. Committee on Ways and Means (House)
Sudocs: Y4. W36:
Established: January 7, 1802, having been preceded by a select committee (Entry 1482).
Annals, (7-1): 697.
Authority: Res. of the House (7-1)
Terminated: Still in existence at the end of the 97-2.

1482. Select Committee on Ways and Means (House)
Sudocs: Y4. W36:
Established: July 24, 1789
Annals, (1-1): 697.
Authority: Res. of the House (1-1)
Terminated: January 7, 1802, when it was made a standing committee (Entry 1481).
Annals, (7-1): 412.
Authority: Res. of the House (7-1)

1483. Select Committee on Charges Against Daniel Webster (House)
Established: April 27, 1846
H. J. (29-1): 727.
Authority: Res. of the House (29-1)
Terminated: June 9, 1846
H. rpt. 684 (29-1) 490.

1484. Select Committee on Weights and Measures (House)
Established: December 4, 1816
H. J. (14-2): 25.
Authority: Res. of the House (14-2)
Terminated: March 3, 1817
Ibid. 558.

1485. Select Committee on Weights and Measures (House)
Established: January 7, 1808
H. J. (10-1): 113.
Authority: Res. of the House (10-1)
Terminated: April 25, 1808, at the end of the 10-1.

1486. Select Committee on Weights and Measures (House)
Established: December 26, 1821
H. J. (17-1): 90.
Authority: Res. of the House (17-1)
Terminated: March 11, 1822
H. rpt. 44 (17-2) 86.

1487. Select Committee on Weights and Measures (Senate)
Established: December 10, 1816
S. J. (14-2): 45.
Authority: Res. of the Senate (14-2)
Terminated: March 3, 1817, at the end of the 14-2.

1488. Select Committee on Memorial of Auctioneers, Commission Merchants, etc. of Philadelphia on Weights and Measures (House)
Established: February 2, 1835
H. J. (23-2): 310.
Authority: Res. of the House (23-2)
Terminated: February 27, 1835
H. rpt. 132 (23-2) 276.

1489. Select Committee on the
Annexation of West Florida to the
Mississippi Territory (House)
  Established: April 28, 1812
    H. J. (12-1): 644.
  Authority: Res. of the House
    (12-1)
  Terminated: May 1, 1812
    Ibid. 660.

1490. Select Committee on the
Military Academy at West Point
(House)
  Established: March 18, 1808
    H. J. (10-1): 499.
  Authority: Res. of the House
    (10-1)
  Terminated: February 27, 1810
    H. J. (11-2): 292.

1491. Select Committee on West
Point Academy (House)
  Established: December 8, 1834
    H. J. (23-2): 46.
  Authority: Res. of the House
    (23-2)
  Terminated: March 1, 1837
    H. rpt. 303 (24-2) 306.

1492. Select Committee to Further
Exploring the Western Waters
(House)
  Established: December 2, 1806
    H. J. (9-2): 13.
  Authority: Res. of the House
    (9-2)
  Terminated: December 22, 1806
    Ibid. 70.

1493. Select Committee on Breach
of Privilege, Assault, Wheeler vs.
Codd (House)
  Established: June 11, 1836
    H. J. (24-1): 985.
  Authority: Res. of the House
    (24-1)
  Terminated: June 14, 1836
    H. rpt. 762 (24-1) 295.

1494. Select Committee on Investi-
gation of Charges Against Burton K.
Wheeler (Senate)
  Sudocs: Y4. W56:
  Established: April 9, 1924
    65 CR 5949.
  Authority: S. Res. 206 (68-1)

Terminated: May 19, 1924
  S. rpt. 537 (68-1) 8223.

1495. Select Committee on Whiskey
Trials in Saint Louis (House)
  Established: March 6, 1876
    H. J. (44-1): 521.
  Authority: Res. of the House
    (44-1)
  Terminated: July 25, 1876
    H. misdoc. 186 (44-1) 1706.

1496. Select Committee to Conduct
an Investigation and Study of
Financial Position of White County
Bridge Commission (House)
  Sudocs: Y4. W58:
  Established: May 25, 1955
    101 CR 7043.
  Authority: H. Res. 244 (84-1)
  Terminated: April 25, 1956
    H. rpt. 2052 (84-2) 11898.

1497. Select Committee on a Report
of the Post-Master General on the
Petition of Samuel Whiting (House)
  Established: January 9, 1808
    H. J. (10-1): 245.
  Authority: Res. of the House
    (10-1)
  Terminated: February 3, 1808
    Ibid. 333.

1498. Select Committee on Petition
of Children of Eli Whitney (House)
  Established: January 31, 1848
    H. J. (30-1): 322.
  Authority: Res. of the House
    (30-1)
  Terminated: August 14, 1848, at
    the end of the 30-1.

1499. Select Committee to Make
Further Provision for Widows and
Orphans of Volunteers and Militia
(House)
  Established: December 13, 1815
    H. J. (14-1): 50.
  Authority: Res. of the House
    (14-1)
  Terminated: January 3, 1816
    Ibid. 122.

1500. Special Committee on Wildlife
Resources (Senate)
  Sudocs: Y4. W64:

Established: April 17, 1930
  72 CR 7209.
Authority: S. Res. 246 (71-2)
Terminated: January 21, 1931
  S. rpt. 1329 (71-3) 9324.

1501. Select Committee on Con-
servation of Wildlife Resources
(House)
  Sudocs: Y4. W64/2:
  Established: January 29, 1834
    78 CR 1505.
  Authority: H. Res. 237 (73-2)
  Terminated: August 2, 1946, at
    the end of the 79-2.

1502. Select Committee on Purchase
of Property at Wilkins' Point, New
York for Fortification Purposes
(House)
  Established: February 9, 1858
    H. J. (35-1): 359.
  Authority: Res. of the House
    (35-1)
  Terminated: June 8, 1858
    H. rpt. 549 (35-1) 968.

1503. Select Committee to Inquire
into the Conduct of General James
Wilkinson (House)
  Established: April 4, 1810
    H. J. (11-2): 491.
  Authority: Res. of the House
    (11-2)
  Terminated: May 1, 1810
    Ibid. 641.

1504. Select Committee on Monument
to David Williams, one of the
Captors of André (House)
  Established: April 25, 1836
    H. J. (24-1): 754.
  Authority: Res. of the House
    (24-1)
  Terminated: January 18, 1838
    H. rpt. 428 (25-2) 334.

1505. Select Committee to Investi-
gate Certain Statements Made by
Dr. Wm. A. Wirt (House)
  Sudocs: Y4. W74:
  Established: March 29, 1934
    78 CR 5818.
  Authority: H. Res. 317 (73-2)
  Terminated: May 2, 1934
    H. rpt. 1439 (73-2) 9782.

1506. Committee on Woman Suffrage
(House)
  Established: September 24, 1917
    55 CR 7385.
  Authority: H. Res. 12 (65-1)
  Terminated: December 5, 1927
    69 CR 14.
  Authority: H. Res. 7 (70-1)

1507. Select Committee on Woman
Suffrage (House)
  Established: February 25, 1882
    13 CR 1448.
  Authority: Res. of the House
    (47-1)
  Terminated: March 3, 1883, at
    the end of the 47-2.

1508. Select Committee on Woman
Suffrage (Senate)
  Sudocs: Y4. W84:
  Established: January 9, 1882
    S. J. (47-1): 162.
  Authority: Res. of the Senate
    (47-1)
  Terminated: April 18, 1921
    61 CR 404-05.
  Authority: S. Res. 43 (67 -
    Special)

1509. Special Committee to Investi-
gate Production, Transportation and
Marketing of Wool (Senate)
  Sudocs: Y4. W88:
  Established: July 10, 1935
    79 CR 10944.
  Authority: S. Res. 160 (74-1)
  Terminated: May 29, 1946
    S. rpt. 1398 (79-2) 11016.

1510. Committee on World War
Veterans Legislation (House)
  Sudocs: Y4. W89:
  Established: January 14, 1924
    H. J. (68-1): 162.
  Authority: H. Res. 146 (68-1)
  Terminated: January 2, 1947
    60 Stat. 812.
  Authority: PL 79-601

1511. Select Committee on the
World's Fair (House)
  Established: January 16, 1890
    21 CR 650.
  Authority: Res. of the House
    (51-1)

Terminated: March 3, 1891, at
the end of the 51-2. Replaced
by Select Committee on Columbian Exposition.

1512. Select Committee on Memorial
of William Wright Against the
Commonwealth Bank of Boston (House)
Established: December 23, 1841
H. J. (27-2): 93.
Authority: Res. of the House
(27-2)
Terminated: August 20, 1842
Ibid. 1374.

1513. Select Committee on Charges
Against Judge Wylie (House)
Established: May 13, 1876
H. J. (44-1): 947.
Authority: Res. of the House
(44-1)
Terminated: August 15, 1876, at
the end of the 44-1.

1514. Select Committee on the Yazoo
Claimants (House)
Established: March 9, 1814
H. J. (13-2): 414.
Authority: Res. of the House
(13-2)
Terminated: January 7, 1815
H. J. (13-3): 483.

1515. Select Committee on Erecting
Marble Columns at York, Virginia
(House)
Established: December 23, 1848
H. J. (30-2): 147.
Authority: Res. of the House
(30-2)
Terminated: March 3, 1849, at
the end of the 30-2.

1516. Select Committee on Memorial
from Yorktown, Virginia for Monu-
ment on Battle Ground (House)
Established: May 13, 1834
H. J. (23-1): 620.
Authority: Res. of the House
(23-1)
Terminated: January 5, 1836
H. rpt. 82 (24-1) 293.

PART II

BIBLIOGRAPHY

Books:

Andriot, John L. Guide to U. S. Government Publications. 2 vols.
McLean, Va.: Documents Index, 1980.

Baker, Richard A. The United States Senate: A Historical Bibliography.
Washington: Government Printing Office, 1977.

Checklist of United States Public Documents, 1789-1909. Washington:
Government Printing Office, 1911.

Congressional Globe, 23rd-42nd Congress, 1833-1873.

Congressional Record, 43rd-97th Congress, 1873-1982.

Davidson, Roger N. and Oleszek, Walter J. Congress Against Itself.
Bloomington: Indiana University Press, 1977.

Debates and Proceedings in the Congress of the United States (commonly
cited as Annals of Congress), 1st-22nd Congress, 1789-1833.

Deschler, Lewis. Deschler's Precedents of the House of Representatives
Including References to Provisions of the Constitution and Laws, and
to Decisions of the Courts. House Document 661, 94th Congress, 2nd
sess., 1976--. 7 vols.

Goldman, Perry M. and Young, James S., eds. The United States
Congressional Directories, 1789-1840. New York: Columbia University
Press, 1973.

Harlow, Ralph Volney. The History of the Legislative Methods in the
Period Before 1825. New Haven: Yale University Press, 1917.

Hinds, Asher Crosby and Cannon, Clarence. Hinds' Precedents of the
House of Representatives of the United States Including References to
Provisions of the Constitution, the Laws, and Decisions of the United
States Senate. 11 vols. Washington: Government Printing Office,
1907-1941.

Riddick, Floyd Millard. The United States Congress; Organization and Procedure. Manassas, Va.: National Capital Publishers, 1949.

U. S. Congress. Congressional Commissions, Committees, etc., Alphabetical List Showing Commissions and Select, Special, Joint and Standing Committees. 79th Congress, 1st session, 1945.

U. S. Congress. House. Journal of the House of Representatives of the United States. 1st-96th Congress, 1789-1980.

U. S. Congress. Joint Committee on Congressional Operations. Abolish the Joint Committee on Congressional Operations. S. Rept. 316, 95th Cong., 1st sess., 1977.

U. S. Congress. Joint Committee on the Organization of Congress. Organization of Congress. Hearings before the Committee pursuant to H. Con. Res. 18, 79th Cong., 1st sess., 1945.

U. S. Congress. Joint Committee on the Organization of Congress. Organization of Congress. Hearings pursuant to S. Con. Res. 2, 89th Cong., 1st sess., 1965.

U. S. Congress. Senate. Committee on Armed Services. Establish a Senate Select Committee on Intelligence. Hearings to Consider S. Res. 400, 94th Cong., 2nd sess., 1976.

U. S. Congress. Senate. Committee on Rules and Administration. Committee System Reorganization Amendments of 1977. Hearings to Consider S. Res. 4, 95th Cong., 1st sess., 1977.

U. S. Congress. Senate. Committee on Finance. History of the Committee on Finance. S. Doc. 27, 95th Cong., 1st sess., 1877.

U. S. Congress. Senate. Committee on Rules and Administration. Legislative Authority for the Select Committee on Small Business. Proposed Select Committee on Committees. Hearings before the Committee, 94th Cong., 2nd sess., 1976.

U. S. Congress. Senate. Committee on Rules and Administration. Proposed Standing Committee on Intelligence Activities. Hearings to Consider S. Res. 400, 94th Cong., 2nd sess., 1976.

U. S. Congress. Senate. Journal of the Executive Proceedings of the Senate of the United States of America. 27th Congress, 2nd session-28th Congress, 2nd session, December 6, 1841-March 20, 1845.

U. S. Congress. Senate. Journal of the Senate of the United States. 1st-96th Congress, 1789-1980.

U. S. Congress. Senate. Special Committee on the Organization of Congress. Amendments made to the Legislative Reorganization Act of 1946 by S. 355. Committee Print, Washington: Government Printing Office, 1967.

U. S. Congress. Senate. Special Committee on the Organization of Congress. Legislative Reorganization Act of 1946. A Report to Accompany S. 2177. S. Rept. 1400, 79th Cong., 2nd sess., 1947.

U. S. Congress. Senate. Temporary Select Committee to Study the Senate Committee System. First Report with Recommendations of the Committee. S. Rept. 1395, 94th Cong., 2nd sess., 1976.

U. S. Congress. Senate. Temporary Select Committee to Study the Senate Committee System. Senate Committee System. Committee Print, Washington: Government Printing Office, 1976.

U. S. Congress. Senate. Temporary Select Committee to Study the Senate Committee System. Senate Committee System. Hearings before the Committee on S. 586, 94th Cong., 2nd sess., 1976.

Article:

Gould, James W. "The Origins of the Senate Committee on Foreign Relations," Western Political Quarterly 12 (September 1959): 670-682.

DATES OF CONGRESSIONAL SESSIONS

Congress	Session	Date of Beginning	Date of Adjournment
1st	1	Mar. 4, 1789	Sept. 29, 1789
	2	Jan. 4, 1790	Aug. 12, 1790
	3	Dec. 6, 1790	Mar. 3, 1791
2d	1	Oct. 24, 1791	May 8, 1792
	2	Nov. 5, 1792	Mar. 2, 1793
3d	1	Dec. 2, 1793	Jun. 9, 1794
	2	Nov. 3, 1794	Mar. 3, 1795
4th	1	Dec. 7, 1795	Jun. 1, 1796
	2	Dec. 5, 1796	Mar. 3, 1797
5th	1	May 15, 1797	Jul. 10, 1797
	2	Nov. 13, 1797	Jul. 16, 1798
	3	Dec. 3, 1798	Mar. 3, 1799
6th	1	Dec. 2, 1799	May 14, 1800
	2	Nov. 17, 1800	Mar. 3, 1801
7th	1	Dec. 7, 1801	May 3, 1802
	2	Dec. 6, 1802	Mar. 3, 1803
8th	1	Oct. 17, 1803	Mar. 27, 1804
	2	Nov. 5, 1804	Mar. 3, 1805
9th	1	Dec. 2, 1805	Apr. 21, 1806
	2	Dec. 1, 1806	Mar. 3, 1807
10th	1	Oct. 26, 1807	Apr. 25, 1808
	2	Nov. 7, 1808	Mar. 3, 1809
11th	1	May 22, 1809	Jun. 28, 1809
	2	Nov. 27, 1809	May 1, 1810
	3	Dec. 3, 1810	Mar. 3, 1811

Congress	Session	Date of Beginning	Date of Adjournment
12th	1	Nov. 4, 1811	Jul. 6, 1812
	2	Nov. 2, 1812	Mar. 3, 1813
13th	1	May 24, 1813	Aug. 2, 1813
	2	Dec. 6, 1813	Apr. 18, 1814
	3	Sept. 19, 1814	Mar. 3, 1815
14th	1	Dec. 4, 1815	Apr. 30, 1816
	2	Dec. 2, 1816	Mar. 3, 1817
15th	1	Dec. 1, 1817	Apr. 20, 1818
	2	Nov. 16, 1818	Mar. 3, 1819
16th	1	Dec. 6, 1819	May 15, 1820
	2	Nov. 13, 1820	Mar. 3, 1821
17th	1	Dec. 3, 1821	May 8, 1822
	2	Dec. 2, 1822	Mar. 3, 1823
18th	1	Dec. 1, 1823	May 27, 1824
	2	Dec. 6, 1824	Mar. 3, 1825
19th	1	Dec. 5, 1825	May 22, 1826
	2	Dec. 4, 1826	Mar. 3, 1827
20th	1	Dec. 3, 1827	May 26, 1828
	2	Dec. 1, 1828	Mar. 3, 1829
21st	1	Dec. 7, 1829	May 31, 1830
	2	Dec. 6, 1830	Mar. 3, 1831
22d	1	Dec. 5, 1831	Jul. 16, 1832
	2	Dec. 3, 1832	Mar. 2, 1833
23d	1	Dec. 2, 1833	Jun. 30, 1834
	2	Dec. 1, 1834	Mar. 3, 1835
24th	1	Dec. 7, 1835	Jul. 4, 1836
	2	Dec. 5, 1836	Mar. 3, 1837
25th	1	Sept. 4, 1837	Oct. 16, 1837
	2	Dec. 4, 1837	Jul. 9, 1838
	3	Dec. 3, 1838	Mar. 3, 1839
26th	1	Dec. 2, 1839	Jul. 21, 1840
	2	Dec. 7, 1840	Mar. 3, 1841
27th	1	May 31, 1841	Sept. 13, 1841
	2	Dec. 6, 1841	Aug. 31, 1842
	3	Dec. 5, 1842	Mar. 3, 1843

Congress	Session	Date of Beginning	Date of Adjournment
28th	1	Dec. 4, 1843	Jun. 17, 1844
	2	Dec. 2, 1844	Mar. 3, 1845
29th	1	Dec. 1, 1845	Aug. 10, 1846
	2	Dec. 7, 1846	Mar. 3, 1847
30th	1	Dec. 6, 1847	Aug. 14, 1848
	2	Dec. 4, 1848	Mar. 3, 1849
31st	1	Dec. 3, 1849	Sept. 30, 1850
	2	Dec. 2, 1850	Mar. 3, 1851
32d	1	Dec. 1, 1851	Aug. 31, 1852
	2	Dec. 6, 1852	Mar. 3, 1853
33d	1	Dec. 5, 1853	Aug. 7, 1854
	2	Dec. 4, 1854	Mar. 3, 1855
34th	1	Dec. 3, 1855	Aug. 18, 1856
	2	Aug. 21, 1856	Aug. 30, 1856
	3	Dec. 1, 1856	Mar. 3, 1857
35th	1	Dec. 7, 1857	Jun. 14, 1858
	2	Dec. 6, 1858	Mar. 3, 1859
36th	1	Dec. 5, 1859	Jun. 25, 1860
	2	Dec. 3, 1860	Mar. 28, 1861
37th	1	Jul. 4, 1861	Aug. 6, 1861
	2	Dec. 2, 1861	Jul. 17, 1862
	3	Dec. 1, 1862	Mar. 3, 1863
38th	1	Dec. 7, 1863	Jul. 4, 1864
	2	Dec. 5, 1864	Mar. 3, 1865
39th	1	Dec. 4, 1865	Jul. 28, 1866
	2	Dec. 3, 1866	Mar. 3, 1867
40th	1	Mar. 4, 1867	Dec. 2, 1867
	2	Dec. 2, 1867	Nov. 10, 1868
	3	Dec. 7, 1868	Mar. 3, 1869
41st	1	Mar. 4, 1869	Apr. 10, 1869
	2	Dec. 6, 1869	Jul. 15, 1870
	3	Dec. 5, 1870	Mar. 3, 1871
42d	1	Mar. 4, 1871	Apr. 20, 1871
	2	Dec. 4, 1871	Jun. 10, 1872
	3	Dec. 2, 1872	Mar. 3, 1873
43d	1	Dec. 1, 1873	Jun. 23, 1874
	2	Dec. 7, 1874	Mar. 3, 1875

Congress	Session	Date of Beginning	Date of Adjournment
44th	1	Dec. 6, 1875	Aug. 15, 1876
	2	Dec. 4, 1876	Mar. 3, 1877
45th	1	Oct. 15, 1877	Dec. 3, 1877
	2	Dec. 3, 1877	Jun. 20, 1878
	3	Dec. 2, 1878	Mar. 3, 1879
46th	1	Mar. 18, 1879	Jul. 1, 1879
	2	Dec. 1, 1879	Jun. 16, 1880
	3	Dec. 6, 1880	Mar. 3, 1881
47th	1	Dec. 5, 1881	Aug. 8, 1882
	2	Dec. 4, 1882	Mar. 3, 1883
48th	1	Dec. 3, 1883	Jul. 7, 1884
	2	Dec. 1, 1884	Mar. 3, 1885
49th	1	Dec. 7, 1885	Aug. 5, 1886
	2	Dec. 6, 1886	Mar. 3, 1887
50th	1	Dec. 5, 1887	Oct. 20, 1888
	2	Dec. 3, 1888	Mar. 3, 1889
51st	1	Dec. 2, 1889	Oct. 1, 1890
	2	Dec. 1, 1890	Mar. 3, 1891
52d	1	Dec. 7, 1891	Aug. 5, 1892
	2	Dec. 5, 1892	Mar. 3, 1893
53d	1	Aug. 7, 1893	Nov. 3, 1893
	2	Dec. 4, 1893	Aug. 28, 1894
	3	Dec. 3, 1894	Mar. 3, 1895
54th	1	Dec. 2, 1895	Jun. 11, 1896
	2	Dec. 7, 1896	Mar. 3, 1897
55th	1	Mar. 15, 1897	Jul. 24, 1897
	2	Dec. 6, 1897	Jul. 8, 1898
	3	Dec. 5, 1898	Mar. 3, 1899
56th	1	Dec. 4, 1899	Jun. 7, 1900
	2	Dec. 3, 1900	Mar. 3, 1901
57th	1	Dec. 2, 1901	Jul. 1, 1902
	2	Dec. 1, 1902	Mar. 3, 1903
58th	1	Nov. 9, 1903	Dec. 7, 1903
	2	Dec. 7, 1903	Apr. 28, 1904
	3	Dec. 5, 1904	Mar. 3, 1905
59th	1	Dec. 4, 1905	Jun. 30, 1906
	2	Dec. 3, 1906	Mar. 3, 1907

Congress	Session	Date of Beginning	Date of Adjournment
60th	1	Dec. 2, 1907	May 30, 1908
	2	Dec. 7, 1908	Mar. 3, 1909
61th	1	Mar. 15, 1909	Aug. 5, 1909
	2	Dec. 6, 1909	Jun. 25, 1910
	3	Dec. 5, 1910	Mar. 3, 1911
62d	1	Apr. 4, 1911	Aug. 22, 1911
	2	Dec. 4, 1911	Aug. 26, 1912
	3	Dec. 2, 1912	Mar. 3, 1913
63d	1	Apr. 7, 1913	Dec. 1, 1913
	2	Dec. 1, 1913	Oct. 24, 1914
	3	Dec. 7, 1914	Mar. 3, 1915
64th	1	Dec. 6, 1915	Sept. 8, 1916
	2	Dec. 4, 1916	Mar. 3, 1917
65th	1	Apr. 2, 1917	Oct. 6, 1917
	2	Dec. 3, 1917	Nov. 21, 1918
	3	Dec. 2, 1918	Mar. 3, 1919
66th	1	May 19, 1919	Nov. 19, 1919
	2	Dec. 1, 1919	Jun. 5, 1920
	3	Dec. 6, 1920	Mar. 3, 1921
67th	1	Apr. 11, 1921	Nov. 23, 1921
	2	Dec. 5, 1921	Sept. 22, 1922
	3	Nov. 20, 1922	Dec. 4, 1922
	4	Dec. 4, 1922	Mar. 3, 1923
68th	1	Dec. 3, 1923	Jun. 7, 1924
	2	Dec. 1, 1924	Mar. 3, 1925
69th	1	Dec. 7, 1925	Jul. 3, 1926
	2	Dec. 6, 1926	Mar. 3, 1927
70th	1	Dec. 5, 1927	May 29, 1928
	2	Dec. 3, 1928	Mar. 3, 1929
71st	1	Apr. 15, 1929	Nov. 22, 1929
	2	Dec. 2, 1929	Jul. 3, 1930
	3	Dec. 1, 1930	Mar. 3, 1931
72d	1	Dec. 7, 1931	Jul. 16, 1932
	2	Dec. 5, 1932	Mar. 3, 1933
73d	1	Mar. 9, 1933	Jun. 15, 1933
	2	Jan. 3, 1934	Jun. 18, 1934
74th	1	Jan. 3, 1935	Aug. 26, 1935
	2	Jan. 3, 1936	Jun. 20, 1936

Congress	Session	Date of Beginning	Date of Adjournment
75th	1	Jan. 5, 1937	Aug. 21, 1937
	2	Nov. 15, 1937	Dec. 21, 1937
	3	Jan. 3, 1938	Jun. 16, 1938
76th	1	Jan. 3, 1939	Aug. 5, 1939
	2	Sept. 21, 1939	Nov. 3, 1939
	3	Jan. 3, 1940	Jan. 3, 1941
77th	1	Jan. 3, 1941	Jan. 2, 1942
	2	Jan. 5, 1942	Dec. 16, 1942
78th	1	Jan. 6, 1943	Dec. 21, 1943
	2	Jan. 10, 1944	Dec. 19, 1944
79th	1	Jan. 3, 1945	Dec. 21, 1945
	2	Jan. 14, 1946	Aug. 2, 1946
80th	1	Jan. 3, 1947	Dec. 19, 1947
	2	Jan. 6, 1948	Dec. 31, 1948
81st	1	Jan. 3, 1949	Oct. 19, 1949
	2	Jan. 3, 1950	Jan. 2, 1951
82d	1	Jan. 3, 1951	Oct. 20, 1951
	2	Jan. 8, 1952	Jul. 7, 1952
83d	1	Jan. 3, 1953	Aug. 3, 1953
	2	Jan. 6, 1954	Dec. 2, 1954
84th	1	Jan. 5, 1955	Aug. 2, 1955
	2	Jan. 3, 1956	Jul. 27, 1956
85th	1	Jan. 3, 1957	Aug. 30, 1957
	2	Jan. 7, 1958	Aug. 24, 1958
86th	1	Jan. 7, 1959	Sept. 15, 1959
	2	Jan. 6, 1960	Sept. 1, 1960
87th	1	Jan. 3, 1961	Sept. 27, 1961
	2	Jan. 10, 1962	Oct. 13, 1962
88th	1	Jan. 9, 1963	Dec. 30, 1963
	2	Jan. 7, 1964	Oct. 3, 1964
89th	1	Jan. 4, 1965	Oct. 23, 1965
	2	Jan. 10, 1966	Oct. 22, 1966
90th	1	Jan. 10, 1967	Dec. 15, 1967
	2	Jan. 15, 1968	Oct. 14, 1968
91st	1	Jan. 3, 1969	Dec. 23, 1969
	2	Jan. 19, 1970	Jan. 2, 1971

Congress	Session	Date of Beginning	Date of Adjournment
92d	1	Jan. 21, 1971	Dec. 17, 1971
	2	Jan. 18, 1972	Oct. 18, 1972
93d	1	Jan. 3, 1973	Dec. 22, 1973
	2	Jan. 21, 1974	Dec. 20, 1974
94th	1	Jan. 14, 1975	Dec. 19, 1975
	2	Jan. 19, 1976	Oct. 1, 1976
95th	1	Jan. 4, 1977	Dec. 15, 1977
	2	Jan. 19, 1978	Oct. 15, 1978
96th	1	Jan. 15, 1979	Jan. 3, 1980
	2	Jan. 3, 1980	Dec. 16, 1980
97th	1	Jan. 5, 1981	Dec. 16, 1981
	2	Jan. 25, 1982	Dec. 23, 1982

CHRONOLOGICAL LIST
OF COMMITTEES

Congress	House Committee (** denotes standing committee)
01-07	Ways and Means
01-46	Rules
01-54	Elections **
03-40	Revisal and Unfinished Business **
03-79	Claims **
04-16	Commerce and Manufactures **
07-97	Ways and Means **
08-79	Accounts **
09	Army Regulations
09	Cession Act of North Carolina
09	Circuit Court in the District of North Carolina
09	Compensation of the Officers of the Senate and House
09	Courts of the U.S., Laws Regulating
09	Duty on Vessels in Charleston, S.C.
09	Elections of the House, Contested
09	Granger, Gidion, Post-Master General
09	Indiana Territory, Letter from William H. Harrison
09	Injunction Power to Judges of the District Courts
09	Invasion of our Territory by Troops of Spain
09	Jurors Serving in Federal Courts, Compensation
09	Letter and Two Printed Books in German
09	Lewis and Clark Compensation
09	Marine Corps Pay Bill
09	Marshalls, Further Security Required of
09	Michigan Territory Laws
09	Michigan Territory, Letter from A.B. Woodword
09	Michigan Territory, Letter from William Hull, Gov.
09	Michigan Territory, Report from Governor and Judge
09	Militia in the District of Columbia
09	Naval Peace Establishment
09	Non-Importation Act
09	Patent Laws
09	Philadelphia, Services Rendered to the Frigate

Congress	House Committee (** denotes standing committee)
09	Post Roads, Bill to Establish Certain
09	Refugee Acts, Report of the Commissioners under the
09	Revenue Surpluses
09	Revenues, State of
09	Roads, Money Appropriated for Public
09	Salaries of Secretaries and Judges of Indiana, etc.
09	Slave Trade, Prohibition of the
09	Slaves, Explain the Act to Prohibit the Importation of
09	State Public Records, Act, and Judicial Proceedings
09	Supreme Court, Altering the Terms of the
09	Western Waters, Further Exploring the
09-10	Crimes against the U.S.
09-10	Fortifications and Protection of Ports, etc.
09-10	Gun Ships, Building
09-10	Peace and Safety of the Union, Combination against
09-10	Public Buildings, Report of the Surveyor of the
09-10	Statute of Limitations
09-11	Cumberland Road Commissioners
09-12	Indian Tribes, Trade Regulation with
09-24	Militia
09-79	Library **
09-82	Public Lands **
10	Algiers Dey and Regency
10	Arms, etc Export
10	Army Unauthorized Advances of Moneys
10	Arts, Useful
10	Bruin, Peter J.
10	Clothing of the Militia
10	Courts in Vermont
10	Courts of Kentucky, Tennessee and Ohio, Jurisdiction of
10	Courts of the U.S., Rules of Proceedings
10	Courts of U.S.
10	Debt Imprisonment Relief
10	Fortification near Portland, Maine
10	Georgia Post Roads
10	Inaes, Harry
10	Indiana Territory Division
10	Indiana Territory Judges
10	Indiana Territory, Right of Suffrage Extension
10	Infirm and Superannuated Soldiers Relief
10	Jay, James Memorial
10	Judges and State Courts Jurisdiction
10	Merchant Vessels, Regulation and Conduct
10	Military Establishment, the Marine Corps, and Seamen . . .
10	Militia Laws of the U.S.
10	Mint, Report of the Director
10	Mississippi Territory, Right of Suffrage
10	Naturalization, Uniform Rule of
10	Orleans Territory Proposing an Amendment
10	Post Offices and Post Roads
10	Present, Emolument, Office, or Title . . .
10	Refugees from the British Provinces of Canada

Congress	House Committee (** denotes standing committee)
10	Salt Can Be Supplied from within the U.S., Extent
10	Seamen, Provision for the Benefit of
10	Territories of the U.S., Repealing a Part of the Ordinance
10	Tripoli, Communication from Hamet Bashow Camameli of
10	Virginia, Defense of the Eastern Frontier of
10	Volunteer Troops for the U.S., Raising and Organizing
10	Weights and Measures
10	Whiting, Samuel
10-11	Military Affairs and Naval Establishment
10-11	Mississippi Territory, Additional Judge and Jurisdiction
10-11	Pike Expedition, Compensation for
10-11	West Point, Military Academy at
10-79	Post Offices and Post Roads **
10-97	District of Columbia **
11	Army State and Disposition
11	Capitol Moneys Appropriated
11	Census Returns Deficiencies
11	Census, Third
11	Coles, I.A. Letter of
11	Courts of Maryland, Altering Time
11	Courts of New Jersey, Altering Time
11	Courts of New York, Vermont, and Connecticut
11	Courts of North Carolina
11	Domestic Manufactures Reported by the Sec. of Treasury
11	Engineers Corps
11	Fugitives from Justice in the Indiana Territory
11	General Assemblies Prolonged
11	Jury, Securing the Right to an Impartial
11	Land Laws Distribution
11	Laws of the U.S., an Index to the
11	Madison County, Mississippi, a Rep. in Gen. Assembly
11	Maritime Precincts, and a Maritime League
11	Marshalls in Certain Cases, Proceeding against
11	Merchant Vessels, Convoying
11	Mobile River Free Navigation
11	Mortality of the Army at New Orleans
11	National Bank Establishment
11	Navy Department, Expenditure of Moneys Appropriated
11	New Orleans Batture, Attorney General on Claims
11	Public Records, State of the Ancient
11	Recognizances and Bail
11	Seamen, American
11	University, National
11	Vincennes to Dayton, Opening a Road from
11	Vincennes to Dearborn County, Indiana Territory, Road from
11	Wilkinson, James
11-12	Court in Maine, Altering Time
11-12	Florida, West
11-12	Lambert, William, Letters on the First Meridian
11-12	Libel, Inquire What Prosecutions Have Been Commenced for
11-17	Military Affairs
11-17	Naval Affairs

Congress	House Committee (** denotes standing committee)
12	Apportionment of Representatives
12	Bankruptcy
12	Cannon and Small Arms Munitions of War
12	Chesapeake and Delaware Canal
12	Compensation of the Officers of the Congress
12	Compensation to Witnesses in Criminal Cases
12	Consuls and Vice-Consuls, Alteration of Laws Concerning
12	Court in Connecticut and Virginia, Altering Time
12	Courts in Vermont
12	Courts of New York and Virginia
12	Fines and Forfeitures from the Treasury Department
12	Illinois Territory, Res. of the Legislature
12	Illinois Territory, Right of Suffrage
12	Impressments
12	Indian Affairs
12	Indiana Territory Division
12	Indiana Territory, Division and Government for Michigan
12	Judges Compelled to Reside within Their Districts
12	Judges from Holding Other Offices Disqualified
12	Judges of Territorial Courts, Extending Jurisdiction
12	Judicial System Alteration
12	Jurisdiction over White Persons within Indian Lines
12	Lands for the Officers and Soldiers of the Revolution
12	Louisiana, Constitution of the Territory of
12	Mint at Philadelphia
12	Mississippi Territory Admission to the Union
12	Missouri Territorial Government
12	Moneys Drawn from the Treasury since the Year 1801
12	Naturalization Laws
12	Navy Department, Retrenchments in the Expenses of the
12	Navy Hospitals, Report of the Secretary of the Navy on
12	Ohio, Boundaries
12	Patent Office, Estimate of the Expense of Finishing the
12	Printing, Public
12	Public Acts of the State Shall Be Authenticated
12	Retaliation
12	Road for the Greenville Treaty Line to the North Bend
12	Security on Appeals from District to Circuit Courts
12	Sheriffs in the Indiana Territory, Election of
12	Spanish American Colonies
12	Superintendent of the Indian Trade
12	West Florida to the Mississippi Territory, Annexation of
13	Army Supply Contracts
13	Congress Meeting Earlier than Permitted by Constitution
13	Copper Coins Alteration
13	Court in Mississippi Territory, Establishing a District
13	Discipline for the Army, Establishing a Uniform Mode of
13	Electing Senators, Representatives, etc.
13	Flags and Standards Taken from the Enemy
13	Fugitives from Justice
13	Indiana Territory, Protest of Legislative Council
13	Laws To Be Published in the Several Territories

Congress	House Committee (** denotes standing committee)
13	Lead Mines in Missouri, Leasing
13	Magruder's Letters
13	Mississippi Territory Extension of Suffrage
13	National Bank
13	Naval Reform
13	Northwestern Frontier, More Effectual Defense of
13	Ports to Armed Vessels of Foreign Nations, Use of Our
13	Portsmouth, New Hampshire Petition
13	Post Office, Petition to Revise the Law Regulating
13	Public Buildings in the City of Washington, Rebuilding
13	Revenue Cutters
13	Roads in Tennessee and Mississippi Territory, Repairing
13	Seat of Government, Removal of the
13	War Has Been Waged by the Enemy, Manner in Which the
13	Washington, Capture of the City of
13	Water Communication from the Chesapeake to St. Mary's
13	Yazoo Claimants
13-14	Cumberland Road
13-14	Mississippi Territory, Petition of Legislature
13-19	Pensions and Revolutionary Claims
13-46	Public Expenditures **
13-97	Judiciary **
14	Assent of Congress to Virginia Act
14	Attorney General's Office Establishment
14	Banks Incorporated in the District of Columbia
14	Berkshire Association
14	Bible Society of Philadelphia
14	Bonus of the National Bank
14	Bounty Lands Commutation
14	Canadian Volunteers Relief
14	Claims Commissioner R.B. Lee
14	Clerk of the House Increase in Salary
14	Compensating Members of Congress
14	Flag of the U.S.
14	Georgia, Interference with the Rights of
14	Ghent, Peter B. Porter as Commissioner
14	Harrison, General, Accounts
14	Illegal Traffic of Negroes in the District of Columbia
14	Indian Trade
14	Indian Tribes, Condition
14	Indiana Territory Petition for a State Government
14	Indiana Territory, Western Limits of
14	Indiana, Knox County Petition
14	Mail on Sunday, Practice of Opening
14	Militia Expenses
14	Mississippi Territory Admission to the Union
14	Mississippi Territory Counties Admission to the Union
14	Missouri Territory on the Erection of Forts
14	Missouri Territory, Petition of Inhabitants
14	National Currency
14	Niagara Frontier, Petition of the Inhabitants of
14	North Carolina, Petition of the General Assembly

Congress	House Committee (** denotes standing committee)
14	Offices Are Useless, What
14	Post Office, Fiscal Concerns of the General
14	Register of All Officers of Government
14	Reynoldsburgh Road
14	Road from Washington, Pennsylvania to the Sandusky River
14	Road in Virginia, Turnpiking a
14	Roads, Petition of Washington Inhabitants for
14	Rodgers, Commodore
14	Slavery, Convention for Promoting the Abolition of
14	Society for Propagating the Gospel
14	Tallmadge, Judge
14	Thomas, James Settlement of the Accounts of Quartermaster
14	Unsettled Balances
14	Virginia Land Warrants, Further Time for Locating
14	Weights and Measures
14	Widows and Orphans of Volunteers and Militia, Provision
14-15	University, National
14-19	Slave Trade, Prohibition of the African
14-62	Private Land Claims **
14-70	Expenditures in Public Buildings **
14-70	Expenditures in the Navy Department **
14-70	Expenditures in the Post Office Department **
14-70	Expenditures in the State Department **
14-70	Expenditures in the Treasury Department **
14-70	Expenditures in the War Department **
15	Alabama Admission to Union
15	Arkansas Territorial Establishment
15	Bank of U.S.
15	Coins, Foreign and Weights and Measures Regulation
15	Connecticut Asylum for the Deaf and Dumb
15	Cranch's Code of Laws
15	Fugitive Slaves
15	Georgia and Survey of Lands in Big Bend of Tenn.
15	Illinois Constitution
15	Michigan Territory Delegate to Congress
15	Property Lost in the War with Great Britain
15	Slaves from Amelia Island
15-16	Officers and Soldiers of the Revolution
15-17	Indian Affairs
15-20	Roads and Canals
16	Apportionment of Representatives under 4th Cen
16	Army Appropriations Inquiry
16	Brownstown Treaty
16	Clothing of Domestic Manufacture for the Services
16	Debt Imprisonment
16	Ghent Treaty, Fifth, Sixth and Seventh Articles
16	Johnson, Colonel James
16	Laws in Newspapers, Publication of
16	Missouri Admission to the Union
16	Missouri Constitution
16	Mohican or Stockbridge Indians
16	Powder and Lead to Individuals, Loan of

Congress	House Committee (** denotes standing committee)
16	Salaries, Reduction of
16	Slavery in the Territories, Prohibiting
16	States Jurisdiction in Selecting Sites for Forts
16	Vaccine Institute, Petition of the National
16-17	Bank of U.S.
16-17	Coins, Foreign and Currency Regulation
16-17	Post Office Department, Affairs
16-20	Columbia River Settlements
16-52	Commerce **
16-62	Manufactures **
16-97	Agriculture **
17	Accountability of Public Moneys
17	Arkansas Territorial Limits
17	Banking Institutions in Charleston, S.C.
17	Executive Departments Affairs
17	Field Services and Police of the Army, Pub. Error
17	Florida, Petition of Residents
17	Ghent Treaty, Fifth Article
17	Land Offices, Examination
17	Mix, Elija
17	Pennsylvania Militia Fines
17	Suppression of Part of the Document from Sec. of Treas.
17	Tompkins, Daniel D.
17	Vaccination, Modifying the Act to Encourage
17	Virginia Militia, Fines Imposed on
17	Weights and Measures
17-18	Creek and Cherokee Indians Treaties
17-18	Cumberland Road
17-18	Roads and Canals Leading to Illinois, Indiana, and Miss.
17-18	Washington, D.C., Sales of Public Lots in
17-21	Retrenchment of the Expenses of the Government
17-79	Indian Affairs **
17-79	Military Affairs **
17-79	Naval Affairs **
17-94	Foreign Affairs **
18	Arms, etc Contracts
18	Canal around the Falls of the Ohio
18	Charges against Sec. of Treasury by Ninian Edwards
18	Charges Preferred by George Kremer against Speaker
18	Chesapeake and Ohio Canal Proposal
18	Columbian Institute
18	Deaf and Dumb, Granting Assistance to Certain Assns.
18	Electing President of the United States, Rules
18	Illinois Canal
18	Lafayette, General, Sacrifices of
18	Louisiana, Aliens in the State of
18	North Carolina on Tennessee Lands, Petition
18	Ohio and Mississippi Rivers, Obstructions in the Navigation
18	Ohio, Lands Lying between Robert's and Ludlow's Line in
18	Ordnance and Ordnance Stores
18	Peale's Portrait of Washington, Purchase
18	Police for the Capital

Congress	House Committee (** denotes standing committee)
18	Property Lost in the War of 1812
18	Public Lands, New Regulations for the Sale of
18	Tennessee between the Tennessee and Big Pigeon Rivers
18	United Brethren for Propagating the Gospel among Heathen
18-19	Columbia River Military Post Establishment
18-19	Deaf and Dumb Institution in Kentucky
18-19	Electing the House, President, etc. Amendment
18-19	Monroe, James Accounts
19	Apportionment of Representatives Next Census
19	Bills of Exchange
19	Calhoun, John C. and His Conduct as Sec. of War
19	Deaf and Dumb Associations in New York and Pennsylvania
19	Educational and Internal Improvements Fund
19	Election Laws of the Several States
19	Executive Department Reorganization
19	Exploration of the Polar Regions
19	Land Offices, Rigid and Strict Accounting of Receivers of
19	Observatory, National University and National
19	Officers of the War of 1812 for Bounty Lands
19	Ohio and Territory of Michigan, Boundary between
19	Patent Office
19	Public Buildings
19	Revolutionary Officers
19	Revolutionary Pensions **
19	Supreme Court, Proceedings of the
19	Tennessee, Grant of Certain Vacant Lands to
19	Vaccination
19	Washington Monument
19-21	Military Pensions
19-22	American Colonization Society
19-43	Revolutionary Claims **
19-79	Territories **
20	Assault on the President's Secretary
20	Laws, Stereotyping
20	Mint
20	Missouri Boundary
20	Revolutionary Bounty Lands
20-21	Retrenchment
20-21	Deaf and Dumb, Asylum for the Instruction of
20-22	Census, Fifth
21	Blind Asylum in New England
21	Legal Tender, Making Five Franc Pieces, etc.
21	Mint in North Carolina, Establishing
21	Ohio and Mississippi Rivers, Improvement of Navigation of
21	Patents with the Names of the Patentees, List of
21	Public Lands for Education, Appropriating Proceeds of
21	Roanoke Inlet, Opening
21	Surplus Revenue, Distribution
21	Washington, General, Entombment of
21-22	Internal Improvements
21-22	Transylvania University
21-23	Assay Office in the Gold Region

Congress	House Committee (** denotes standing committee)
21-46	Revolutionary Pensions **
21-79	Invalid Pensions **
22	Blind Asylum
22	British Depredations of the Northern Frontier
22	Debt Imprisonment
22	Fasting, Prayer and Humiliation
22	Fraud in Contract to Supply Indians
22	Houston, Samuel Trial
22	Journals and Laws Distribution
22	Live Oaks in Florida
22	Maryland, Claim
22	Massachusetts Resolutions
22	Public Accounts, a System of
22	Revolutionary Claims, Memorial for Virginia
22	Transylvania University and Brown University, Endow
22-23	Bank of U.S. Affairs
22-23	Biennial Register
22-23	Steam Boilers, Explosion of
22-24	Coins
22-24	Rhode Island Brigade of the Revolution
22-25	Patents and Patent Laws
22-70	Railways and Canals **
23	Boundary of the Chickasaw Indians
23	Erie and Wabash Canal
23	Ewing, John
23	Foundry, National
23	Pay of Officers of the Army and Navy
23	Post Office Department Affairs
23	Salaries of Officers of the Government
23	Tennessee Lands
23	Treasury Department, Reorganize the
23	Washington, General, Publication of the Works of
23	Weights and Measures
23-24	Ohio, Establish the Northern Boundary Line of the State
23-24	West Point Academy
23-24	Yorktown, Virginia for Monument on Battle Ground
23-25	Pension Law of 1832 to Troops Employed against Indians
24	Amendment to the Constitution on Elections
24	Banks Employment of Agents
24	Banks of the District of Columbia
24	Elections, Contested
24	Executive Departments Administration
24	Loans from Deposit Banks to Members of Congress, etc.
24	Pay of Members of Congress and Contingent Expenses
24	Reilly's Vapor Bath
24	Slavery
24	Smithsonian Legacy and Institution
24	State Banks, Constitutionality of
24	Steam Navigation, and Causes of Disasters
24	Tobacco, High Duties on
24	Truss in the Army and Navy, Right to Use an Improved
24	Wheeler vs. Codd

Congress	House Committee (** denotes standing committee)
24-25	Williams, David, One of the Captors of Andre
24-27	Hale, Nathan, Monument
24-36	Roads and Canals **
24-62	Militia **
25	Amendment to the Constitution on Appointment
25	Cilley's Death in a Dual Investigation
25	Dental Surgery
25	Duelling Prohibition
25	Elections, Bill to Secure Freedom of
25	Elliott, Commodore
25	Flag Carried at the Battle of Wyoming
25	Lawrence, P.K.
25	Laws of the U.S., Duff Green's Memorial to Stereotype
25	Mexican Correspondence
25	Naturalization Laws
25	Officers of the U.S., Appointment of
25	Portraits of Presidents of the U.S.
25	Public Lands, Past Donations and Plans for Distributing
25	Sergeant-at-Arms Communication on Error in Paying Members
25	Steam Engines
25	Sub-Treasury Plan of R.M.T. Hunter
25	Swartwout, Samuel
25	Tuscaloosa, Alabama, Establishment of a Pension Office at
25	Virginia Claims
25	Virginia Land Warrants and Returning Surveys, Repealing
25	Virginia Military District Land in Ohio
25-26	Fourth Regiment
25-26	Georgia Memorial for the Payment of Revolutionary Debt
25-26	Meteorology
25-26	National Foundry
25-26	Public Press, Separation of Patronage of Government from
25-26	Tobacco Trade
25-27	Blair and Rives
25-27	Smithsonian Bequest
25-27	Steam Boilers
25-70	Mileage **
25-79	Patents **
25-79	Public Buildings and Grounds **
26	Claims Prosecutions by Officers of the House
26	Commonwealth Bank of Boston, Claims against
26	Fight in the House between Messrs. Bynum and Garland
26	Forms of Returns Necessary for Members of the House
26	Franking Abuses
26	Pay of Members of Congress and Other Officers of Government
26	Printing
26	Stationary
26	Stationary Furnished to Persons Not Entitled
27	Agricultural Bank of Mississippi
27	Apportionment of Representatives
27	Census Bill
27	Coast Survey
27	Currency

Congress	House Committee (** denotes standing committee)
27	Fight between Mr. Wise and Mr. Stanly
27	Finance and Currency
27	Foundry, National
27	Grain Growing Interest
27	Gulf of Mexico Charts and Surveys
27	Hemp, Inspection and Manufacture of Water-Rotted
27	Jackson County, Illinois Petition on Inundated Lands
27	Lawrenceville, Pa. Pike Street Highway
27	Maps of Boundary between Texas and the U.S.
27	New York Custom House, Finishing and Furnishing
27	Retrenchment of the Expenses of the Government
27	Soldiers Who Served under Generals St. Clair and Wayne
27	Sylvester, Henry H.
27	War Steamer on Lake Erie, Construction of a
27	Wright, William against the Commonwealth Bank of Boston
28	Army Pay
28	Banks in the District of Columbia
28	Census, Sixth Errors
28	Copyright
28	Engraving, Lithography etc.
28	Franking Violation by Post Office
28	Maps of Exploring Expeditions
28	National Institute Memorial
28	Quarrel between White and Rathbun
28	Rhode Island Legislature, Memorial of Democratic Members
28	Statistics
28	Virginia Resolutions
28	Wabash and Erie Canal, Grant of Land for
28	Washington, Remove the Building over the Statue of
28-29	Smithsonian Fund
28-36	Engraving **
29	Blind
29	Congress, Selling of Books by Members to
29	Consular System
29	Courts in Alabama
29	Indians, Expenditures by Butler and Lewis
29	Lands Sold, Three Percent to Ohio, Indiana, Illinois, etc.
29	Laws of the U.S., Purchase of Tenth Volume
29	Madison's Writings
29	Marine Corps Pay of Officers
29	Pay Bill for Non-Commissioned Army Officers
29	Post Office Contract for Blanks, Paper, Twine, etc.
29	Reporters for Union Newspapers
29	Revolution, Relief of Officers and Soldiers of the
29	Webster, Daniel
29-30	Morton's, W.T. Petition on Prevention of Pain in Surgery
30	Cedar Bluffs, Alabama Petition
30	Coins Value
30	Drugs, Inspection of Imported
30	Indian Department Corruption Charges
30	Jay, James on Copyright Law
30	Mail, Arrangement with Railroads for Carrying the Mail

Congress	House Committee (** denotes standing committee)
30	Mexican Ports, Duties on during the War
30	Mexican War Prosecution
30	Mexico, Families of Those Who Have Died in
30	Mexico, Protection of Friends of Peace in
30	Panama, Canal or Railroad across
30	Patenting Medicines
30	Penitentiary System of District of Columbia, Revising
30	Swamp or Submerged Lands, Reclaiming
30	Tobacco Trade
30	Whitney, Eli
30	York, Virginia, Erecting Marble Column at
31	Bounty Land Act of 1850
31	Election of General Taylor
31	Ewing, Thomas
31	Galphin Claim and G.W. Crawford's Connection
31	Giddings, J.R. and Abstraction of Papers from Post Office
31	Horner, Doorkeeper
31	Speaker on Mutilating Journal, Charges against
32	Corwin, Thomas and the Gardiner Claim
32	Ether Discovery
32-33	Crimes, Abuses, Bribery, or Fraud in the Prosecution of
32-33	Revenue, Frauds on the
33	Bayley, Thomas H.
33	Civil Works Superintendence by the Military
33	Collins and other Mail Steamers
33	Colt's Patent
33	Courthouses
33	Electing President and Vice President
33	Guano Trade
33	House, Number and Composition of Employees of the
33	Memphis Navy Yard
33	Minnesota Land Bill
33	Mississippi River from Hickman to Obion River, Leveeing
33	Smithsonian Institution, Reinvesting the Funds of the
33	Smithsonian Institution, Rufus Choate on the Management of
33	Washington National Monument
33-38	Pacific Railroad
34	Corrupt Combinations of Members of Congress
34	Granager, Amos P.
34	Kansas Territory, Election Fraud in the
34	Ohio, Granting Lands for the Improvement of the
34	Sumner, Senator, Alleged Assault
35	Artist of the United States
35	Charges against a Member of the Committee on Accounts
35	Cullon, William, Late Clerk of the House
35	Doorkeeper of the House, Accounts and Conduct
35	Expenditures, Navigation Laws, and Duties on Imports
35	Fort Snelling Reservation
35	Kansas (Lecompton) Constitution
35	Kentucky and Tennessee Surveys
35	Matteson, O.B.
35	Naval Contracts and Expenditures

Congress	House Committee (** denotes standing committee)
35	Niagara Ship Canal, Grant of Lands to the
35	Post Office in Philadelphia, Purchase of a Bank for
35	Printing Laws
35	Stone, Lawrence and Company
35	Superintendent of the Public Printing
35	Virginia Military District Land in Ohio
35	Wilkins' Point, New York for Fortification Purposes
36	Abstraction of Books
36	Condition of the Country
36	Corruptions in Government
36	Fort Sumter Surrender
36	Franking Abolition
36	Indian Trust Bonds Abstraction
36	Interference by the Executive with the Action of the House
36	Message of the President of January 8, 1861
36	Protest of the President of June 22, 1860
36	Public Stores in New York, Contract for Rent of
36	Thirty Three on the Disturbed Condition of the Country
36	Tobacco Trade, Present Condition of the
36-70	Expenditures in the Interior Department **
37	Abstraction of Report
37	Ashley, J.M.
37	Charges of Corruption in the New York Tribune
37	Government Contracts
37	Government Employees Interest in Banking Institutions
37	Government Expenditures Reduction
37	Loyalty of Government Employees
37	Military and Post Roads from New York to Washington
37	Niagara, Ship Canal around the Falls of
37	Patent Office, D.P. Holloway's Management of the
37	Rebel Property, Confiscation of
37-38	Armory
37-38	Emancipation
37-39	Bankrupt Law
38	Anderson, Lucien
38	Blair, F.P.
38	Chemist of the Agriculture Department
38	Congressional Annals and Debates Purchase
38	Defenses of the Northwestern Frontier
38	Emigration
38	Field, A.P., Assault on the Honorable W.D. Kelley
38	Indian Affairs
38	Patents, Charges against the Commissioner of
38	Pensions
38	Rebellious States
38	Treasury Department, Alleged Frauds in the
38-39	Railroad from New York to Washington
38-62	Pacific Railroad **
38-79	Coinage, Weights and Measures **
38-93	Banking and Currency **
38-97	Appropriations **
39	Atwater, Dorence

Congress	House Committee (** denotes standing committee)
39	Civil Service of the U.S.
39	Corrupt Bargain with the President
39	Direct Taxes and Forfeited Land
39	Education Bureau
39	Freedmen
39	Internal Revenue Frauds
39	Lincoln, President, Death of
39	Loyal States, Reimbursement of
39	Memphis Riot
39	Military and Postal Railroad from Washington to N.Y.
39	New Orleans Riots
39	Paynter, U.H.
39	Provost Marshall's Bureau
39	Rousseau, Assault upon Mr. Grinnell
39	South Carolina, Murder of Soldiers in
39-40	District of Columbia System of Common Schools
39-40	Southern Railroads
39-43	Freedmen's Affairs **
39-79	Mines and Mining **
40	Clothing Destitute Soldiers
40	Contingent Fund of the House Disbursement
40	Donnelly, Ignatius
40	Missouri Delegation on a Letter to Senator Harrison
40	New York Election Frauds
40	Niagara Ship Canal
40	Pay Department
40	Prince Edward's Island
40	Prisoners, Treatment of Union
40	Soldiers' and Sailors' Bounty
40-41	Reconstruction
40-48	Education and Labor **
40-79	Laws Revision **
41	Brooks, James
41	Postal Telegraph
41	Smith, W. Scott, Expulsion from the Reporters Gallery
41	Tonnage, Cause of Reduction of American
42-43	Civil Service Reorganization
42	Credit Mobilier--Poland Committee
42	Credit Mobilier--Wilson Committee
42	Louisiana, Investigate Condition of Affairs in
42	Message of the President on the Condition of the States
42	Navy Department, Affairs of
42	Stamps in the Sub-Treasury of New York, Loss of
42	Washington Monument
42-44	Centennial Celebration and the National Census of 1875
42-44	Mississippi River Levees
43	Alabama Affairs
43	Arkansas Affairs
43	Central Pacific Railroad
43	Mississippi Affairs
43	Reid, at the Suit of A.R. Shepherd
43	Salaries, Reduction of

Congress	House Committee (** denotes standing committee)
43	Washington Monument, Completion of the
43-70	Expenditures in the Justice Department **
43-79	War Claims **
44	Civil Service Reform **
44	District of Columbia Board of Police Commissions Charged
44	Election in Florida
44	Election in Louisiana
44	Election in South Carolina
44	Electoral Vote
44	Freedman's Bank
44	House Clerk
44	Powers, Privileges, and Duties of the House
44	Real Estate Pool and the Jay Cooke Indebtedness
44	Southern States
44	Texas Frontier Troubles
44	Voting in the Cities of New York, Philadelphia, etc.
44	Whiskey Trials in Saint Louis
44	Wylie, Judge
44-62	Mississippi River Levees and Improvements **
44-79	Engrossed Bills **
45	Election Frauds Alleged in Presidential Election
45	Randall, Samuel J.
45-46	Elections of the President and Vice-President, Declaration
45-53	Civil Service Reform
46	Congressional Elections in Cincinnati
46	Donnelly vs. Washburn Contested Election
46	Epidemic Diseases
46	Labor Depression
46-48	Pensions, Bounty and Back Pay
46-53	Alcoholic Liquor Traffic
46-79	Pensions **
46-97	Rules **
47	Bailey, John
47	Woman Suffrage
47-48	Census, Tenth
47-48	Public Health
47-50	Newburg, N.Y., Monument and Centennial Celebration
47-53	Election of President and Vice President
48	Boynton Investigation
48	Ordnance and Gunnery
48-49	American Ship Building **
48-49	Indian Schools and Yellowstone Park
48-79	Education **
48-79	Labor **
48-79	Rivers and Harbors **
49	Admission to the Floor
49	Labor Troubles
49	Telephone Investigation
50	Contract Labor, Convicts, and Paupers Importation
50	Library Building
50	Library Investigation
50	Railroad Strike, Reading

Congress	House Committee (** denotes standing committee)
50-51	Indian Depredation Claims
50-52	Census, Eleventh
50-79	Executive Papers Disposition **
50-79	Printing **
50-97	Merchant Marine and Fisheries **
51	Ballot Box Purchase
51	Leedom, John P., Late Sergeant at Arms
51	World's Fair
51	Silver Pool Investigation
51-53	Immigration and Naturalization
51-53	Irrigation of Arid Lands
51-70	Expenditures in the Department of Agriculture **
52	Columbian Exposition
52	New York Elections
52	Panama Canal Company
52	Pension Bureau Investigation
52	Watson's Charges
52-93	Interstate and Foreign Commerce **
53	Capitol Sanitary Conditions
53-68	Civil Service Reform **
53-68	Irrigation of Arid Lands **
53-70	Alcoholic Liquor Traffic **
53-79	Election of President and Vice **
53-79	Immigration and Naturalization **
54	Leavenworth Soldiers' Home Investigation
54-79	Elections **
54-79	Elections No. 1 **
54-79	Elections No. 2 **
54-79	Elections No. 3 **
55	District of Columbia Gas and Telephone Companies
55-57	Census, Twelfth
56	Louisiana Purchase, Centennial
56	Military Academy, Investigation of Hazing
56	Roberts, Brigham H.
56	Washington City Centennial
56-57	Documents, Examination and Disposition
56-57	House Employees, Appointment and Payment of
56-79	Insular Affairs **
57	Danish West Indies Purchase
57-70	Industrial Arts and Expositions
57-79	Census **
58	Post Office Departments, Relations of Members with
58	Swayne, Charles
59	Government Hospital for the Insane
59-70	Expenditures in the Department of Commerce **
60	Bills and Resolutions Introduced in the House
60	Frauds and Depredations in Public Service
60	House Office Building Rooms Distribution
60	Lilley, George L.
60	Public Service, Prevention of Fraud in
60	Pulp and Paper Investigations
60	Record, Expunging Remarks from the

Congress	House Committee (** denotes standing committee)
60	Secret Service
60-70	Election of President, Vice-President, and Rep. **
61	Oklahoma, Indian Contracts in
61	Ship Subsidy Lobby
62	American Sugar Refining Company
62	Taylor and Other Systems of Shop Management
62	United States Steel Corporation
63	Sims, Representative
63	Cotton Situation in the South
63	Lobby Investigation
63-79	Roads **
64	Callaway and the Congressional Record
64	Congressional Record Alleged Inaccuracies
64	Marshall, Snowden
64-65	Indian Service Conditions
64-79	Flood Control **
65	Heflin, Charges by
65	National Security League
65	Ordnance and Ammunition
65-66	Water Power **
65-70	Woman Suffrage **
66	Berger, Victor L.
66	Budget
66	Expenditures in the War Department
66	Shipping Board Operations
67	Bergdoll, Grover Cleveland
67	Budget
67	Readjustment of Service Pay
68	Air Services
68	Government Bonds and Other Securities
68	Members of Congress, Charges against
68	National Disabled Soldiers League Inc.
68-69	English, George Washington
68-69	Shipping Board Emergency Fleet Corporation
68-79	Civil Service **
68-79	Irrigation and Reclamation **
68-79	World War Veterans Legislation
69	Langley, John W.
70	Federal Penal and Reformatory Institutions
70-79	Memorials **
70-82	Expenditures in the Executive Departments **
70-93	Campaign Expenditures
71	Communist Propaganda
71-72	District of Columbia and the U.S. Fiscal Relations
72	Government Competition with Private Enterprise
72-73	Economy **
73	House Restaurant, Management and Control of
73	Wirt, William A.
73-74	Real Estate Bondholders' Reorganizations
73-74	Un-American Activities
73-79	Wildlife Resources, Conservation of
74	American Retail Federation

Congress	House Committee (** denotes standing committee)
74-75	Executive Agencies of the Government
74-75	Old Age Pension Plans
74-75	Un-American Activities
75-76	Government Organization
76	Anthracite Emergency Program
76	National Labor Relations Board
76-77	Interstate Migration of Destitute Citizens
77-78	Air Accidents
77-78	National Defense Migration
77-93	Small Business
78	Executive Agencies
78	Indian Conditions of America
78	Montgomery Ward Company Seizure
78-79	Post-War Economic Policy and Planning
78-79	Post-War Military Policy
79	Food Shortages
79	Food Shortages, Particularly Meat
79	National Defense Program and Its Relation to Small Bus.
79	Surplus Property, Disposition of
79-91	Un-American Activities **
79-93	Public Works **
79-97	Armed Services **
79-97	Education and Labor **
79-97	House Administration **
79-97	Post Office and Civil Service **
79-97	Veterans Affairs **
80	Commodity Transaction
80	Foreign Aid
80	Newsprint
81	Lobbying Activities
81	Veteran's Education and Training Program
81-82	Food Products, Use of Chemical in
81-82	GI Bill
82	Katyn Forest Massacre
82	Pornographic Materials
82-83	Tax-Exempt Foundations and Comparable Organizations
82-97	Government Operations **
82-97	Interior and Insular Affairs **
83	Baltic States Incorporation in USSR
83	Communist Aggression
83-84	Benefits for Armed Services Veterans
83-84	Survivors Benefits
84	White County Bridge Commission
84-97	House Recording Studio
85	Astronautics and Space Exploration
85-93	Science and Astronautics **
85-97	Science and Technology **
87	Export Control
88	Government Research
88	Pages, Welfare and Education of Congressional
89	Standards and Conduct
90	House Resolution 1 on the Seating of Adam Clayton Powell

Congress	House Committee (** denotes standing committee)
90-91	House Beauty Shop
90-97	Standards of Official Conduct **
91	Southeast Asia, All Aspects of U.S. Military in
91-93	Crime
91-93	House Restaurant
91-94	Internal Security **
93	Committees
93-95	Banking, Currency and Housing **
93-97	Aging
93-97	Budget **
93-97	Public Works and Transportation **
93-97	Small Business **
94	Missing in Action in Southeast Asia
94	Sports, Professional
94-95	Intelligence
94-96	International Relations **
94-96	Outer Continental Shelf
94-97	Interstate and Foreign Commerce **
94-97	Narcotics Abuse and Control
95	Assassinations
95	Congressional Operations
95	Energy
95	Ethics
95	Population
95-97	Banking, Finance and Urban Affairs
95-97	Intelligence
96	Committees
96-97	Foreign Affairs **
97	Children, Youth and Families

JOINT COMMITTEES

Congress	Joint Committee (** denotes standing committee)

01-44	Enrolled Bills **
09-79	Library **
19	Police and Preservation of the Capital **
20	Laws for the District of Columbia, Prepare a Code of **
22	Laws for the District of Columbia, Code of **
25	Smithsonian Bequest **
29-97	Printing, Public **
33	Amending Constitution in Election of Pres
33	San Francisco Disaster
36	Washington's Statue, Inaugurating **
37-39	War, Conduct of the **
38	Senate Chamber and Hall of the House of Representatives **
38-39	Indian Tribes, Conditions
39	Reconstruction **
39	Confederate States, Former Condition
39-41	Retrenchment
40	Civil Service in the Departments Reorganization
40	Executive Mansion Repairs and Furnishings **
40	Ordnance
40	Pay of the Employees of Each House, Revise and **
42	Insurrectionary States, Condition of Affairs in Late
43	District of Columbia Affairs
44	Chinese Immigration
44	District of Columbia Framing a Form of Government
45	Army Reorganization
45	Indian Bureau Transfer **
47	Shipbuilding, American
47	State, War and Navy Department Building
48-49	Scientific Bureaus **
50	Washington Aqueduct Tunnel, Work on the
50-78	Executive Papers Disposition **
53	Capitol Cornerstone Laying Centennial
53	Naval Affairs **
53	Naval Personnel **
53-54	Chickamauga and Chattanooga National Military Park
53-54	Ford's Theater Disaster **
54-55	Alcohol in the Arts
55	District of Columbia Charities and Reformatory
59	District of Columbia Public Parks
59	Mail Matter, Second Class **
59-61	Laws, Revision and Codification
61	Interior Department and Forestry Service Investigation **
61-62	Alaska Conditions
62-63	Federal Aid in Construction of Post Roads
62-63	Mail Matter, Second Class and Compensation for Railways **
62-63	Parcel Post, General **
62-63	Postage on 2nd Class Mail Matter, etc. **
63	Armor Plant Cost
63-64	District of Columbia and the U.S. Fiscal Relations **
63-64	Rural Credits **

Congress	Joint Committee (** denotes standing committee)
64-65	Interstate and Foreign Commerce **
64-65	Interstate Commerce **
65-66	Postal Salaries **
65-66	Reclassification of Salaries **
66	Pacific Coast Naval Bases **
66-67	Readjustment of Service Pay
66-67	Rural Credits, System of Shortime **
66-68	Postal Service **
66-68	Reorganization **
66-68	Reorganization of the Admin. Branch of the Government **
67	District of Columbia and the U.S. Fiscal Relations **
67-68	Banking and Currency **
67-68	Congressional Salaries **
67-68	Federal Prisoners Employment **
67-68	Federal Reserve System **
68-71	Northern Pacific Railroad Land Grants **
69	Muscle Shoals **
69-70	Harriman Geographic Code System
69-94	Internal Revenue Taxation **
70-71	Aircraft for Seacoast Defense
70-71	Salaries of Officers and Employees of the Senate **
72-73	Veterans Affairs **
73	Dirigible Disasters **
75	Hawaii **
75	Government Organization **
75	Tax Evasion and Avoidance **
75-76	Tennessee Valley Authority **
75-77	Forestry **
75-77	Phosphate Resource of the U.S. **
76	Safety of Capitol Roofs
76-77	Mediterranean Fruitfly, Eradication **
77-93	Reduction of Non-Essential Federal Expenditures **
78	Federal Communications Commission **
78	Selective Service Deferments **
78-79	Congress Organization **
78-91	Executive Papers Disposition **
79	Pearl Harbor Attack **
79-84	Economic Report **
79-84	Economics, Temporary National **
79-91	Legislative Budget **
79-95	Atomic Energy **
80	Housing **
80	Pacific Islands **
80-81	Foreign Economic Cooperation **
80-81	Labor Management Relations **
81-93	Navajo-Hopi Indian Administration **
81-95	Defense Production **
82-83	Railroad Retirement Legislation **
82-91	Immigration and Nationality Policy **
84-89	Smithsonian, Construction of Building for **
84-97	Economic **
85-86	Washington Metropolitan Problems **

Congress	Joint Committee (** denotes standing committee)
89	Congress Organization **
91-95	Congressional Operations **
92-93	Budget Control
94	Bicentennial Arrangements
94-97	Taxation **

SENATE COMMITTEES

Congress	Senate Committee (** denotes standing committee)
09-79	Library **
10-79	Senate, Audit and Control the Contingent Expenses of **
10-11	Outrages in Southern States, Alleged
14	Attorney General's Office Established
14	Compensation of Congress, Constitutional Amendment
14	Compensation of Members of Congress, Law Repeal on
14	Indiana Admission to the Union
14	Mississippi Territory Admission to the Union
14	Roads and Canals
14	University, National
14	Weights and Measures
14-15	Slave Trade
14-19	Commerce and Manufactures **
14-35	Militia **
14-67	Public Lands **
14-79	Claims **
14-79	Military Affairs **
14-79	Naval Affairs **
14-79	Pensions **
14-79	Post Offices and Post Roads **
14-95	District of Columbia **
14-97	Finance **
14-97	Foreign Relations **
14-97	Judiciary **
15	Indian Title to Certain Lands Extinguishment
15	Mississippi Admission to the Union
15-16	Seminole War
16	Alabama Constitution
16	American Colonization Society
16	Congressional Salaries Reduction
16	Fire Engine Purchase
16	Land Commissioners Reports
16	Missouri Admission to the Union
16	Public Buildings
16-17	Roads and Canals **
16-18	Amendments Proposed to the Constitution
16-67	Senate Contingent Expenses **
16-79	Indian Affairs **
16-79	Public Buildings and Grounds **
17	National Road from Cumberland to Wheeling
17	Tariff Regulation
17-20	Debt Imprisonment Abolition
17-21	Roads and Canals
18	Arkansas Legislative Memorial
18	Banks in Which Deposits Have Been Made
18	La Fayette, Marquis de
18	Peale's Portrait of Washington
19	Bankruptcy
19	Georgia and the Creek Indians
19-21	Revenue among the States, Distributing a Part of Public

Congress	Senate Committee (** denotes standing committee)
19-23	French Spoliations
19-33	Manufactures **
19-34	Agriculture **
19-67	Private Land Claims **
19-79	Commerce **
20	Alabama Land Purchase
20	Revolutionary Officers
20	Vaccination
21	Amendment to the Constitution on Elections
21	Coins
21	Duelling
21	Iron Manufacturers Memorials
21	Kendall, Amos
21	Monroe, James Accounts
21	Peck, James H.
21	Post Office Department, Investigation
21-26	Mileage of Members of Congress, Uniform Rule
21-34	Roads and Canals **
22	Bank of U.S.
22	Ohio Michigan Boundary
22	Tariff, Bill to Modify the
22-47	Revolutionary Claims **
23	Amendment to the Constitution
23	Mint, Establishing Branches of the
23	Patronage, Executive
23	Poindexter, Letter from
23	President's Message Refusing to Furnish a Paper to Senate
23-25	Reilly's Gas Apparatus
24	Arkansas Constitution
24	Incendiary Publications
24	Ohio Michigan Boundary
24	Patent Office
24	Public Lands and the Means of Preventing Their Monopoly
24	Quinby, A.B. for His Steam Engine
25	Columbia River Occupation
25	Georgetown, D.C. Memorial on Retrocession
25	Green, Duff
25	Ruggles, Mr.
25	Steam Vessels, Danger of
25	Tippett, Edward D.
25-27	Oregon Territory
25-79	Patents **
26	Bank Note Circulation
26	Bankruptcy
26	Debts of the States, Assumption by the General Government
26	Fishing Bounties and Allowances
26	Florida and Its Admission to the Union
26	Washington June 5, 1840, Modifying the Charter of
27	Fiscal Agent Employment
27	Fiscal Corporation of the U.S.
27-79	Printing **
28	Michigan and Arkansas Admission to the Union

Congress	Senate Committee (** denotes standing committee)
28	Niles, John W.
28	Secrecy, Violation of the Injunction of
28-42	Retrenchment **
28-67	Territories **
29	Copyright Law
29	Corruption Charges in the Daily Times
29	French Spoliations Prior to 1801
29	Memphis Convention
29	Morton, W.T.G. Memorial
29	Smithsonian Institution
30	California Admission to the Union
30	Cherokee Claimants
30	Fremont, John C., Publication of Results
30	Monuments to Deceased Senators
30	Oregon Railroad
30	Retired List for the Army and the Navy
30	Rivers and Harbors of the U.S., Chicago Convention on
30	Shields, James
30	Tariff Bill of 1828, Repealing the First Section of
30-32	Census, Seventh
31	Disorder in the Senate of April 17, 1850
31	Mexican Boundary Commission, Scientific Corps Attached to
31-33	French Spoliations Prior to 1801
32	Catlin's Collection of Indian Scenes Purchased
32	Emigrant Route and Telegraphic Line to California
32	Ether Discovery
32	Insane, Grant Land to States for Relief of Indigent
32	Insane, Grant Land to States for the Indigent
32	Mallory, R.S. and D.L. Yullee
32	Mexican Boundary Commission, Report to the Sec. of Int.
32	Mexican Boundary, Irregularities in Running and Marking
32-33	Mexico, Proceedings of the Board of Commissioners
33	Bean, Richard and Mark
33	Mitchell, Professor, Construction of a Machine
33	Private Claims Commission, Establishing
33	Ships, Protection of Life and Health in Passenger
33	Sickness on Emigrant Ships
33	Telegraph between Washington and Baltimore
33-38	Pacific Railroad
34	Sumner, Charles Assault upon
35	Banks of the District of Columbia
35	Military Asylum near Washington, D.C.
35-36	French Spoliation Claims
36	Amendments Proposed to the Constitution
36	Comptroller William Medill
36	District of Columbia, Circulation of Bank Notes
36	Duties on Imports
36	Harpers Ferry Seizure
36	Houmas Lands Settlers
36	Order in the Galleries, Preservation of
36	Printing, Certain Alleged Abuses Connected with the
36	Printing, Investigate Public

Congress	Senate Committee (** denotes standing committee)
36	Thirteen on the Disturbed Condition of the Country
36-37	Senate Chamber, Alter and Improve
37	Armory and Foundry
37	Army Efficiency
37	Banks Expedition
37	Harpers Ferry Invasion
37	Humphreys, West H.
37	Military Claims Originating in West Virginia
37	Pensacola Navy Yard Surrender
37	Rebels, Confiscate Property and Free the Slaves of
37	Stark, Benjamin
37-48	Agriculture **
38	Naval Supplies
38	Overland Mail Service, Condition of the
38	Slavery and the Treatment of Freedmen
38-42	Pacific Railroad **
38-79	Manufactures **
39	Banks, National
39	Coins, Weights and Measures
39	Compensation
39	Interior Department Reorganization of Clerical Pay
39	Mississippi River Levees
39	Mississippi River, Reconstruction of Levees
39	National Telegraph Company
39-79	Mines and Mining **
40	Census, Ninth
40	Impeachment of the President
40	Impeachment Trial
40	Representative Reform
40	Treasury Printing Bureau, Examine the Management of the
40-41	Education **
40-43	Senate, Revise the Rules of the
40-97	Appropriations **
41	Hatch, Davis
41	Texas, Alleged Traffic with Rebels in
41-42	Disabilities, Removal of Political
41-45	Mississippi River Levee System
41-70	Laws Revision **
41-79	Education and Labor
42	Arms to French Agents
42	Clayton, Powell
42	Investigation and Retrenchment **
42	Ordnance Stores by the Government of the U.S., Sale of
42	Pomeroy, Senator
42	Senate, Evidence Affecting Certain Members of the
42	Treaty of Washington Made Public, How and by Whom
42-46	Transportation Routes to the Seaboard
42-67	Railroads **
42-79	Privileges and Elections **
43-67	Civil Service and Retrenchment
43-79	Rules **
44	Electoral Vote

Congress	Senate Committee (** denotes standing committee)
44	Mississippi, Alleged Frauds in Recent Elections
44-67	Civil Service, Examination of the Several Branches
44-67	Engrossed Bills **
44-79	Enrolled Bills **
45	Hot Springs, Arkansas, Omission of a Clause in a Bill
45	Louisiana, Late Presidential Election
45	Mexico, Relations between the U.S. and
45-46	Elections of 1878, Alleged Frauds and Violence
45-46	Indian Territory, Removal of Northern Cheyennes to
45-46	Treasury Department, Books and Accounts of the
45-49	Census, Tenth
45-50	Epidemic Diseases
45-53	Nicaraguan Claims
46	Emigration of Negroes from the South to North
46	Freedman's Savings and Trust Company
46	Pluero-Pneumonia among Animals
46-47	Cabinet Officers on the Floor of the Senate
46-67	Mississippi River and Its Tributaries, Improvement
46-67	Transportation Routes to the Seaboard **
47	Distilled Spirit Tax Bill
47	North Carolina, Revenue Collections in
47	Ordnance and Projectiles, Heavy
47	Patterson, Carlisle P., Service Rendered by
47-48	Ordnance and Gunnery
47-48	Sioux and Crow Indians, Condition of the
47-61	Potomac River Improvement
47-67	Library of Congress, Additional Accommodations for
47-67	Woman Suffrage
48	Senate, Compensation of Employees of
48	Steel Producing Capacity of the U.S.
48-49	Interstate Commerce
48-49	Ordnance and War-Ships
48-67	Fisheries **
48-95	Agriculture and Forestry **
49-50	Centennial of the Constitution and the Discovery of Am.
49-50	Indian Traders
49-51	Executive Departments Methods
49-67	Coast Defenses **
50	Civil Service Operations
50	Government Printing Office
50-52	Canada Relations
50-52	Irrigation and Reclamation of Arid Lands
50-52	Pacific Railway Commission
50-54	Epidemic Diseases **
50-61	Indians, Five Civilized Tribes
50-67	Census **
50-67	Meat Products, Transportation and Sale of
50-79	Interstate Commerce **
51	Senate, State of the Administrative Service of the
51-52	Armed Strikebreakers
51-53	Immigration and Naturalization
51-53	Indian Depredations

Congress	Senate Committee (** denotes standing committee)
51-53	Quadro-Centennial
51-54	University of the United States
51-67	Revolutionary Claims **
51-79	Immigration **
52	Cherokee Nation's Complaints of Invasion of Terr.
52-53	Banks, Failed National
52-53	Forest Reservations in California
52-54	District of Columbia Corporations
52-56	Geological Survey
52-67	Canada Relations **
52-79	Irrigation and Reclamation **
53	Bribery Attempts Investigation
53	Ford Theater Disaster
53	Public Distress
53-54	Forest Reservations
53-67	Banks, National
53-67	Indian Depredations **
53-67	Pacific Railroads **
53-79	Immigration and Naturalization **
54	Tennessee Centennial Exposition
54-56	International Expositions
54-56	Nicaragua Canal Construction
54-65	University of the United States **
54-67	District of Columbia Corporations **
54-67	Forest Reservations and Protection of Game **
54-67	Public Health and National Quarantine **
55	Omaha Exposition
55-56	Washington City Centennial
56-60	Executive Departments Expenditures **
56-66	Pacific Islands and Puerto Rico **
56-67	Coast and Insular Survey **
56-67	Cuban Relations
56-67	Geological Survey **
56-67	Industrial Expositions
56-67	Philippines **
56-79	Interoceanic Canal **
57-61	Standards, Weights and Measures
58	Swayne, Charles
59	Indian Territory, Affairs in
59	Indian Territory, Affairs of Five Civilized Tribes in
59-61	Documents, Examination and Disposition
59-67	Indian Lands Trespasses
60-61	Expenditures in the Department of Agriculture
60-61	Expenditures in the Interior Department
60-61	Expenditures in the Justice Department
60-61	Expenditures in the Navy Department
60-61	Expenditures in the State Department
60-61	Expenditures in the Treasury Department
60-61	Expenditures in the War Department
61	Indian Contracts
61	Public Expenditures **
61	Wages and Prices of Commodities

Congress	Senate Committee (** denotes standing committee)
61-62	Third Degree Ordeal
61-67	Expenditures in the Department of Agriculture **
61-67	Expenditures in the Interior Department **
61-67	Expenditures in the Justice Department **
61-67	Expenditures in the Navy Department **
61-67	Expenditures in the Post Office Department **
61-67	Expenditures in the State Department **
61-67	Expenditures in the Treasury Department **
61-67	Expenditures in the War Department **
61-67	Indians, Five Civilized Tribes **
61-67	National Resources Conservation
61-67	Papers in the Executive Department, Disposition of Useless
61-67	Standards, Weights and Measures
62	Archibald, Robert W.
62	Lorimer, William
62-63	Expenditures in the Department of Commerce and Labor **
63	District of Columbia Excise Board
63	Telepost
63-64	Ship Purchase Lobby
63-67	Expenditures in the Department of Commerce **
63-67	Expenditures in the Labor Department **
63-91	Banking and Currency **
64	Attorney General Investigation
64	Senators, Clerical Assistance to
65	Washington Railway and Electrical Company
66	Budget
66	Budget Consideration of National
66	District of Columbia School System
66	Reconstruction and Production
66-67	Pacific Islands, Puerto Rico, and the Virgin Islands **
67	Civil Service Commission Examining Division
67	Crop Insurance
67	Ex-Servicemen, Bureaus etc. Dealing with Welfare of
67	Execution without Trial in France
67	Haiti and Santo Domingo **
67	Readjustment of Service Pay
67-68	Nine Foot Channel from the Great Lakes to the Gulf
67-68	Reforestation
67-68	Veterans Bureau Investigation
67-79	Civil Service **
67-79	Public Lands and Surveys **
67-79	Territories and Insular Affairs **
67-82	Expenditures in the Executive Departments **
68	Campaign Expenditures
68	Propaganda Affecting Taxation and Soldiers' Bonus
68	Wheeler, Burton K.
68-69	Internal Revenue Bureau
68-69	War Finance Corporation, Certain Loans Made by the
69	Alien Property Custodians Office
69-70	Expenditures in Senatorial Elections **
69-70	Senatorial Elections
69-70	Tariff Commission

Congress	Senate Committee (** denotes standing committee)
70	Civil Service Illegal Appointments
70	Mexican Propaganda Investigation
70	Presidential Campaign Expenditures
70	Propaganda or Money Alleged Used by Foreign Governments
71	Heflin on Intermarriages in New York
71	Wildlife Resources
71-72	Alaska Railroad
71-72	Expenditures in the 1930 Senatorial Campaign
71-72	Post Office Leases
71-72	Unemployment Insurance **
72	Foreign Currencies
72	Reconstruction Finance Corporation, Loans Made by
72-74	Air Mail and Ocean Mail Contracts
72-85	Campaign Expenditures Investigation
73	Shiloh National Park, Superintendent of the
73-74	Bankruptcy and Receivership
73-74	Philippines, Economic Condition in the
73-74	Presidential and Senatorial Campaign Expenditures
73-75	Munitions Industry
74	Land and Water Policies of the U.S.
74	Virgin Islands, Administration of Government of the
74-75	Executive Agencies of the Government
74-75	Lobbying Activities
74-79	Silver
74-79	Wool, Production, Transportation, and Marketing
75	Mississippi Flood Control Project, Labor Conditions
75	Unemployment and Relief
75-76	American Merchant Marine
75-76	Civil Service System
75-76	Court Reorganization and Judicial Procedure
75-76	Government Organization
75-76	Merchant Marine, American
75-76	Taxation of Government Securities and Salaries
75-78	Senatorial Campaign Expenditures
75-79	Civil Service Laws
76-81	American Small Business
77	Farm Labor Conditions in the West
77	Fiscal Affairs of the Government
77	Old-Age Pension System
77-78	Fuel Situation in the Middle West
77-78	Gasoline and Fuel Oil Shortages
77-79	Fuels in the Areas West of the Mississippi
77-80	Defense, National Program
77-80	National Defense Program
78	Centralization of Heavy Industry in the U.S.
78-79	Presidential, Vice-Presidential, and Senate Camp. Expend.
78-80	Petroleum Resources
78-80	Post-War Economic Policy and Planning
79	Atomic Energy
79-80	Public Lands **
79-87	Interstate and Foreign Commerce **
79-95	Labor and Welfare **

Congress	Senate Committee (** denotes standing committee)
79-95	Post Office and Civil Service **
79-95	Public Works **
79-97	Rules and Administration **
79-97	Armed Services **
80-95	Interior and Insular Affairs **
81-82	Crime in Interstate Commerce
81-97	Small Business
82-95	Government Operations **
83	Censure Charges against Senator McCarthy
83	Mail Cover on Senators
83	McCarthy, Censure Charges against Senator
84	Contribution Investigation
84-85	Foreign Aid Program
84-85	Political Activities, Lobbying, and Campaign Contributions
85-86	Labor Management Field, Improper Activities in the
85-86	Memorabilia of the Senate
85-86	Space and Astronautics
85-95	Aeronautical and Space Sciences **
86	Unemployment Problems
86-87	National Water Resources
87-95	Aging
87-95	Commerce **
88-95	Standards and Conduct
89-90	Congress Organization
90-95	Nutrition and Human Needs
91-93	Equal Educational Opportunity
91-97	Banking, Housing and Urban Affairs
91-97	Veterans Affairs **
92-93	Secret and Confidential Government Documents
93	National Emergency Termination
93	Presidential Campaign Activities
93-97	Budget **
94	Intelligence Activities
94-95	Senate Committee System
94-97	Intelligence Activities
95	Conduct, Official
95-96	Human Resources **
95-97	Aging **
95-97	Agriculture, Nutrition, and Forestry **
95-97	Commerce, Science and Transportation
95-97	Energy and Natural Resources **
95-97	Environment and Public Works **
95-97	Ethics
95-97	Governmental Affairs **
95-97	Indian Affairs
96-97	Labor and Human Resources **
97	Law Enforcement Undercover Activities of the Justice Dept.

SUBJECT INDEX

ARMY (Cont.)
  regulations, 74, 345
  reorganization, 71
  supplies, 225-227
  supply contracts, 69
  unauthorized advances of monies,
    70
ART AND ARTIST, 76
ASHLEY, J. M., 78
ASSASSINATIONS, 79
  Lincoln, 788
  Poindexter plot, 1075
ASSAULT
  Bynum vs. Garland, 497
  on John Ewing, 436
  A. P. Field vs. W. D. Kelley, 494
  on Amos P. Granager, 589
  on U. H. Paynter, 1052
  on President's secretary--1828,
    80
  Rousseau vs. Grinnell, 1247
  on Sims, 1300
  on Charles Sumner, 1357-1358
  Wise vs. Stanly, 496
ASSAY OFFICES, 81
ASTRONAUTICS, 83
ASTRONOMICAL OBSERVATIONS, 913
ATOMIC ENERGY, 84-85
ATTORNEY GENERAL, 86-88
ATWATER, DORENCE, 89
AVIATION ACCIDENTS AND SAFETY, 16

BACK PAY, 1067
BAIL, 1184
BALLOT BOXES, 91
BALTIC STATES, 92
BANK FAILURES, 111-113
BANK OF THE U.S.
  affairs, 93
  bonus, 136
  conduct and management, 96
  memorials, 95, 104
  national bank, 931-932
  recall of deposits, 1116
BANKRUPTCY, 105-109
BANKS AND BANKING
  Agricultural Bank of Mississippi,
    10
  Commonwealth Bank of Boston, 255
  and currency, 94, 98-100
  District of Columbia, 115-118
  employment of an agent, 110
  failed, 111-113
  Federal Reserve System, 493
  finance and urban affairs, 102-103

BANKS AND BANKING (Cont.)
  and housing, 101
  institutions, 104
  liquidation of deposits, 119
  loans to members of Congress, 790
  national, 111-113
  state banks constitutionality,
    1341
BANKS EXPEDITION, 114
BARTLETT, J. R., 841
BATTLE OF WYOMING, 508
BAYLEY, THOMAS H., 120
BEAN, RICHARD AND MARK BEAN, 121
BENTON, THOMAS HART, 346
BERGDOLL, GROVER CLEVELAND, 123
BERGER, VICTOR L., 124
BERKSHIRE ASSOCIATION, 125
BIBLE SOCIETY OF PHILADELPHIA, 126
BICENTENNIAL CELEBRATION, 127
BIENNIAL REGISTER, 128
BILLS AND RESOLUTIONS, 129
BILLS OF EXCHANGE, 130
BLAIR, FRANK P., 131
BLAIR AND RIVES, PRINTERS, 132
BLIND
  asylum, 133
  New England asylum, 134
  petition for benefit of, 135
BONDS, 574
BOUNDARY DISPUTES
  Chickasaw Indians, 137
  Ohio-Michigan, 993, 996-998
BOUNTY
  military, 1067, 1324
BOUNTY LANDS
  Act of 1850, 138
  commutation of, 139
  for Virginia rev. army, 756
  revolutionary, 1216
BOYNTON, H. V., 140
BREACH OF PRIVILEGE
  assault of Rosseau, 620
  assault, Wheeler vs. Codd,
    1493
  Samuel Houston, 620
BRIBERY
  campaign contribution in the
    Senate, 286
  charges against Lucien Anderson,
    45
  charges against Senator Pomeroy,
    1080
  in prosecution of crimes, 319
  in Senate, 141
BROOKS, JAMES, 143
BROWN, JOHN, 597-598

About the Compiler

Walter Stubbs is Documents Librarian at Southern Illinois University at Carbondale. His articles have appeared in *Library Resources and Technical Services* and *Illinois Libraries.*